SOUTHEAST ASIA BETWEEN AUTOCRACY AND DEMOCRACY

IDENTITY AND POLITICAL PROCESSES

Edited by
Mikael Gravers, Peter Wad
Viggo Brun and Arne Kalland

Nordic Association for Southeast Asian Studies
Aarhus University Press
1989

Copyright: Aarhus University Press, 1989
Word-processed at the University of Copenhagen
Printed in Denmark by Werks Offset, Aarhus
ISBN 87 7288 217 4

AARHUS UNIVERSITY PRESS
Aarhus University
DK-8000 Aarhus C, Denmark

CONTENTS

Irene Nørlund
Women in Socialist Reform Policy:
Vietnamese Textile Workers

The Nordic Association for Southeast Asian Studies (NASEAS) was formed in 1983 to promote social science research on Southeast Asia, as well as related problems in South and East Asia, to extend and strengthen contacts between researchers, students and institutions, and to support the dissemination of research results.

To achieve these goals, the association has arranged annual conferences since 1984 rotating between the various Nordic countries, and these conferences have become the most important forum for presentation and discussion of the ongoing research on Southeast Asia in the nordic countries.
Up till now five conferences have been held:

- The state in Southeast Asian development Copenhagen, Denmark, 1984
- Rural Transformation in Southeast Asia. Kungälv, Sweden, 1985
- Ethnicity, class and gender in the perspective of national development in Southeast Asia. Oslo, Norway, 1986
- Southeast Asia between autocracy and democracy. Pindstrup, Denmark, 1987
- The time dimension in Southeast Asian Studies. Lammi, Finland, 1988

The articles in this book are revised versions of papers presented at two of these conferences, i.e. the conference on "Ethnicity, class and gender in the perspective of national development in Southeast Asia" held in Oslo,

1986 and the conference "Southeast Asia between autocracy and democracy" held near Århus 1987. These conferences brought together Nordic academics (Danish, Finnish, Norwegian, and Swedish) from various disciplines (history, anthropology, sociology, cultural sociology, political science, economics, geography, linguistics) specializing in Southeast Asian studies.

The editors would like to express their gratitude to:

- The **Nordic Council**, the **Norwegian Agency for International Development (NORAD)** and the **Danish International Development Agency (DANIDA)** for funding the conferences in Oslo 1986 and Århus 1987;
- **Aarhus University Research Fund** for funding this publication;
- **Lisbeth Egerod** and **Bruce Hubbard** for correcting and improving the language;
- **Jens Østergaard Petersen** and **Mette Thunø** for formatting the manuscript;
- **Keld Hansen** and **Ole F. Jensen**, Institute of Informatics, University of Copenhagen, for technical assistance;
- **Aarhus University Press** for lay-out and patience.

THE DEBATE ON "EVERYDAY FORMS OF PEASANT RESISTANCE": A CRITIQUE

Mikael Gravers
University of Aarhus

INTRODUCTION

In a discussion of the political processes "between autocracy and democracy" in Southeast Asia it is impossible to cover all central issues, and it is also difficult to isolate an overarching problematic. In this paper I have selected for a discussion a recent and an extremely important debate on "everyday forms of resistance among peasants in Southeast Asia"[1]. But before I attempt a critical evaluation of the theoretical concepts of this current debate, I venture a few and very general observations concerning the theme of the conference.

Southeast Asia and the liberation from colonial rule and capitalist exploitation by revolution have almost been synonymous since 1945. The general concepts of liberation and revolution were based on the idea of a combined struggle for national liberation and a socialist revolution founded on the absolute power of an alliance between peasant and workers.

This process and the outcome of the struggle in the different countries has now unveiled some fundamental and very complicated contradictions between the concepts of a common national liberation (coined with one foreign enemy in mind and with "freedom" for everyone as a reward) and the liberation from the exploitation by one class (based

---

[1] J. C. Scott and J.T.Kerkvliet, 1986.

on the thesis of a "liberating" dictatorship of a worker-
-peasant alliance). The double meaning of liberation was
- and is perhaps still - based on the concept of a
political struggle ending with the single and decisive
blow against the head of the monster and the centre of
the oppressing power, national and international.

After more than forty years of struggle with varying
outcomes, we are now able to conclude that not only has
this strategy caused much suffering in some countries in
Southeast Asia, but it has perhaps not always rewarded
the supporters with the fruits of liberation in terms of
better living conditions and a freer participation in the
political processes.

Problems of human rights, political and economic mar-
ginality, isolation from the international relations and
cultural deprivation are certainly not compatible with
the original ideas of liberation and revolutions and
their contention of progress and freedom.

Thus the question of democracy and autocracy is not only
about support of or resistance to a regime and its policy
and ideology. It is also about the possibilities of
groups and individuals of participating in the economic
and political processes in order to improve their conditions of life. Ideas about reforms and "glasnost" have
created world-wide discussions and seem to be the top
item of the agenda in many countries - although with
great variations. Regimes, systems and ideologies are now
measured by their ability to deliver this kind of freedom.

Thus democracy/autocracy is a question of the participation of the population in accumulation and distribution
of power on various levels. During this process the

actors and their evaluation of the situation naturally depend on the local historical and social conditions. This very superficial diagnosis is of course not sufficient to cover all aspects regarding democracy/autocracy. I only want to emphasize that the rural population in Southeast Asia and other areas can no longer be considered to be living in a kind of segregation from the rest of the social hierarchy and its economic and political interests. It is high time we stop referring to the rural population as exclusively being in favor of or against revolutions or in endless resistance to the rulers, as is the basis of the debate of "everyday forms of peasant resistance".

To a much larger extent we should seek to emphasize the various possibilities of the rural population and its ability to participate in political alliances, and we should evaluate the economic and political aspirations of this population along with those of the growing urban middle-class. These aspirations imply larger individual freedom to accumulate, to consume, to organize, and to voice their political opinion. Altogether, a higher standard of living and an increased consumption in abroad sense seem to play a more important part than the type of regime and the form of government. This implies a clear disparity since on one hand the state has to give greater possibilities and on the other to ensure law and order for very different interests.

I believe that it is important to see the peasants as co-actors in this double process, and not just as the eternal passive victim of outside forces like the world market, the state and unpredictable rulers. The way in which they participate need not be in the role of the completely marginated, subjected and individualistic person who offers an almost atavistic resistance to any relation of power. Resistance in specific social and historical contexts is, of course, an important part of peasant society, but not necessarily as 'the essence' of their social existence.

Peasants have been analyzed in terms of a passive and individualistic mentality, or their revolutionary potential, "moral economy" and now "every day forms of resistance".

Instead of confirming or affirming such essential qualities we need to focus on the very processes by which an agrarian population participate in or are excluded from political power. The degree of participation is closely connected with the relative welfare of peasants (and farmers). The degree of welfare measured against the urban population, on the other hand, is an important indication of the state of democracy and thereby of the possibilities of peasants to improve their conditions of living.

In 1986 a special issue of the "Journal of Peasant Studies" called "Everyday Forms of Peasant Resistance in South-East Asia" was published by J. C. Scott and J. T. Kerkvliet. This issue and a succeeding flow of books and articles have provided a much needed and important renewal of the debate on the political role of peasants - and have especially focused on the subjective conditions by analyzing everyday forms of resistance.

The debate includes several complex theoretical considerations which deserve a thorough discussion. However, my intention here is only to emphasize a few important points for a discussion. What I intend to do is to give a index of some essential serious theoretical problems and to ask some critical questions.

I will solely concentrate on Scott's contribution which has inspired the debate and Turton's theoretical considerations which have a more general perspective.

I shall warn the reader, however, that it is a partisan presentation where the shades have often been omitted and where my basis is the anthropological part of the debate.[2]

The central theme of the debate is how the peasants are able to gain political power and achieve influence on their living conditions - on everything from land, interest on loans and prices, to the cultural forms of every day life. The debate is more concerned with the day to day struggles than with the structures of power and classes. What question will such a debate try to answer? How are the theoretical questions formulated, and how is the analysis carried out?

These are the central questions. But the first problem we must deal with is the category of peasants.

A BRIEF OUTLINE OF THE ORIGIN OF THE PEASANT DEBATE

Seen as a whole we are dealing with a continuation of a long theoretical tradition within and outside anthropology, a tradition comprised by that broad and problematic category of PEASANTS.

---

[2] It is important to emphasize that the detailed and thorough analysis of data from peasant communities in Malaysia and Thailand - especially in Scott's impressive book from 1984 - is not discussed in this paper. My aim is exclusively the theoretical issue in Scott & Kerkvliet, 1986 while I am aware that the empirical findings are extremely important in the discussion.

Within anthropology, peasants were really brought up for discussion after World War II. During colonial times the traditional object of anthropology were "the primitives" (who would disappear according to the law of evolution), but after the war the object changed to the greater part of mankind who was the most important colonial subjects, that is the peasants, who at that time became a threat to the colonial powers. Therefore it was important to analyze their actions. Within the tradition of anthropology the most important factor has been to emphasize a strange, different and an irrational object which is seldom awarded a subjective place in the arena of global history. "Peasants" were a suitable extension of the traditional primitive object but with the one difference that peasants played a more active part in the transformation and development of societies. Still, the early analysis focused on the special, almost statically rationality and mentality of peasants. Furthermore they were mostly regarded as oppressed, passive victims - whereas the oppressors and the oppression making processes were often absent in the analysis or reduced to abstract representations.[3]

It is necessary to bear this in mind in order to consider the present debate - and also of course in order to be able to see it as a movement away from the above mentioned classification of peasants.

---

[3] "Primitive" societies and peasants in anthropological theory have one thing in common: They must always be represented - cf. Marx's words from the 18th Brumaire: "They (peasants) cannot represent themselves they have to be represented". What they are, what they can do or cannot do is ascribed and emphasized by powerful others. Their "qualities" and "reality" is reproduced in the theories as an essence outside history.

The category PEASANTS was created as a type in a continuum of traditional and modern societies (undeveloped/developed etc.). At this point it comes natural to refer to Redfield's famous and still frequently applied dichotomy between the little and the great tradition, folk society/-culture - urban society/culture as the basis of the debate. In Redfield's view the peasant is a type between the primitive man and the proletarian in the continuum of development - i.e. a special HUMAN TYPE.

It is striking that the treatment in anthropology of an abstract human essence and types often coincides with the emphasizing of the different, the irrational and the ahistorical aspect of the object. That is also the case of the analyses of peasants in this period. In the debate they were somewhat reduced to a merely formalistic essence with Foster's "Image of the Limited Good".[4]

In Foster's analysis peasants act as the result of a cognitive/mental essence where they individually try to maximize the scarce goods ranging from food to a place in heaven. According to Foster they cling to traditions and are afraid of changes, except if these are to their individual advantage.

With the central works of Eric Wolf (1966, 1969), history was gradually introduced into the debate. Now peasants acted as an "agent" in revolt and revolution. They were placed in economically and politically defined classes. However, the category peasants including its special qualities and the attempts on comparative studies continued. The compatibility/incompatibility of this kind of

---

[4] For the classical peasant debate, see e.g. Potter, J.M. Diaz, M.N. and Foster, G.M. (eds.): Peasant Society. A Reader. Boston 1967.

essence seeking analysis on one hand and a historical analysis of classes on the other were not questioned. The category peasant developed into a very contradictory concept for the analysis of the complex relations in the anti-colonial and revolutionary struggles.

The many valuable and systematic, concrete analyses and theoretical discussions did not remove the basic problems around the object. The debate on the modes of production - especially feudal/Asiatic modes of production - resulted in new terms which made it possible to define production and economy as social conditions. It maintained, however, an evolutionary logic and did not manage to remove built-in ideas of stagnation and the picture of peasants as passive victims of a development and of the logic of a way of production - either in tributary conditions or as small producers.

The criteria of the debate continued on the whole to have a negative connotation i.e. peasants are not primitive tribal societies, they are not farmers, not workers ... They have a special economic rationality - in periods they work for less profit with a smaller effort, they measure surplus and working hours in a different rationality (cf. the Chayanow-debate) - they try to be "working the system to their minimum disadvantage" (Hobsbawm's famous words). These and many other more or less supported general assertions often led to a continuous reductionism in which a certain quality of this extensive part of mankind was exaggerated ("minimizing risk" etc.). In spite of the fact that many analyses emphasized historical, social and cultural differences the debate looked for a general essence and dealt with peasants as the expression of a dichotomous understanding of global development.

New variants supervened for instance "proletarians in disguise" (S. Amin 1977), small producers inside or outside the capitalist mode of production (J.S.Kahn 1980). A special and different rationality was to be found and peasant society was still relatively static: "blocked" or "underdeveloped". Only under special circumstances and in special alliances did they have a potential for freeing themselves. This model was, however, usually a poor-peasant strategy and an imitation of China's experiences and Mao's theory. It was the same problems of the heterogeneity of the category which showed themselves in the specific historical conjunctures.

When in 1976 J. C. Scott resumed the discussion of "the moral economy", it was somewhat a return to the basis of the debate and the specific rationality of "the small tradition" - especially the right to reciprocity and subsistence as the moral essence of a universal "peasant culture". The debate on the moral and rational (Scott and Popkin et al.) can be seen as a continuation of Redfield, Foster and others. A common paradigm where a HUMAN TYPE and its economic/political cultural and mental essence is the real object in a comparative project. Peasants often act undifferentiated and ahistorical in the superior theoretical aspect of the debate. And when peasants act they generally play the part of victims who are often politically seduced.

This is a very short and perhaps an extremely one-sided characteristic of a very comprehensive debate. An unpleasant characteristic - but I think it is the crucial problem of the debate - and the place where to put one's questions. That's precisely why the debate on "EVERYDAY RESISTANCE" is so important.

"EVERYDAY RESISTANCE" - RESISTANCE AGAINST WHAT?

The importance of this debate is that it does not reduce the discussion of peasants to their part either in a revolutionary project, a revolt or in passive subjection. The intention, then, of this debate seems to be the possible avoidance of such a reduction of peasants to mere objects of an investigation of a common grand rationale.

Scott refers to the debate about peasant revolt and revolution as a "left wing romance". It was one-sided when characterizing the peasant as a rebel and a revolutionary, and peasant rebellions and revolutions are few and far between, according to Scott (1986:5) In very few revolts and revolutions throughout history have peasants actually been the prime mover. And often they were defeated or ended by getting the peasants another repressive government (Scott 1986:6).

The debate on revolution forgot the everyday resistance which according to Scott has great importance to peasants who are often not in a position to organize and perform collective actions. Please notice that this old negative determination reappears as a phrase from the early debate and that the participants in the debate are still looking for some common essence ending in the following definition of EVERYDAY RESISTANCE:

"The prosaic but constant struggle between the peasantry and those who seek to extract labour, food, taxes, rents .... from them". (Scott 1986:6)

The forms are as follows: "Foot-dragging, dissimulation, false-compliance, pilfering, feigned ignorance, slander, arson, sabotage and so forth". (Ibid. p. 6).

This is the description of the everyday life of peasants. At first sight one might be tempted to understand the above as if peasants were criminal by instinct, provided you read this general quotation out of its context. But these descriptive terms are specifically defined in the examples and throw light on both historical and current forms of resistance in this small everyday guerrilla tactics - or the "little class struggle" which I feel tempted to call it in line with Redfield. Class conditions in the village are complicated by many alliances and loyalties, kinship and patron - client relations which apart from creating interdependence obstruct the collective and organized resistance by the peasants.

What Scott emphasizes is that peasants try to counteract the exploitation and to live as advantageous as possible by stealing a little, cheating or sabotaging. They test some limits before an open and costly confrontation but do not disapprove of the structure and the system. Class and class-consciousness is the last stage of the process according to E. P. Thompson. Thus self-interests take precedence over solidarity-type actions. The arguments are not very far from Foster's "image of the limited good" by implying a common calculation by the peasants as if it is a general social function.

The individual acts are altogether the core of the analysis. The state, structure, and system are being underplayed in favor of individual choices. In this respect the debate is very much in accordance with more general theoretical trends. It tries to create a general view. At the same time it has a great resemblance to the early debate on peasants where they were depicted as either individualists if and when they act, or as people who cannot act or participate on their own initiative. For instance, Scott writes in an article from 1987:

... almost by definition, peasant involvement in a social movement occurs only through the meditation of non-peasant allies. (Scott 1987:421 - my emphasis).

In the everyday resistance they can act themselves, however, - according to Scott they calculate on their small influence on the rulers. According to Scott they survive and they only engage in class struggle over culture and tradition - but not over laws and power. Redfield's vocabulary seems more obvious in connection with the mention of the small uncoordinated fight in terms as "folk culture of the peasants little tradition". And in the mentioning of the cheating of the peasants and of their avoiding military service Scott says that it is "embedded in the peasant subculture". (Ibid. 452).

So we are back to the search for an essence in the category of peasant - something underlying embodied in their "subculture" and which controls their acts and mentality. This essence seems to REPRESENTS PEASANT CULTURE AND RESISTANCE according to Scott et al.

In the following part I am going to examine this line of thought - establishing though that even if my criticism is not constructive when pointing out this tendency to reductionism, the critique is not aimed at the many concrete observations which originate from the analysis of the empirical context. My criticism is exclusively aimed at the general theoretical and the more fundamental aspects of the debate.

PROBLEMS, QUESTIONS, AND COUNTER-QUESTIONS

Quite informally we ought to ask ourselves first: WHAT IS THIS DEBATE LOOKING FOR - WHICH QUESTIONS IS IT TRYING TO

ANSWER? Which questions are asked compared to the answers given?

Obviously there is a desire to formulate general theoretical questions and to perceive them in concrete empirical connections. There is also a clear showdown with system oriented analyses (modes of production - the state) and a focus on individual acts as an expression of a general development. Three points are based on axiomatic assumptions:

1) peasants have some common social and cultural traits.
2) they offer resistance - and even as a part of their everyday forms of life.
3) they act according to the same pattern regardless of historical, political connections.
1+3) combined they constitute a category of a common essence: socially, culturally and mentally.

Critical questions:

1) What do peasants do when they do not offer resistance? It is a very problematic assumption that peasants in almost everything they do offer resistance as a conduct which is exclusively aimed at surviving with as small expenses as possible.

2) Which acts are political, then? Are theft, swindle and evasions always a resistance against those who collect interest and tax?

REFUTATION

Peasants are an integrated part of the struggle for power and the display of force in society. In this way they are an active element in the determination of the relative

15

strength of the different parties in the struggle - and therefore peasants cannot be reduced to the mere victims who are only trying to survive. What is described as resistance in the debate is, in my opinion, neither exclusively political nor necessary in order to survive. (Notice Christine White's critical comments in "Journal of Peasant Studies", op.cit.) These actions may be directed towards a neighbor or an equal, even though Scott does not include such actions towards those similarly disposed. The conditions mentioned by Scott may be part of a trial of strength between classes and alliances - but they may be seen as individual opportunism (which he admits in some passages). And how do we make out what is significant to the general problems in question?

Against whom or what is this resistance directed? Not the system but the persons who extract the peasants work and exploit them. But peasants as political beings are hardly fixed on persons alone, neither can any action against a person be regarded as the expression of resistances in an abstract sense (we shall return to this later).

Finally, Scott calls any obstruction among peasants in Tanzania, Malaysia, Vietnam etc. resistance. Thereby he evades taking a position on historical, political and cultural differences. What is common to the object PEASANTS then? They belong to a different category than primitive societies, workers, bureaucrats landowners, bourgeoisie etc. Peasants do something which these other categories and classes do not - they offer everyday resistance! But don't the others offer resistance?

The peasants in Scott's opinion are small land-owners, tenants and farm workers with something in common: the resistance which is "embedded in their culture".

To sum up, the theory is therefore <u>essence oriented</u> ,that is, it postulates a specific defined quality as the incentive and explanation of all conditions. It is eo ipso <u>subjective</u>, placing the essence with individuals and their actions and it <u>formalizes</u> since it refers to the uniformity and to the quality a priori. Finally it is <u>metaphysical</u> since it tries to place the essence as "embedded" in a sub-culture like another primitive force beyond physical manifestation, and human intervention and organization.

Such a theoretical basis will always involve the risk of ending in cliches and repetitions of eternal truths. However, the debate is certainly not just negative seen in a wider perspective. It emphasize a number of important aspects in connection with the general conditions of the peasants, their political participation and especially their necessary cynicism in relation to autocracy and democracy in a world where power seems to be metaphysical and placed in distant and amorphous systems such as the world market - systems towards which it is difficult to offer resistance. Usurer and civil servant can be hit directly, however. That is part of the reality of peasants.

A good thing about the debate is that it has opened the analysis in relation to more limited examinations of economic and political systems and their internal logic and functions. The debate is also trying to avoid economy - but has it become too much of a reduction, nevertheless?

To begin with we ought to question the use of the type/-category of 'peasant'; or at least only use it in a descriptive way - even though that would complicate the whole basis of the debate.[5] But at least we have to qualify who is offering resistance and towards what and whom. The social, political and historical conditions must not be forgotten in favor of a merely empirical identification of forms of resistance classified in types ad infinitum. It is important to establish the social and cultural context before we discuss the general, and accordingly the specifics of the general.

What Scott et al. describes and generalizes as everyday forms of resistance is therefore different ways in which the relative strengths between the rulers (landlords, civil servants, army, police etc.) and small producers and farmers are submitted to the struggle for power and the test of social forces. The debate emphasizes, however, that alliances and interdependence often cut across this fact. It means that the same people who offer everyday resistance may also be supporting autocratic rulers who reduce their political and economic space. And precisely this difference is extremely important to analyze, i.e. who participate in alliances with politicians, bureau-crats, big landowners, etc.

For this purpose we need a more thorough analysis of the political field and of power.

---

[5] A peasant is a "worker on the land" in the literal sense. But the term is often used to designate a traditional non-capitalist agricultural producer (a petty commodity producer, tenant, sharecropper etc.) In contrast a farmer is involved in a modern, capitalist agricultural production, owner of his land, wealthy by comparison. This wide descriptive distinction is used here.

Andrew Turton (1986, 1984) discusses "everyday resistance" in connection to power and the anatomy of the relations of power. He involves Foucault (1980) in the debate - obviously trying to avoid a mechanical materialistic view.

According to Turton, peasants do not only react to exploitation and oppression and they are not passive victims between the great revolts. These collective actions are rare and Turton rejects terms which generalize such actions: militarism, "image of the limited good", "moral economy" etc. - they belong to the past. On the contrary Turton tries to ask a number of questions relevant to an analysis of power (in the wide sense of Foucault) combined with an analysis of the "power bloc" (in the wide sense of Gramsci), as to class, ideology and the discourse of power including the cultural forms of life.

I neither can nor will reproduce Foucault's extensive and complex work in this context. I shall only point out what is Turton's 'basic ideas'. First and foremost this is Foucault's idea of power as being present in all situations - not only in structures, institutions and persons but as complex strategic relations in society. Power is concatenated to knowledge and truth and finally with the forms of subjection and discipline. Power is never to be found in one particular place, never appropriated by anybody. The result of this idea of power is that resistance always has to be decentralized. Everybody uses his will for power and his knowledge to offer resistance where he works and lives. The distinction between the political and non-political is revoked - that is, Turton uses it for defining the daily battle field of the peasants as "the middle-ground" - an endless stationary

19

warfare in a no man's land where peasants resist exploitation and subjection including attacks on their culture,
customs, identity and dignity.

Quite naturally, Turton ends in a confrontation between
his use of Foucault's anti-essence theory where power
circulates endlessly everywhere also outside the institutions, and the attempt to analyze power in a political
systemic sense with regard to classes. Here it is limited
to the power over institutions and the use of these for
creating hegemony. Precisely this difference, however,
may be crucial in order to develop the debate: That the
fighting and resistance are not only actions against
power or means of obtaining power - they are both.

Foucault maintains that we can fight against the hegemonic
forms of power - but we cannot abolish power. It may be
revealed but will never disappear. And his theory implies
the same intrinsic discrepancy: it claims not to be a
universal theory (total theory) of systems and it only
applies in the analysis of the local empirical conditions.
At the same time, however, Foucault uses power in an
abstract, almost metaphysical sense, as a universal
primitive force in human beings and superior to historical
and material connections.

Thus Turton can only make use of Foucault for making an
index of outward forms of power and resistance - not for
the purpose of throwing light on the strategic contents
of the relations. The important thing is, however, that
Turton is in quest of the concrete mechanisms of power,
the microphysics of power and its modes of operation in
society as a whole.

Turton's open analysis will of course be put to a serious
test when the social system and its power relations are

to be examined. Then the weaknesses will show themselves. We are left with an index of abstract, self-valid terms and categories: fear, violence, consensus, surveillance - as conceptions of both power and the purpose of resistance.

Turton uses Thailand as an example and maintains that the Thai state is relatively autonomous and that the power bloc is not yet dominated by the bourgeoisie (Turton 1986:40). That is why the "local power blocs" have to be investigated, including the local alliances of big landowners, bureaucrats, and the police among others. Between these people and the poor peasants the contradictions are manifest and here we find "the middle-ground":

This opened up a perspective on 'local powers', power blocs and coalitions which were seen as an important mediation and localization of contradiction between state and capitalist spheres on the one hand and the rural producers on the other. (Ibid., p. 40).

This is the localization of the main social contradictions and the field of resistance. The higher spheres of the state and its institutions constitute a relatively autonomous centre of power, while the local battlefield holds complex economic social and cultural conditions and various interests and interpretations according to Turton. Here peasants offer resistance to power.

Power seems mostly to be represented by the state apparatus though, and its use of physical power, ideology (it creates fear), surveillance, and subjection.

Resistance manifests itself in sabotage, evasion of laws etc. (cf. Scott) and in various symbolic expressions, in songs or in the practice of religion and in work. Turton thinks that the Thailand everyday resistance expresses a stationary warfare after the open resistance offered by

21

the peasants in 1973-80. The murders of some 30 of their
leaders checked their organization - but according to
Turton it gave them the self-confidence which they now
use in a "hit and run" tactic.

Turton asks many relevant questions in spite of the
theoretical differences between power as a system and
power as a quality in every social form but not localized.
Particularly in the thorough and seminal article from
1984 there is much important information and many points
which cannot be discussed here. It is very inspiring. In
its openness, however, it also ends by being a big index
of more or less abstract and self valid ideas - often
amounting to the metaphysical and without our always
getting a concrete preciseness and localization of the
acting subject - and without arriving at a precise
identification of the contents of resistance i.e. what
resistance consists of and towards what it is directed:
the local coalitions and persons or the state and the
regime?

RESISTANCE AND PARTICIPATION IN THAILAND

Thailand, of course, cannot exemplify all aspects of this
discussion, but it can serve as a brief illustration, and
the recent political development in Thailand can be used
to elaborate some of the central issues of the debate.

However Thailand is a good example of the incompatibility
in Scott, namely that local resistance may coincide with
support of a regime which mobilizes against the same
resistance. From the middle of the 1970s the power bloc
thus succeeded in mobilizing at least 3 million peasants
to para-military organizations. These organizations were
not only nationalist and anti-Communist but demand a
subjection in accordance with the existing conditions of

property and local alliances which do not only act as an independent power bloc but are clearly connected with the army, the royal house, big landowners, the owners of the rice mills on the national political level. 90% of the participants in these para-military organizations were and are still "poor peasants" according to Morell and Chai-anan (1982). This mobilization of a power and for a power can not only be reduced to pretended resistance or be due to fear. Turton (1984) clearly shows that fear of reprisals and ostracism have pressed many people into the organizations (Village Scouts, National Defence Volunteers). But we may also be dealing with a resistance towards the Communist Party and its strategy. In this way the mobilization to para-military groups may have played an important role in the debacle of the Communist party (CPT) as a part of the army's strategy of placing amnesty ahead of military force.

In this connection it is really important with a thorough analysis of the relative strength of the different powers. The real organizer of these para-military corps was the army and its intelligence organ (ISOC). In this context Turton and others forget that the army is not only an apparatus of power in itself measurable by its organization and its ability to use force – it only has the power which corresponds to the support of the population and especially the classes and social strata from which soldiers and non-commissioned officers are being recruited. This recruitment basically takes place among the rural population i.e. in all classes, and power reaches further than its organized form – a soldier, a "village scout" or a so-called Ranger also exercises and represents a power in the local social relations which the person forms a part of.

It is very important to examine the rural population's understanding of the relative strength of the different powers and the way in which they operates - especially in the grey sphere between civilian and military domain. Turton's contribution from 1984 is an important clue to such an analysis - but is still based on the general presumptions of the thinking and acting of (the category) peasants.

In Thailand for instance with the current political trends it is essential to assess how the ideas of the army and the Internal Security Operation Command (ISOC) on "peaceful revolution from above" are being understood and what is at the bottom of these thoughts. Terms such as "mass democracy" (and sovereignty of the masses"), "democracy from above" and the abolition of "dark influences" in the shape of corruption and capitalist power (here is often referred to the great family-owned capitals) have been mentioned:

The present form of democracy in our country - I mean the present form of elections - promotes capitalist dictatorship. It is necessary in terms of capitalism. Only those who own capital have the right and power in our political situation. They (the wealthy) make use of the constitution in order to control power for their own benefit ....
(High-ranking officer in "Far Eastern Economic Review", June 19, 1986).[6]

In the article quoted above the Thai officer refers to the extensive use of the purchase of votes at elections and the change of parties for payment. According to the

------

[6] Recently an analysis of the Thai economy was published by the Bangkok newspaper, the Nation, June 18, 1988 saying that: "Over 10 million people still suffer in poverty;..but still the upper classes who account for 20 percent of the Thai population (53 million) control half of the national wealth and income".

officer in question politicians and capitalists engender poverty and injustice.

"Democracy from above" does not only appeal to the middle class with ideas of a corporate state. It also aims at mobilizing a large part of the rural population around "an absolute democratic rule" where the masses are not led by the nose with purchase and sale of votes, and where the army should guarantee that the differences between those who possess and those who work are equalized. This "Thai-way of democracy" - which also seems to have been inspired by Golkar - is a construction of a new division of powers with a controlled parliament and a powerful royal house. Veiled in a revolutionary vocabulary an autocratic, oligarchic and paternalistic rule seems to be lurking. Add to this the ideas of a corporate state and the result is indeed a political syncretism constructed by the army.

The Thai army not only organizes power and seeks control of the rural population. The rural population is part of the basis of power, its reservoir and mandate. Furthermore the army supervises the communication of these ideas and their cultural symbols. The army speaks on behalf of everybody and wants to represent everybody. It has already, however, obtained a real and direct control of a large part of the rural population by way of the para--military organizations.

These matters are important to examine. And this is precisely what Turton is trying to do. He goes behind the forms of resistance to the anatomy of power and with Foucault he looks at the instruments of power, its methods and tactics. To this we should add the theories of power as mentioned in the example above. These must be analyzed before we can decide whether some peasant's theft or

25

evasion from military service has a significance in a wider context as resistance towards "power".

The levels of the analysis must therefore be dissociated and more carefully delineated - better than in Turton (1986) with the dichotomy between the great power bloc and the local power bloc - between state - "middle-ground" and village. It may be a good topographic description of political domains and battle fields but the categories need more precise contents.

In order to exemplify local resistance it might be interesting to have a thorough analysis of the many NGO projects in Thailand - especially in the poor northeast provinces. Do these projects for instance indicate a strengthening of a "traditional moral economy" and local resistance? The peasants have formed co-operatives with rice banks, buffalo banks and fertilizer banks (Reiko 1985:67). Buddhist monasteries are often the managing centres of the co-operatives and the monks are active in organizing these. Such a mutual aid is clearly a resistance to loan-sharks and usurers.

The co-operatives are based on Buddhist ideals and ideas of self-reliance (Reiko 1985 and Hirsch 1986). They may very well exemplify that focus has changed from the poor peasant revolution of the Communist Party in the 1970s to local attempts to organize themselves and secure a reasonable welfare. A "rural activist" expresses himself so:

Once back in the 70s we were eager to change the structure, but we failed. Now we are going to stress more people's awareness about how they can participate; change the consciousness of people rather than change the structure. (Reiko 1985:68).

Even though this statement may not apply to all peasants it is significant that participation is emphasized. This statement may also be read as an expression of the present political conjuncture - but not as an evidence that all peasants now only offer "everyday resistance" instead of "structural resistance and change".

The rural population will also measure its political-demo-cratic possibilities in the shape of welfare. This means that political participation does not only concern franchise and influence through elections. At previous elections in Thailand the rural vote was very small and many people knew little about party-political conditions. The typical vote was cast for persons - candidates of whom people in the villages hoped would forward their matters. The purchase of votes, however, to a large extent decided these person-oriented alliances. When you receive money you must also repay with your vote. Said a villager:

If you take something from someone and don't give him something in return, then you are committing a sin. (McBeth 1986:45).

A "sin" (bap in Thai) means negative merit in Buddhism.

Often the local population is disappointed with their MPs who do not always consider the welfare of the electorate when participating in a game of power in the power bloc, whose complex hierarchy of personal patron-client rela-tions dominate the power relations in Thailand.

No wonder therefore that many people in Thailand are in sympathy with thoughts in sections of the army of "sover-eignty of the masses" and "absolute democratic rule" through a "peaceful revolution". A "strongman" lurks in the background and decades of autocracy in the shape of personal power relations still dominate the political life. Seeking protection and achieving welfare through patron-client relations are deep rooted in Thailand and are hardly removed by revolutions from "above" or from "below".

The low price of rice paid to the peasants and the farmers throughout the last 30 years has almost been synonymous with the low standard of living for a large part of the agrarian population. Low incomes, high interest, high prices of fertilizers and pesticides have contributed to a stagnation of agriculture and an expansion which has ruined the forests. Landlessness and a life in poverty as tenant, sharecropper, farm worker or farmer in debt are symptoms of threatened welfare and the lack of democratic participation in the power relations.

No wonder therefore that some peasants have now picked up ideas of ecological farming and co-operative farming where they <u>minimize</u> the consumption of fertilizers and pesticides as well as their private consumption. Apparently they apportion a lower income but avoid getting into the clutches of the loan-sharks and go bankrupt. Others prefer to draw up a contract with multinational agribusiness companies, like Pokphand. For instance they become managers of a hog farm where the firm supplies hogs, feed etc. and secure an income which is immediately above the average income.

Both examples express the attempts of the agrarian population of obtaining welfare by participating in the system and by recognizing its relations of power. But at the same time the participation is a kind of resistance to the forces which control the conditions of their life. The participation and the resistance of the peasants and the farmers is developing as diversified as their urban counterparts of a growing middle class. Resistance and participation are complementary parts of the political process.

I therefore agree with the following lines:

..the degree of democracy in Thailand can simply be measured by the welfare of rice farmers. So long as the Thai rice farmers are still in constant difficulties, there will be no hope for true democracy in Thailand. (Apichai Puntasen and Montri Chenvidayakarn 1986:72)

That does not mean, however, that increased welfare only is a question of equal economic distribution and political participation. Democracy also means freedom to express oneself through various cultural activities. For instance, a revival of traditional Thai dances and songs forms part of some of the co-operatives in the north east and Buddhism is also an important medium in this connection. Buddhism and its ethics have proven to play a crucial part in the political development of recent years - in more autocratic forms about the role of the king, national unity and harmony as well as an expression of a local organization and mobilization (Gravers 1985/86 and 1988).

The analysis of the cultural and ideological conditions and forms is therefore an important element in the debate of democracy/autocracy. The problem is, not to reduce culture or ideology to simply being reflections of the economy or inversely to raise culture or ideology to dominant factors which give meaning to all human actions a priori as a metaphysical code.

This problem is obvious in Turton's wide application of ideology and culture - often making the two concepts almost synonymous. It is problematic to continue the discussion of ideology implying one dominant ideology and a "false" consciousness. In this sense ideology is often described as a superjacent substance or independent instrument deciding people's consciousness and twisting it. This tendency is found in Turton's article, but he seems to be aware of the problem:

Ideology, dominant discourse, may set limits to our thinking, but do not determine the internal elaboration of our thoughts or responses. (Turton 1984:63).

Ideology appears to have a dominant access to individuals' mind and consciousness. However, no concept or theory, no idea or ideology is constructed outside social relations or independent of these.

Therefore it seems extremely difficult to apply the term ideology versus reality etc. uncritically and widely about culture, religion and cosmology (Gravers 1985/86). On the other hand religion is often an important political medium and a field where both power and resistance are being used.

CONCLUSION

Instead of applying Scott's somewhat abstract or totally empirical types and terms I think Turton has many good points and concentrates on doing the right thing: he perceives the relative strength of the different power relations and power as something which is not only seen in structures but which <u>circulates and is being exchanged</u>. In that way we can avoid banal repetitions about this, and that action of peasants = resistance according to an abstract index which is evident in both Scott and Turton's articles.

Should attempts be made, however, to give a kind of definition of power in connection with the contents of the debate it must specify the relative strengths in the social relations, that is between and within classes and alliances at the local and at the national level. The relative strengths must be "measured" in accordance with the ability to mobilize people and resources in the current trends and the ability to control these processes including the communications and its cultural contents and forms.

In these processes the agrarian populations are active participants but with varying identities and loyalties. The peasant or the farmer may seek influence whether he joins a cooperative or the Village Scouts, and he may at the same time resist corruption or the destruction of the environment by pesticides. But the experience by participating - and not some a priori and metaphysical essence or index - is the foundation of his identity, loyalty and alliances within struggles locally or on a larger scale. The resistance of today may be turned into the new alliances of tomorrow. In this connection it is extremely important to have in mind that class identity or even solidarity is crosscut by many other identities and relations.

The historical background must also be included in the analysis so that power is not reduced to function or metaphysical energy. (This trend is clearly to be found in Foucault). More detailed analyses of the empirical development of the processes also seem more relevant than creating new categories, maintaining the old ones or making a dichotomy between "big and small" - violence and consensus etc. The "everyday resistance" debate is heavily burdened with these kinds of concepts which have simply outlived their days. It does not ask the relevant questions but ritually repeats concepts belonging to the description of peasants as a human type.

However, it is always easier to criticize than to add new knowledge. The purpose of this paper is to create a debate.

It is an extremely important debate whether it is about South-east Asia or any other part of the world. But to anthropology it is also a caveat: too often we try to make anthropology by reinterpretations of old eternal truths - typologies or dichotomizing the rationality of "others" - instead of formulating new questions and analyzing the processes of social life. (Gravers 1988).

The old concepts are too easily confirmed - like the following words of a village headman from the Uthaithani province in Thailand:

No one will listen to us (peasants) because we are so stupid. (McBeth 1986)

Do we in this statement find the reproduction of the "image of the limited knowledge/power of peasants", a self-subjection and/or the exclusion from participation in "the dominant discourse"?

BIBLIOGRAPHY

Amin, S: **Imperialism and Unequal Development** (Hassocks, 1977).

Apichai Puntasen & Montri Chenvidyakarn: **Policy of Rice in Thailand. Policies, Issues and Conflicts** (forthcoming) (Bangkok: Ms Thammasat University, 1986).

Foucault, M: **Power/Knowledge. Selected interviews and other writings 1972-77** (New York: C. Gordon (ed), 1980).

Gravers, M: "Buddhismen mellem kapitalisme og socialisme - udviklingsstrategier og den politiske kamp i Thailand siden 1960", **Den ny verden** (Copenhagen), vol. 19, 3, 1985/86.

Gravers, M: "Antropologien efter "primitivismen"- Buddhisme og politik i Thailand som eksempel"; in Torsten Madsen (ed.): **Bag Moesgårds Maske,** (Aarhus: Aarhus University Press, 1988), pp. 31-46.

Hirsch, Ph: "Which Route to Prosperity", **Inside Asia,** no. 8, pp. 23-25, 1986.

Kahn, J.S: **Minagkabau Social Formations. Indonesian Peasants and the World-Economy** (Cambridge: Cambridge University Press, 1980).

McBeth, J: "Political Crossroads", **Far Eastern Economic Review,** June 19, pp. 40-49, 1986.

Morell, D. & Chaianan Samudavanija: **Political Conflict in Thailand. Reform, Reaction, Revolution** (Cambridge, Mass., 1982).

Potter, J.M. et al.: **Peasant Society** (Boston, 1967).

Reiko, Inoue: "Organizing for real Development", **AMPO Japan-Asia Quarterly,** vol. 17, 4, 1985.

Scott, J.C: **The Moral Economy of Peasants** (New Haven, 1976).

Scott, J.C: **Everyday Forms of Peasant Resistance** (New Haven, 1984).

Scott, J.C. & B.J.T. Kerkvliet (eds.): "Everyday Forms of Peasant Resistance in South-east Asia", special issue of **The Journal of Peasant Studies**, vol. 13, 2, 1986.

Scott, J.C: "Resistance without Protest and without Organization. Peasant Opposition to the Islamic Zakat and the Christian Tithe", **Comparative Studies in Society and History**, vol. 29, 3, 1987.

Turton, A: "Patrolling the Middle-Ground. Methodological Perspectives on Everyday Peasant Resistance", **The Journal of Peasant Studies**, vol. 13, 2, 1986.

Turton, A: "Limits of ideological Domination and the Formation of Social Consciousness"; in Turton & Tanabe: **History and Peasant Consciousness in South East Asia** (Osaka, 1984).

Wolf, E.R: **Peasants** (New Jersey: Englewood Cliffs, 1966).

Wolf, E.R: **Peasant Wars of the Twentieth Century** (New York, 1969).

RURAL LEADERSHIP IN 19TH CENTURY WEST JAVA

Hans Antlöv
Gothenburg University

Most 19th and early 20th century accounts of Javanese
leadership and administration regarded indigenous community politics as static and undeveloped, positioned in
some kind of timeless vacuum. Rural political behaviour
was generally ignored and the political performance of
community leaders regarded as unproblematic. Rural society
was culturally and socially homogenous. In their self-
legitimizing efforts, most Dutch colonial observers as
well as indigenous elite historiography neglected the
dynamics of community leadership. The native literate
nobility painted a picture of society in which no authority beside their own was rightful. And the Dutch were,
as a rule, too ignorant of rural conditions to appreciate
the position of local leaders in village life. In either
case, little analytical attention was paid to regional
variations and to the transformation of rural political
life following colonial intervention. The result was the
long-established notion of Javanese society as tradition-
bound and communal. A parallel image of the administrative
structure placed the regent as the righteous ruler and
peasants as naturally subordinated to him.

These conceptions have often been carried over in
post-colonial studies of politics and administration of
Java. Viewed from the historical impression of a customary
and rigid Javanese administrative polity, a traditional
Javanese political culture has been constructed, valid

for all, or most, parts of Java.[1] At centre of this perception is a patrimonial state, composed of the regent and his subjects, stratified in clusters of patron-client relationships (Anderson 1972:34). Power is held to be obtained and exercised through the control over loyal clients, who in turn receive power from being related with a power-holder. The concentration of power at the core of the state (i.e. regent or sultan) is the ultimate sign of the well-being of the whole society. From this centre, power is believed to radiate and "wear off" onto the dependents. Power and status can only be obtained in relation to the potent centre. The powerful are characterized by what Jackson (1980) calls "traditional authority" - authority recognized solely on the basis of who the holder is. A powerful person, in a sense, invites a voluntary submission.

The picture drawn of village society in Java is a miniature version of the all-empowered patrimonial state, where "the subordinate obeys the superior...without questions about morals, religion, values or ideology" (Jackson 1980:xx). The acquisition and execution of power and authority require neither persuasion nor exploitation; it is acquired through the dependency of the servile subjects, without public voice, bound by eternal subordination to the will of the patron.

In this view, there exist neither local autonomy nor internal dynamics in village politics. The rural elite, in charge of dormant communities and upholding a cultural-

---

[1] This is a common notion held by many of the "culturalistic" inspired social scientists. Moertono (1968) and Anderson (1972) are perhaps the two most well-known; recent authors include Jackson (1974 and 1980), Koentjaraningrat (1984), Keeler (1985) Suparlan (1977), Mudjanto (1986), Ali (1986) and the debate on the nature of the present Indonesian government (for a review see King 1982). For critics, see Robison (1981), Slamet (1985) and Quarles van Ufford (1987).

ly defined authority, is only a pale shadow of its patron, the ruler. They are merely puppets of the Powerful Ones, unable to accumulate power but in relation to the Centre. This picture of Java - a vertically structured, centralistic but yet patrimonial replica of the Great Oriental Despotism - has also been used to explain contemporary national politics (e.g. Ali 1986 and Reeve 1985). The traditional patrimonial state is seen as timeless and unchanging, also capable of explaining late 20th century politics, as if it still existed; if not "out there" then in the minds of the natives.

It is the argument of this article that the attempts to create a generalized prototype of the political culture of Java and then extrapolate it to contemporary conditions do not contribute to an understanding of leadership and authority in Java. A more profound analysis must take into account regional differences as well as community-level dynamics. A recent trend towards regional historical studies has highlighted the dynamics of local leadership.[2] A conclusion that can be drawn from these studies is that regional variations of leadership and bureaucratic polities historically have been greater than is generally believed. Java cannot be seen as a single administrative system with uniform patterns of leadership and one single conception of power. Regional variations of indigenous cultural properties, partly concomitant with the different ways Dutch colonial rule transformed native society, suggests another approach: one where different patterns of leadership have emerged from distinct regional structures.

---

[2] For east Java, see Elson 1984; for Cirebon, Breman 1983; for the present case of Priangan, Svensson 1980. While Svensson concentrates on the historical development of the agro-economic system in order to understand political and religious movements, the present work which utilizes Svensson's material, focuses on local-level political organization.

Let us now look more closely at the administrative structure of 19th century Priangan, trying to discover the circumstances under which the present administrative polity was formed. This will be done by investigating the specific conditions and properties of local leadership in the area. It will be demonstrated that leadership formation was associated with both ecological and nation-state developments. As a result, the indigenous and colonial history of West Java has prohibited the development of patrimonial conceptions of power and authority.

Ecological conditions

Priangan is a highland region of West Java, consisting of the seven regencies (kabupatens) Cianjur, Sumedang, Bandung, Sukabumi, Ciamis, Garut, and Tasikmalaya. The population is Sundanese with a distinct language and ethnic identity. In the literature it has often been treated as the "little brother" of its more well known eastern neighbour, the Javanese. These two ethnic groups clearly belong to the same cultural tradition in terms of cosmology, rituals, and the structure of kinship.

In the 19th century, however, the highlands of Priangan were still a frontier region. The area was sparsely populated and had few roads and was difficult to colonize. Up until the 1870s, the Dutch governed Priangan through a very indirect rule. Taxation and coffee cultivation for the government were largely the responsibility of the local regents. Tax-cultivation was organized around the individual household. By contrast, the densely populated Javanese plains were easy to govern. The indigenous nobility and later the Dutch were able to control the people without much difficulty. The Javanese plains were opened up to wet-rice cultivation as early as the 5th century; by the 1870s thousands of Dutch officials supervised forced cultivation of sugar-cane on communal fields.

Considering the remoteness and low population density of many parts of Priangan it is understandable that a majority of Priangan's peasants remained swidden cultivators up to the early 19th century. Still at the beginning of the 20th century, pockets could be found were swidden cultivation was practiced. As this agricultural method did not allow for a dense population, settlements were small, dispersed and rarely integrated into larger corporate types of village administrations.

Eventually, fields were made permanent and an irrigation system introduced.[3] Although starting in the late 17th century, the real boom of sawah construction (irrigated ricefields) began much later. In the five year period of 1862 - 1867 alone, about 57 000 ha of sawah is said to have been reclaimed in Priangan (Svensson 1987: 22).

When swidden holdings were turned into irrigated rice fields and the population concomitantly grew, permanent settlements were built around the original swidden cultivators.[4] A household could consist of only

---

[3] It is difficult to ascertain under what conditions the shift to wet-rice agriculture took place in Priangan. In a Malthusian argument, population growth is seen as the main reason for the transition. But swidden societies are usually regarded as balanced in terms of population/production ratio. Another thesis proposed is that a strategy of local regents was to expand the areas of sawah cultivation in order to extend their control over larger sections of the population (Vickers 1987:162). This theory is supported by the fact that it was possible for Priangan villagers to get temporary tax-reduction to construct irrigation systems (Svensson 1987:22).

[4] This natural and territorial unit of settlement will be referred to as neighbourhood or lembur below. The administrative unit that consisted of several neighbourhoods, will be labelled village or kalurahan.

one landholding family, but often kinsmen and neighbours joined and formed an "extended family" - the cacah.[5] Several related cacahs made up one lembur. These natural units of settlement were socially separated entities, often located several hundreds meters apart. Strings of ricefields separated the settlements, and a peasant's land was often located close to his home.

Territorial and administrative settlements

The larger, administrative "village" - kalurahan - was a bureaucratic construction, and probably had not existed until native regents and Dutch officials required a village-level administrative unit for taxation purposes. Kalurahans consisted often of only a few neighbourhoods. In the 19th century, according to some sources (de Klein 1931:49), a settlement of 10 households was a large village.

The kalurahan did not constitute an independent social, judicial and administrative unit with its own rights and duties until the 1870s. Sundanese society has thus no tradition of a corporate and communal village community as in the plains of east and central Java.[6] Cultural communal events, such as the Javanese ritual cleaning of the village or voluntary village work, have never been reported to exist among the Sundanese. Still

---

[5] Confusion exists around this category; it is not certain whether it is an able-bodied man, a household, or even a unit taxation that could have been larger than one household.

[6] Irrigation presupposes a tight administrative control, and it has been described (van Setten van der Meer 1979) how central and east Javanese village bureaucracies were moulded out of the need for irrigation control.

today, joint village activities are limited to formal and bureaucratic events (celebration of independence, headman election, village work). There is not, and has never been reported, a close association with village founders, ancestors, guardian shrines or communal graveyards. The social network and belonging was related to the neighbourhood, the lembur. Rural society tended to be atomistic and decentralized, focusing on the immediate family rather than larger kin-groups. If any settlement unit was autonomous in Sundanese society in the 1870s it was not the kalurahan but the lembur.

Land has never been communally regulated among the Sundanese. It is individually held with private hereditary rights of disposal. The small lots controlled by the kalurahan were usually operated by the nobility or village head to provide part of their income. In general these lots were not perceived as collective land, as the right of disposal of these plots was related to a political position. Land has always been an individual concern, whether profitable or burdensome (obligations attached to land could be very heavy).

The village population was not made up of an undifferentiated body of self-sufficient peasants. Already in early 19th century, the rural inhabitants were stratified and ranked primarily according to landownership (de Haan 1910/12 vol IV:339ff, de Klein 1931:42ff, Van Vollenhoven 1931:706ff, Alisjabana 1954:50ff, Breman 1983:11). The bumi were the landholding peasants, i.e. the owners of both ricefields and house compound. They were often descendants of the original settlers of the lembur, and were considered "full" or "nuclear" villagers. A manumpang was a landless but yet independent households head, owning a house but not land. He was as a rule an agricultural labourer, working on the land of a bumi. A third category of villagers were those totally dependent upon another household, i.e. they did not even own a separate house. These were called _bujang_ or _buniaga_ and were normally a newlywed couple or newcomers to the district. One of the few micro-level studies of a 19th century Priangan village (Kinder de Camareque 1861) reveals that of 61 households, only 17 were landholding _bumis_, while the rest, i.e. 44 households, were _manumpangs_. Of the village's 73 bouws (52 ha), 42 were individually held- 16 bouw by the local nobility, 22 bouw by the _bumis_ and 4 bouw by the _manumpangs_. 31 bouw were held by the village, for the use by local _priyayi_ and village officials. Land distribution was already at this date highly unequal, with almost 2/3 of the population in this particular _kalurahan_ not controlling any land. Although only limited information on landownership in this period is available, it is safe to assume that land inequalities were more pronounced in Priangan than in central and east Java.[7]

Thus, the village administrative head - _lurah_ - did not rule a tightly knit homogeneous corporate body. The lack of communal land, as well as collective obligations and duties, meant that the _lurah_ did not exercise a direct authority over everyday matters. The absence of communal land put the Sundanese village head in a different position compared to his Javanese counterpart (van Dijk 1981:380). The corporate village - _kalurahan_ - was merely an agglomeration of individuals under the formal jurisdiction of a _lurah_. The role and rule of the _lurah_ was until the 1870s largely confined to the formal execution of the regent's rule, while the council of nuclear villagers had the popular support of the inhabitants(de Klein 1931:79). Each neighbourhood had its own informal and "decentralized" council of landholding peasants, elders, and religious leaders, who exercised the authority over everyday matters. These were the

---

[7] In 1905, 46% of Java's large landowners lived in Priangan (Svensson 1980:28).

people common villagers regarded as community leaders. Van Vollenhoven (1931:709) writes that "It seems that a single village council for the whole village community cannot be found in Priangan, but as many such councils as there are neighbourhoods". As the authority of the kalurahan officials were limited to pure administrative concerns, the social and cultural space for individuals and households to act independently in other spheres was equally extended.

The leadership of the Priangan lurah was, in short, more authoritarian than communal. It was legal rather than traditional and certainly not charismatic. This is illustrated by a Dutch official in Cianjur who in 1890 reported (quoted in de Klein 1931: 79) that the population by preference chose the most lazy and stupid person to become lurah. In some areas it was still in the early 20th century difficult for the Dutch to find acceptable candidates. It seems as if it was in the interest of the ordinary villagers to be under as little administration as possible. With an incompetent lurah, the real power would remain in the hands of the nuclear villagers' council. No lurah elections took place in Priangan until the 1870s, and then only by decree of the Dutch.

The isolation of the lurah from villagers indicates that the administrative rule of the Sundanese elite almost by nature was more bureaucratic and authoritative; the appointed officials could to a lesser extent than in the plains of central and east Java draw on popular support. Their authority did not, like among the Javanese, rest on the control of communal land, command of important symbolic resources (such as ritual knowledge), and a monopoly on positions as "village elder". The lurah of Priangan was, quite simply, neither in a position nor accustomed to make independent decisions. He was merely the administrative official residing over a number of largely autonomous neighbourhoods, each with its own popular leader. Although there is little information on the process of electing lurahs, it seems that they often were directly appointed by the local regents as their village-level representatives. Consequently, the Sundanese lurah, unable to draw on popular support from the loosely organized kalurahan, was oriented upwards to the supra-village offices from which his authority emerged.

The legal position of the lurah in Priangan, based on contacts with higher administrative offices, gave him the right to collect taxes in money and kind as well as to extract compulsory services from villagers. At least until the 1870s, and in many places up to the early 20th century, their salary consisted solely of these various taxes (Alisjabana 1954:viii). Taxation and forced labour were levied on common villagers. In the late 19th century, most Priangan villagers - rich and poor - were liable for both pancen- and heerendienst-services. Pancen was corvee-labour on the land of the lurah. Heerendienst was the obligation to work for public service to the benefit of the regent. The village head received, furthermore, a part of the regent's land-tax, cukai[8] (de Klein 1931:80). It has been said that hereby the lurah together with other important village officials came to constitute an "exploitative rural class" (Svensson 1980:24), with a disproportionate part of their incomes deriving from direct taxation of fellow villagers.[9]

---

[8] Cukai was an appanage, first in kind and later convertible to cash, levied on individual households, according to their status. The cukai was the extraction of 1/10 to 1/20 of a landowning peasant's rice-harvest. 2/3 of the tax was delivered to the regent, while 1/3 was kept by the local and religious officials.

[9] In 1926, 53% of the Priangan lurah's average income derived from direct taxation, compared with 22% in the district of Cirebon and 18% in Madiun. The income from office land was only 6% of the total lurah-earnings in Priangan, compared with 47% in Cirebon and 54% in

This exploitation also removed him from the affairs of "common villagers". His decisions were not "communal" and not necessarily approved of by his fellow villagers. To carry out the government's instruction would therefore necessitate a certain amount of coercion or even use of force (e.g. de Haan 1910: vol III:376-377).

Islamic influences

Communal support and the "popular" authority of the lurah was limited. This is certainly one of the reasons for the prominent position of religious leaders in Priangan. At least since the late 17th century, Islamic teachers-ulama - have held a central position in rural Sundanese communities. Until 1870, the ulama was responsible for collecting the regent's tax, cukai, as well as taxes prescribed by the Koran. He received parts hereof as salary. It seems that, until the 1870s, the ulama was part of the "exploitative rural class".

However, the ulamas were also spiritual leaders and as such influential in matters of everyday concern. Firstly, they were reported to have been in charge of the regulation of irrigation and agriculture (de Klein 1931:84). Secondly, they managed the spiritual needs of the community. Life-cycle rituals, agricultural ceremonies, spiritual healing, and religious teaching are all profound parts of Sundanese villagers' everyday lives. These are also the traditional realms of religious authority.

Since the early 18th century a close connection exists between religious and material matters in Priangan. In the 19th century Priangan, the ulamas were responsible for collecting taxes as well as supervising agriculture. When this right formally ceased in 1870, Islamic rejuvena-

---

Madiun (Svensson 1980:25).

tion was underway. The main object of the Islamic revivalist movement was to cleanse Islam from pre-Islamic practices, i.e. beliefs based on traditional rules rather than Islamic law. At the beginning, the movement primarily affected educated and wealthy villagers, those who could read Arabic and were in a position to make the pilgrimage. In the early 20th century, many wealthier families were reformed religious officials who parted with the pre-Islamic practices. The leaders of the different rising religious movements in Priangan were in general influential villagers having made their pilgrimage.

It is no coincidence that the Islamic movement had a very strong following among the Sundanese. The ulama, stripped of their rights to tax the population, sought alternative sources of authority and income. One way was to strengthen their spiritual role, a strategy well in line with the religious revivalism. The ulama broke their bonds with the "tradition-bound" regents, and in many areas became leaders for protest and revivalist movements. This was often combined with strategies aimed at securing an economic position. The more commercially oriented religious groups were up front in this process. The prominent spiritual and economic position of the ulamas made them more prosperous than in other parts of Java (de Klein 1931:106). And their prosperity seems to have increased during the 19th century. It has been said that they eventually became a class of wealthy landlords (Ensering 1987:271). The existence of individual ownership of land made it possible for them to acquire impressive landholdings. Apart from being teachers and officials, the ulamas were often also farmers and traders. Islamic leaders acted thus as catalysts for the sharp increase in commercial activities that resulted from the deregulations of the 1870s.

Accumulation of capital, commercial activity and a corresponding ethos of frugality and thrift stood outside the

traditional, Javanese-oriented, collectivistic cultural
pattern. Being an individually-based religion, in contrast
to old Javanese syncretic apprehensions, Islam therefore
became the prime system of values for many within these
new progressive groups (Svensson 1980:44).

Indirect rule and decentralized nobility

Sundanese people have never identified themselves with a
well-organized state or kingdom making its authority and
protection felt by all surrounding vassals and subordinates. There has never been a strong Sundanese government. In the 15th and 16th century, during the height of
the Sundanese kingdom Pajajaran, domination could not be
said to have been more than symbolic. Due to the remoteness of most parts of Priangan, the Pajajaran ruler
controlled only the nearest districts. The autonomy of
small "vassal-states" was great. Networks of lemburs were
grouped together under the supreme guidance of an "independent regional chief" (Sutherland 1975:63) or "war-
lord" (Wilcox Palmer 1959:43). Each regency was autonomous, headed by a regent - dalem - and a body of functionaries. After the fall of Pajajaran in the early 16th
century, and the following domination first by the
Javanese and later the Dutch, this "decentralization" of
power was further manifested. The idea of a Mighty Centre,
so pronounced in the conception of Javanese political
culture, seems never to have been prominent among the
Sundanese.

A consistently realized indirect colonial rule
prevailed in Priangan until 1870. Prior to that, virtually
no foreign or Dutch administrators permanently resided in
the Priangan Highlands. In 1851, there were only 217
Europeans and 281 Chinese settled in the area - out of a
total of 17 000 Europeans and 125 000 Chinese in the
whole of Java (van Doorn and Hendrix 1982:13). The government of the area was left to the regional dalems - regents

47

- who ruled through a rather vast body of bureaucrats. A definite majority of these bureaucrats was of _priyayi_ origin.[10] The _dalem_ directed his subordinates, and was responsible for the forced delivery of cash crops and collection of colonial taxes. To his position as regent was also attached the right to extract _cukai_ (indigenous tributes) and forced labour services. The absence of Dutch officials gave the Sundanese nobility almost unrestricted room of maneuvering. In other parts of Java the independence of the indigenous elite was countered by the presence of the Dutch administrative corps, whereas in Priangan the regent, through the native bureaucratic elite, had sole authority to administer the rural population.

This system of government, called Preangerstelsel (Priangan System) by the Dutch, lasted until 1870. The main source of income was forced cultivation of coffee, administered by native officials who were responsible for the extraction of taxes and crops. All landholding peasants - _bumis_ - were obliged to cultivate a specific number of coffee plants.[11] Coffee was cultivated on

---

[10] The ruling elite constitutes what has been called nobility or aristocracy - _priyayi_ or _menak_, while their subjects, the dominated are the _wong cilik_ or _jelma leutik_, the "small people". This is a most important distinction for any study of leadership and power on Java. The _priyayi_ is a hereditary nobility having titles and names that distinguish themselves from common villagers. The _wong cilik_, on the other hand, are ordinary people, the "commoners" that constitute the subjects of the _priyayi_'s rule. In the eyes of the _priyayi_ they consist of an uneducated mass of poor rural or urban dwellers.

[11] In the 18th century only _bumis_ were liable for compulsory labour services. In 1785, in an attempt to increase coffee revenues, a law was passed by the Dutch, making both _bumi_ and _manumpangs_ responsible for coffee cultivation. Although the _manumpang_ did not control land, he had to participate in the cultivation of the _bumi_'s

unused fields often located hours away from the settlement. The land was cleared and planted collectively - by
bumis and manumpangs - but it was not a communal arrangement; each farmer owned his crop individually. He har-
vested and transported the ripe coffee-beans with the
help of his own family and neighbours (Kinder de Camareque 1861:286).

Individual households were taxed according to their
landholdings and property. The more land a peasant held,
the more services he had to render. The burden of taxation
was in general very heavy. The services laid on the
village population, both by the Dutch and the local
regents and village officials left little time for
peasants to grow rice, a crop necessary for their own
physical survival. In the 18th and 19th centuries, famines
were reported in many areas in Priangan (de Haan 1910/12
vol IV: § 2130). There are many cases of people who could
not endure the hardships. In the reports from colonial
officials these are often referred to as "overloopers" or
"wegloopers" (tramps). Such a person could:

be picked up and sent back to the regent or the headman
they belonged to, and the regent or headman was fined 10
rijksdaalder every time he did not fulfill his responsibilities (de Klein 1931:44).

In the early 19th century the high number of "wegloopers"
made it necessary for the Dutch to take actions. Accordingly, migrants (most of whom had fled from burdensome
taxation) were often relieved of their colonial duties
during their first and second year, in order to assure
that they would not run away again (de Haan vol IV:420).

In the areas of central and east Java, where sugar
cane was grown on communal fields in rotation with rice,
the village as a corporate body was responsible for

---

fields.

cultivation and delivery of the crop. This pushed for collective activities and strengthened communal bonds of both horizontal and vertical kinds. Although social stratification was not completely equalized, this certainly increased cooperation and enforced notions of communal solidarity. _Preangerstelsel_, quite on the contrary, accentuated the importance of the household as the unit of production. Individual taxation reinforced the autonomy of households and neighbourhoods, and prevented the development of communal structures. The _Preangerstelsel_ also resulted in an increased social stratification. People were differentiated according to landownership, the Islamic elite held a strong position, and the _lurah_ and his functionaries were separated from the peasants by the regents. Integrated into the supra-village bureaucratic structure, the latter were exempted from compulsory services and relieved of economic burdens. The ambition of the village bureaucracy to join forces with supra-village power holders rather than with villagers was reinforced (Tjondronegoro 1984:71).

Conclusion

In this short essay it has been shown that in the 19th century the relative authority and domination of the nobility was greater in Priangan than in east and central Java. The native elite could capitalize on the common villagers both through tributes and corvée labour. These exactions were seen by a regent as his "natural rights" over his subjects. The Sundanese villagers have, however, never subscribed to the idea of unquestionable subordination. The regent's ability to draw on an understanding of his righteous rule was limited. The way the nobility was conceptualized by villagers can be illustrated by a widespread belief that one's foremost duty is to respect:

1 - One's parents, sometime one's elder brother, since he takes the place of the father at his death; 2 - One's parents-in-law; 3 - One's teacher; 4 - One's ruler (Snouk Hurgronje: Verspreide Geschriften vol IV,p 117, cited in Alisjabana 1954).

It is no coincidence that a common villager owed more esteem and loyalty to his family and local religious teacher than to the ruler, who for most villagers was a distant and indistinct figure. The nobility was culturally and socially separated from peasant life. Their prime interests did not lie with the subjects. The rural bureaucratic elite - village heads and petty officials - did not have a prominent social position. The nobility and lurah were regarded as authoritarian figures, even exploitative ones. Accordingly, a cultural distance was kept. The common villagers were neither emotionally attached to the nobility as worldly upholders of a god-given state nor bound by eternal subordination. Anderson's (op. cit.) idea of a Lifegiving Centre - the regent and his officials - from which all power flowed and towards which all people must orient themselves, cannot really be found among the Sundanese. The notion of a political culture that, although formally hierarchical, emphasizes patriarchy and solidarity leads to a search for emotional-ly charged patron-client relationships between the powerful (the nobility) and the commoners. In the context of Priangan, this notion has been elaborated by Jackson (1980), a political scientist who presents a picture of a Sundanese political culture based on traditional authori-ty. The relationship between elite and commoners is here regarded as harmonious and reciprocal, and has nothing to do with the actual exercise of power. Peasants accept the authority of their patrons without questions. No force or coercion is needed.

This idea of a "natural and rightful" subordination of commoners stands in glaring contrast to 19th century

Priangan. Jackson's problem is that he has accepted the false and a-historical conception of motionless, tradition-bound peasant communities. As we have seen, insofar as the ruling regent in Priangan had any relationship with the self-regulating communities at all, it was to extract tributes and perhaps exercise a weakly specified symbolic sovereignty. Neither "immemorial subordination" nor the idea of a single ruling centre from which power flows were strongly pronounced in Priangan.

The two conceptual properties of the Sundanese political administration outlined above - the cultural and social separation of nobility from village life, and their decentralized but yet authoritarian rule - are in many ways contrary to what constitutes a patrimonial political culture. Throughout history, the position of Priangan commoners versus nobility has been one of cultural detachment and even active resistance. In the early 20th century a widespread discontent among the peasantry can be found, channeled towards colonial rulers but above all towards the omnipotent regents and their bureaucracies (van Dijk 1981:371). Numerous movements and "affairs" in the late 19th and early 20th century Priangan (Svensson 1980) unveil an unstable relationship between nobility and peasantry.

Some authors (e.g. Ali 1986:155) argue that the conflict between nobility and peasants reinforces the cultural notion of Power, as both parties articulate the conflict in terms of their shared value-system. I argue instead that the political movements in Priangan must be understood in terms of their political messages. In early 20th century, various movements and parties articulated a clear opposition against the traditional nobility. The Communist party and its local branches focused their attention on the oppression and exploitation carried out by the nobles and the village bureaucratic elite. Like-

52

wise, the Islamic organizations opposed the non-Islamic elements of the traditional worldview of the nobilities. The administrative structure that these organizations were resisting was not part of a "Communalistic" or "Solidarity" discourse. On the contrary, they opposed the decentralized but yet exploitative nature of authority in West Java. Individual landownership, indirect colonial rule, the oppressive nature of priyayi rule, the detachment of the lurah, and strong Islamic movements, were all properties of a cultural development responsible for the creation of a local political structure opposed to a patrimonial concept of power.

BIBLIOGRAPHY

Ali, F: Refleksi Paham "Kekuasan Jawa" dalam Indonesia Modern (Reflections on "Javanese Power" in Modern Indonesia) (Jakarta: PT Gramedia, 1986).

Alisjabana, S: A Preliminary Study of Class Structure among the Sundanese in the Priangan (MA Thesis at Cornell University, Ithaca, 1954).

Anderson, B.R.O'G: "The Idea of Power in Javanese Culture"; in Holt, C. (ed.): Culture and Politics in Indonesia (Ithaca: Cornell University Press, 1972).

Breman, J: Control of Land and Labour in Colonial Java (Leiden: Foris Publication, KITLV, 1983).

van Doorn, J. and W.Hendrix: The Emergence of a Dependent Economy. Consequences of the Opening up of West-Priangan, Java (Rotterdam: CASP Publication no 9, Erasmus University, 1983).

Dijk, C. van: Rebellion under the Banner of Islam (The Hague: Martinus Nijhoof, 1981).

Elson, R.E: Javanese Peasants and the Colonial Sugar Industry: Impact and Change in an East Java Residence 1830-1940 (Singapore: Oxford University Press, 1984).

Ensering, E: "De Traditionele en Hedendaagse Rol van Lokale en Religieuze Leiders in de Preanger, West Java", Bijdragen tot de Taal-, Land, en Volkenkunde, vol. 143, 2-3, 1987.

Haan, F. de: Priangan: De Preanger-Regentschappen onder het Nederlandsch Bestuur tot 1811, four volumes (Batavia, 1910/1912).

Jackson, K: Traditional Authority, Islam and Rebellion. A Study of Indonesian Political Behaviour (Berkeley: University of California Press, 1980).

Jackson, K: **Urbanization and the Rise of Patron-Client Relations: The Changing Quality of Interpersonal Communications in the Neighbourhoods of Bandung and the Villages of West Java** (Cambridge, Mass.: Center for International Studies, MIT, 1974).

Keeler, W: "Villagers and the Exemplary Center in Java", **Indonesia,** no 39 (April 1985).

Kinder de Camareque, A.W: "Bijdragen tot de Kennis der Volksinstellingen in de Oostelijke Soenda-Landen", **Tijdschrift Bataviaasch Genootschap,** no 10 (1861).

King, D: "Indonesia's New Order as a Bureaucratic Polity, a Neopatrimonial Regime or a Bureaucratic Authoritarian Regime: What difference does it make?"; in B. Anderson and A. Kahin: **Interpreting Indonesian Politics: Thirteen Contributions to the Debate** (Cornell Modern Indonesia Project, Interim Report Series no. 62) (Ithaca: 1982).

Klein, J.W. de: **Het Preangerstelsel en zijn Nawerking** (Leiden, 1931).

Koentjaraningrat: **Javanese Culture** (Singapore: Oxford University Press, 1984).

Moertono, S: **State and Statecraft in Old Java: A Study of the Later Mataram Period 16th to 19th Centuries** (Cornell Modern Indonesia Project) (Ithaca, 1968).

Mudjanto, G: **The Concept of Power in Javanese Culture** (Yogyakarta: Gadjah Mada University Press, 1986).

Quarles van Ufford, P: "Contradictions in the Study of Legitimate Authority in Indonesia", **Bijdragen tot de Taal-, Land- en Volkenkunde,** vol 143, 1, 1987.

Reeve, D: **Golkar of Indonesia. An Alternative to the Party System** (Singapore: Oxford University Press, 1985).

Robison, R: "Culture, Politics and Economy in the Political History of the New Order", **Indonesia**, no. 31, April 1981.

Setten van der Meer, N.C van: **Sawah Cultivation in Ancient Java: Aspects of Development during the Indo-Javanese period, 5th to 15th century** (Oriental Monograph Series no 22) (Canberra: Australia University Press, 1979).

Slamet, I: **Cultural Strategies for Survival: The Plight of the Javanese** (Rotterdam: CASP, Erasmus Uni.1985).

Suparlan, P: "Democracy in Rural Java", **Prisma**, March, 1977.

Sutherland, H: "The Priyayi", **Indonesia**, no 19, April, 1975.

Svensson, Th: **Peasants and Politics in Early Twentieth-Century West Java** (Unpublished Manuscript, Department of History, Gothenburg, 1980).

Svensson, Th: **Javanese Village Society in Historical-Anthropological Perspective** (Paper presented at the 20th Nordic Historical Meeting, Reykavik, August 10-14, 1987).

Tjondronegoro, S.M.P: **Social Organization and Planned Development in Rural Java** (Singapore: Oxford University Press, 1984).

Vollenhoven, C. van: **Het Adatrecht van Nederlandsch Indie** (Leiden: Van Brill, 1931).

Vickers, A: "History and Social Structure in Ancient Java", **Review of Indonesian and Malaysian Affairs** (1987).

Wilcox Palmer, A: "The Sundanese Village", in G.W. Skinner (ed.): **Local, Ethnic and National Loyalties in Village Indonesia** (Yale University, 1959).

"SAFE IS AMBIGUOUS". IDENTITY MANAGEMENT AND CONDITIONS OF ISLAMIZATION IN A CENTRAL JAVANESE VILLAGE

Eldar Bråten
University of Bergen

1. INTRODUCTION

This paper is to deal with how symbolic statements concerning identity are being produced by ordinary people in religious life. Such statements are supposed to have implications for the working of parts of local political life, and these possible inter-dependencies between religion and politics will be discussed in relation to strategies of Islamization pursued by religious leaders.

I attempt to relate my argument to the comprehensive discussion following Clifford Geertz' many books on Javanese society and culture. In the mid 1950s Geertz carried out an extensive fieldwork in order to arrive at a detailed description of Islamic religious life on the island. One of his works, the encyclopedic The Religion of Java, (Geertz 1960), has in one way or another been the starting point of most subsequent discussions on religious, anthropological and political themes in studies on Javanese life.

According to Geertz there is a particular inter-linking between religious outlook, political commitment and occupational status that constitutes the main principle for social organization on Java. There are, according to him, three distinct cultural streams, (aliran in Javanese), aligning people vertically across class boundaries. This model accounts among other things for the various political parties that emerged prior to the first national election in 1955. Political commitment is, in this view, based more on common religious outlook and lifestyle than on common material interests. This "subculture approach" to the structure of Javanese politics has met criticism from various scholars. (For a succinct summary of this discussion, see Robert W. Hefner 1987).

I will relate to the debate about Geertz' views here, although from a somewhat different perspective. Whereas Geertz himself and most of his critics mainly have discussed the interlinking of religion and politics at the macro level, as the co-variation of religiously and politically significant elements, I will rather try to analyze religion and politics as they seem to be interrelated and interdependent in the operation of daily village life, that is on the micro level of social interaction rather than on the level of overall social form. If it is true, as Geertz so aptly describes, that there is an immense load of political statements couched in peoples' religious praxis, then a study of the management of religious identity in everyday life must be crucial to our investigation into the character and operation of at least some aspects of local political life. Geertz himself explores a case of such religio-political symbol management in his article on a Javanese funeral (Geertz 1959).

I will try to document how ordinary villagers, who in many ways are dependents of two different leadership groups in the village, try to handle symbolic expressions in the religious field thereby potentially conveying political statements. Through such identity management they do more than merely communicate to each other and to the leaders who they are and who they support. I hold that they in fact produce some of the very constraints on the instrumental political games that their administrative and religious leaders play. I would specifically argue that attempts at political mobilization depend on the leaders' capability of predicting possible support among ordinary people, and it is my hypothesis that such anticipation of commitment may prove difficult in the present day Javanese context. This point will be discussed in relation to the religious leaders and their Islamization strategies.

2. JAVANESE SUB-TRADITIONS

The alirans, as outlined by Geertz, are all streams within Javanese Islam. Regarding religious beliefs the **abangans** are animistic and polytheistic Muslims, the **priyayi** Hindu-inspired Islamic mystics, and the **santris** are more genuinely Islamic. In their religious practices they differ in that the abangans are connected to the **slametan** rituals, the priyayis to meditation, fasting and minor asceticism, and the santris to Islamic rituals and characteristically to the five daily prayers, the communal Friday prayer, and the Holy Fast.

The abangans are - or were - villagers and peasants who rallied behind the Communist Party (PKI) just prior to the 1955 national election. The priyayis "proper" were descendants from the old Javanese aristocracy, but as the times changed, the term widened and denoted in the 1950s people occupying all types of administrative positions, i.e. the bureaucrats who mostly lived in towns and cities. Their political ideology was a national one, and their party was mainly the National Party (PNI). The santris were traders, they were struggling for a Muslim state and joined various Islamic parties, the largest of which were NU (**Nahdatul Ulama**) and **Masjumi**.

Aside from these religiously based ideological differences that divided the Javanese cultural landscape into three alirans, there was, according to Geertz, another distinction running through all of them, thereby creating a scheme of six categories. This distinction is the one between **kolot** ("old-fashioned") and **moderen** ("modern"). This split was, following Geertz, profound among the santris, who were clearly divided into a "traditional" and a "modern" faction, but it was also traceable among the priyayis and the abangans.

In The religion of Java Geertz is primarily interested in how the various alirans can be delineated, and he arrives at his distinctions through exploring the local classificatory scheme with which people grouped themselves primarily on the basis of religious beliefs and practices. The social categories thus labeled appeared to be systematically connected to various types of occupations and political groupings, and Geertz tries to convince his readers that this socio-cultural pattern exists through an impressive mass of informant statements, cases and anecdotes. This documentation does not primarily serve analytical purposes, they are meant not to explain but to exemplify a given socio-cultural form. Geertz' study is thus rather phenomenological, and his ambitions are merely to present an "ethnographic report" (Geertz 1960, p.7). Due to such an approach information on the political context of religious life tends to enter the discussion only as it serves the purpose of delineating the streams. The outcome of Geertz' approach is a new and detailed classification of social categories on Java, and his aim, "..to show how much variation in ritual, contrast in belief, and conflict in values [that] lie concealed behind the simple statement that Java is more than 90 per cent Moslem.." is fulfilled. (Geertz 1960, p.7)

My approach is, on the contrary, to pursue some hypotheses about how the fields of religion and politics can be said to interact in the unfolding of local daily life, how for instance symbolic statements can be made in religious praxis in order to comment upon and to constrain local political games. My focus is on the operation of local life rather than on the classification of emerging types of identity, cultural systems and organizational patterns; I am more concerned with the social processes that generate a form than the social form itself.

3. THE VILLAGE

The village under study is situated close to the town of Salatiga in the highland area of North Central Java, and it belongs to the administrative district (**kebupaten**) of Semarang. Its population is slightly more than 4000 people, and it has an impressive population density of more than 1400 persons/km^2. Most of the farm land, which is spread out around a centrally situated housing compound, is **sawah** (wet-rice), but as the village was connected to Salatiga with a road in 1974, income from all sorts of activities in the town of Salatiga and the city of Semarang constitutes an increasingly important part of most household economies.

The area around Salatiga can be regarded as border area in several senses. First of all it was historically and politically on the border between indigenous influence from the court centres in Solo and Yogyakarta to the south and the Dutch influence and power to the north prior to the Java war (1825-1830). Secondly, it is situated at the outskirts of the early Islamic core area in and around the cities on the north coast. Following professor Koentjaraningrat's division of Java into several cultural areas, one can say that Salatiga and its surroundings are on the fringes of the Pasisir area. (Koentjaraningrat 1985, p. 25-29). Islam is supposed to be purer to the north and more syncretistic to the south. Third, Salatiga and some of its nearby villages have a Christian population that far exceeds the average for Java, and there are several active and large churches and missionaries operating in the villages. It is thus also a Christian outpost in Islamic territory, or vice versa from the Islamic activists' point of view. This fact is often referred to by the Muslims in the area.

My fieldwork village is definitely a "frontier village" in the religious sense mentioned above. Its whole daily life is very much a continuous display of Islamic signs, and people, at least the religious leaders, regard the village as "pure" (**suci**) compared to the surrounding areas. They talk consciously about the spreading of Islam and couch their activities in the term **perjuangan** (fight, struggle). For people outside the village, except for its immediate neighbors who are also very much involved in the same struggle, this Islamic image appears rather extreme, and outsiders often talk about these villagers as **fanatic** and **terlalu** (an unspecified "too much"). If we invoke Geertz' distinctions at the level of the village unit, one is tempted to term it a santri village.

It should be mentioned that the village stands out as a frontier post also in another sense. It is one of the most modern villages in the area, and it seems to be regarded as such both by the villagers themselves and outsiders. The very positive term **maju** (advanced) is often used about it.

Given this position of the village at several borders and frontiers at once, nothing is more natural than naming it **Batasan**, "border-country".

4. RELIGIOUS IDENTITIES

4.1 The slametan

According to Geertz the central ritual for the abangans is the slametan, a short, seemingly insignificant communal meal attended by all male household heads in a neighbourhood. It consists of a small introductory speech in formal Javanese stating the reason for arranging the

slametan, then a recitation part normally conducted by an
Islamic teacher or official, and finally a brief meal
where only symbolic amounts of the food served are eaten
in the presence of the others and the rest is brought
home. The slametans occur partly at specific points of
time determined by an old Javanese time system, such as
on several specific days after a person's death, thereby
constituting a predictable ritual sequence clustering
around major life crises, but slametans occur also as a
response to more mundane changes in status, such as on
the occasion of moving into a new house, departing for a
long journey and so on.

Apart from being connected to an old Javanese and
not to an Islamic calendar, the slametans appeared to be
deviant from a purer interpretation of Islam also in that
they were regarded as ways of accommodating the spirit
world. During slametans offerings were put out to please
disturbing spirits, and following abangan interpretations,
the spirits were taking part in the communal meal. The
idea is that "..the incense and the aroma of the food at
the slametan are considered as food for the spirits in
order to pacify them so they will not disturb the living."
In one of Geertz' informants' words: "That is why the
food and not the prayer is the heart of the slametan."
(Geertz 1960 p.14-15)

The form of the slametan in Batasan anno 1985 is
somewhat different from how it appeared in Modjokuto on
East Java where Geertz did his fieldwork in the mid
1950s. Such differences cannot easily be utilized as
cases of ritual and possible cultural change, as ritual
life on Java can be supposed to vary from place to place.
To understand long term processes of change one needs
first of all extensive data on local developments. This
is only to a certain extent possible with my material on
Batasan. From a synchronic point of view, I will in what
follows try to describe the symbolic and social processes

whereby ritual forms and changes in ritual forms are generated. I will present a Batasan slametan in some length, and rather than taking for granted that the slametan is an identifier of "abanganness", I will discuss how <u>various </u>categories and groups of people seem to utilize these ritual occasions to make religious, political and other statements.

One night, about the time it was suspected, my landlady started having labor pains and was rushed to the clinic in Salatiga on the back of a motorbike. Less than one hour later she gave birth to a boy, their third, and last, since she and her husband had decided to join the family planning program. This being their last child, the whole occasion was special, and they wanted to give a really big **resepsi** (reception) this time. The husband works as a driver and had almost doubled his work hours for two months to earn as much as possible before this birth. In addition to the money he borrowed, he had saved a lot by the time the child came, and the money was put into new clothes for the two sons, a brand new luxurious bed, a radio, a large TV (in addition to the small one they already had) and lots of new kitchen utensils. Already the following evening about 50 household heads had gathered in the front room which was emptied of furniture and where bamboo mats were spread on the floor. There was a kind of slametan in the evening with lots of chanting followed by a rice meal and after that coffee and snacks. Nobody brought food home, however. The next evening about 50 new household heads appeared, but I recognized a few of them from the day before. This time there was no chanting, but lots of food, and we sat in a circle like the day before, eating and drinking. The real big party came on the third day, however, when all the household heads from the days before and a few new men appeared. Altogether more than one hundred household heads were present, more than 10% of all the households in Batasan. Among them were some prominent **kyais** (Islamic leaders) and the village secretary. The **lurah** (village chief) himself was busy arranging a **wayang kulit** performance (a shadow play) at his place. The host proudly showed me the list of invited guests. Only five of them couldn't come, he said, as they had some other urgent business to do.

In the afternoon, just a few hours before the party was to begin, my landlord brought me a note with the suggested name of the boy written on it. He wanted me to type it out 120 times on my typewriter. These pieces of paper were to be put in the baskets of food that the guests would bring home. The name was Javanese and contained the usual part Tri, indicating that the boy was the third child. The previous days there had been a big discussion about the boy's proper name. The newborn's eldest brother (10 years old) thought it would be proper to name him after the month in which he was born (according to the modern calendar), and his father agreed. Together they came up with a Javanese name, the month (August) and Tri being part of it. A young brother of the newborn's mother, however, suggested something more modern; maybe a name derived from Jimmy Hendrix or Michael Jackson, like Jimmy, Henry, Jack or something like that. (Others suggested the anthropologist's name, but it did not find common support..)

I started to write out the Javanese name and was almost half finished when the father appeared again. He said, slightly embarrassed, that the boy's name had been changed, and the piece of paper he gave me showed that the boy's young uncle (16 years old) had won in the end. The name now contained a popstar part, Tri and another Javanese name, this one also being the choice of the mother's side of the family. They wanted me to write the name, the date and a few formal phrases in Indonesian. I asked, "What date is it today in **pasaran** (the Javanese five day week)", but they laughed and said, "Oh, you do not need that any longer. Use the date only!" I put it down once and went to Salatiga to photocopy it 120 times.

Around nine o'clock in the evening a stream of people started to flow in, all of them men, apart from a few women slipping in through the kitchen door to join the lively group who had been working since early morning to prepare the food. The men all wore **sarung** except the host himself and a few others, all of them apparently close neighbors. They formed two big circles in the front room, and when that was full, filled the wide porch and the front yard where bamboo mats had been laid out. I noticed that some people chose to sit outside, and, when people had seated themselves, it was apparent that some of the eldest and most prominent villagers were placed inside. The most respected kyai, a young devout man, had taken the innermost seat together with his much older "right hand" man. The host himself was on the fringes of the whole company outside. People seemed to enjoy themselves. The first men to arrive, a few hours before it started, had already been in the kitchen to look at the food and been invited to a first serving. And the more than hundred men, who by nine o'clock were spread around the front part of the house, chatted lively, commenting on the layout of the garden, discussing how the host had been able to get all those patterns in his wall decoration, talking about the next harvest and so on and so forth. In the emptied main room there was a big cupboard left, where a dozen solid, expensive and newly bought glasses were on display, lit up by a small lamp inside the cupboard itself. They made up a prominent part of the emptied room and much interest focused on them.

The pleasant chatting came to an end when a friend of the host held his brief opening speech stating the reason for this slametan, but revived again when he finished. The chanting which followed immediately rooted itself after a second or two and drowned out the hearty talking. That continued for about half an hour. A few young trained Muslims lead the chanting, one of them reading whole passages on his own, awaiting bursts of "Allahu akbar" and "Amen" from the audience, sometimes passing the task to his neighbor to continue, sometimes letting the audience drop in and take over the chanting. During one sequence the people were uttering the Confession with steadily increasing speed, resulting in an astonishingly perfect performance. An impressive feature of this chanting was that it was carried out without the slightest outward sign of emotional commitment, both on the parts of the leaders and the audience. Here and there someone dropped out for a moment to whisper something to neighbour, who responded smilingly, and now and then the chanting leaders sent a quick glance in the direction of the drop-outs. They didn't seem to have a fixed time or a point at which to stop chanting, and none of them seemed willing to make that decision. (During the chanting two days ago there was a small dispute between two of the leaders, an old man who after close to an hour felt that it was time to stop, and a younger man who grabbed his book and continued for a few chapters more).

After the chanting was over, the jovial humming atmosphere picked up again, and the food was soon passed through the circles of men. It was chicken, quality rice and vegetables, and it was served on plates. Everyone got a spoon. People ate rapidly, yet some did not get time to finish before the "take home food" arrived in grand bamboo baskets. They contained probably close to two kilos of rice each, and there were several types of vegetables, chicken and eggs. At once people asked permission to leave, searched out their sandals in the mess in the front yard and hurried away. Not long afterwards a few men came back, however, to continue their chatting. Coffee and snacks and lots of tobacco were served, and later on people started to play cards and dominoes, first for fun, later for fun and money. However, most people went down the road where the lurah's shadow play was in progress.

Later I talked to one of the newborn's uncles (a maternal one) about the boy's name. He smiled and said what was important, was to give a child a modern name so people wouldn't take his parents to be kolot ("old-fashioned"). What kind of names, I wondered, and he made the distinction between national names (**nama national**) and Arabic names (**nama Arab**). I realized that all those involved in the discussion about a proper name, including the young uncle who favored Jimmy Hendrix, had Arabic names and that none of them had ever suggested such a name for the newborn. The mother's side decided on an even more modern (that is Western) name than the father preferred, and the husband was teased because of this pop-name by his neighbors later.

It is obvious from this and other such occasions that the slametan and its constituent symbols carry various meaning and significance for various participants and that details of behaviour involved even can be studied as attempts at identity management.

It seems, for instance, that the parents of the newborn utilized the birth of their third child and the slametan occasions that followed to display their wealth and modernity. The whole arena, their expensive and well-kept brick house of new style architecture, the flowers in pots, their private garden surrounded by a steel fence, their living room with embroideries of natural motifs on the walls and so on, displayed modernity. The same is probably the case with the host himself who wore trousers, not the sarung, the use of my typewriter to make invitations, the use of plates and spoons instead of banana leafs, the dropping of the Javanese calendar in the invitations and not least the newborn's modern, Western name. Throughout the whole occasion, which lasted three days, they constantly used the modern term "resepsi" about the events.

No doubt the social and recreational aspects of the slametan occasion were enjoyed and even highlighted by some. The pleasant and talkative atmosphere surrounding such events indicates that this is the case, sometimes to such an extent that it may interfere with the timing of the ritual. An example of this was a second-day-after-death slametan I witnessed which was scheduled for 8 o'clock but which did not take place before 10.30, and then it became a very brief event, apparently because people seemed to enjoy themselves so much (the dead's son included) that nobody really wanted to start. That the soul of the deceased, according to some informants, was roaming around in the very room we were sitting in begging for the livings' prayer about safety in the hereafter, did not seem to bother the participants much.

As the religious leaders are in charge of recitation, they are able to decide how extensive this part should be. This may be an occasion for stating a point about commitment to Islam, especially in contrast to the restless who are waiting for food or for the gambling sessions later in the evening. It appeared to me that the young devotee's attempt to stretch out the recitation in the slametan above was exactly such a statement.

As a consequence of such symbol production during the slametan I maintain that the emerging occasion (the ritual itself included) is a highly complex entity with several facets of meaning. It is an occasion where various values can be expressed, inclinations enjoyed, and meanings sought and found. This pertains also to the more stable features of such events, such as the special food served, the chanting, the point of time at which it is held, the compulsory attendance of neighbours and so on and also to the overall meaning of the ritual itself. (For a broader discussion of these issues, see Bråten, forthcoming.)

The most conspicuous elements in the emerging ritual forms in Batasan are the Islamic ones. There are no obvious animistic elements, like incense and offerings, left, as was formerly the case in Batasan, the recitation of Arabic texts is definitely the longest single sequence in the slametan ritual, and this part is carried out not only by the leaders but by all the participants, very unlike the situation in Modjokuto in the 1950s. There is, then, no obvious reason to treat the slametan in Batasan today merely as an animistic (or "abangan") ritual. In most of its ritual aspects it is clearly Islamic (or "santri"), although in one interpretation the slametan is still regarded as a ritual device against disturbing spirits (**yang menganggu**, "those who disturb").

This difference in interpretation of symbols and rituals is reflected linguistically as well. There are several terms to denote such ritual instances, and there is very little agreement about the use of these terms. Nevertheless, the terms **slametan** derived from the word **slamet** ("safe" or "well-being"), **syukuran** ("thanksgiving") and **resepsi** (a Dutch word) are the most frequent and indicate some of the different aspects I believe are contained in the same ritual. I suggest that the slametan at least can "be read" (both by the anthropologist and by the Javanese themselves) as a) a ritual to restore or secure states of harmony and peace (slamet), among other things by pleasing disturbing spirits, b) a ceremony of gratitude to Allah, and c) a modern, secular celebration. Various categories of actors seem to have differing interpretations and inclinations, and the emerging ritual sequence cannot easily be categorized.

The slametans in Batasan have a compulsory character. There are cases where invited people do not attend, but they normally provide a good excuse, the best of which is that they have another slametan to attend. Consequently religious life in Batasan seems to be generated by people agreeing much more about the necessity of ritual life and the basic formal procedures of rituals than about the meaning of these rituals.

4.2 Ambiguity

I have indicated above that details of ritual life are open to symbolic manipulations and potential loci for statements of religious identity. Very few attempts at identity management are, however, obvious and clear-cut.

Quite contrary, Batasan religious life is full of ambiguities, and if people make statements as to their inclinations and commitments, they normally do so in very subtle ways.

For instance, when my landlord used trousers instead of sarung in the slametan above, he may have utilized the native distinction between "old-fashioned" and "modern" to state his modern values (as trousers:sarung as modern:old-fashioned) or he may have attempted to secularize the event or even symbolically oppose the religious leadership (as the sarungs, not trousers, are the appropriate clothes at religious occasions). To assume that the fact that many people choose to sit far away from the religious leaders at slametans is a symbol of lacking religious commitment seems logical as distance in physical space usually indicates strained relations. Nevertheless, as prominent persons in Batasan (but not in Modjokuto in the 50s) are accorded the innermost seats, distance in space may as well signal respect for the leaders and a down-grading of one's own social rank.

This is not only a question of methodological problems in our analysis, I believe in fact that such ambiguity often will be produced by the actors themselves in order to conceal one's actual intentions, opinions and commitments. There are still some "unorthodox" rituals left in Batasan religious life, and the symbolic statements produced in such arenas seem to be regarded as problematic both by ordinary people in Batasan and their religious leaders. One such incident occurred in the beginning of my fieldwork when there was a total lunar eclipse. Because my Indonesian was rudimentary and I was in the middle of the initial confusion, I probably did not completely understand what was going on, but here are the events I managed to record:

Nobody wanted to go to bed, and the atmosphere was extraordinary. I did not know there was going to be a lunar eclipse, but I understood that people were waiting for something. They seemed nervous, and there was lot of loud music around in the village. The moon suddenly started to disappear, and the atmosphere on the porch where we were standing, felt rather fragile. Now someone started to call people through the loudspeaker of the mosque in the adjacent kampung. At the moment when the moon disappeared totally, my landlady and a few other women in the neighborhood ran into their houses. My landlord smiled and said his wife had to take a bath so her fetus wouldn't be destroyed, but he joked a little about this, too, and said it was just old tradition. After this we went inside, and the whole thing seemed to be finished. I went to bed and thought the others did so, too. The loud music didn't cease, however, and after an hour or so I got up again to see what was going on. My landlord heard me and got up, too.

In a newly built house up the road there were lots of young men and boys. The walls of the house were in place, but the roof was not put on yet, so the whole group sat under the open sky with the lunar eclipse above their heads. When we arrived, I realized I had missed a slametan. Around 25 people had been there, I counted from the number of plates, and my landlord had in fact gone there, too, without inviting me. People greeted me and brought forward tea and tobacco. The atmosphere was very relaxed, people were listening to wayang (theater recordings) from a tape, and there were enough cassettes to last the whole night. Some young boys were sleeping under a big bamboo mat, and in an adjacent room a group of men were playing cards. The rest just listened, rather absent-minded, nobody was talking, and almost all of them smoked the strong tobacco spread all around the rooms on small plates. The story on the tape changed from heavy fighting scenes to gamelan music, long dialogues, funny clowning and back again to magic sounding gamelan music. This relaxed, untalkative performance went on until early morning, when people started to walk home. I asked my landlord what it had been all about. He didn't want to talk about it, but said finally that they were seeking **keselamatan** ("well-being"). Afterward nobody wanted to talk about the incident and pretended that the ritual bathing had never taken place.

This lunar eclipse slametan which was turned into a house initiation slametan so as to disguise the real intentions of the host, is a brilliant and typical example of the production of complexity in ritual life. What is mani-

71

fested in daily life are complex ritual forms that may be accorded meaning much at the will of the individual participant, and the possible interpretations are numerous. People were in fact invited to a house initiation ceremony, and because of the legitimacy of such a ritual, there were probably Islamic leaders present to carry it out in a proper way. What makes it likely that the other interpretation holds, namely that this in fact was a slametan arranged to protect the neighborhood from celestial forces, is that the slametan was held at one o'clock in the night and not in the evening as usual. Besides, to conduct a slametan in a roofless house just below the disappearing moon must have been a magnificent dramatization of the event.

One may note that the Muslim activists themselves tried to utilize the momentum of the situation by gathering people for an extra prayer meeting in the mosque. The ritual emerging here was probably also highly polysemic.

Aside from this production of complexity in symbolic expressions and ritual forms there are incidents where actual or personal identity is not only concealed but presented actively in a distorted or even opposite way. The next case, where a young, educated and highly respected man from one of the factions of the Islamic leadership in the village meets his much older opponent, illustrates this particular point.

Nahdatul Ulama (NU) is the dominant religious group in Batasan, and both of the men in the following case are members of this group. Formerly NU was part of the Islamic political party PPP, but it withdrew from politics in 1984. This decision was far from accepted by everyone in NU, and some members continued their activities in PPP. These people could, then, hold no leading positions in NU any longer. The young man in the following case is still a party official and seems to be highly respected as such. Among other things he led an important caderization

72

meeting in PPP in Batasan in 1986. In his family there are several influential kyais and some of the leading figures in PPP on Central Java are his relatives.

The old man is autodidact, self-confident and according to Javanese standards a rather fierce-looking, vocative person who carried out the pilgrimage in 1980. His style is rather charismatic, and he is one of the very few persons in the village who wear Arabic styled clothes.

My assistant and I were about to go to interview the old haji about the history of Islam in the village when the young party official wanted to join us. First he said there were other interesting religious leaders in the village, too, we should rather visit, but I insisted on the charismatic **haji** and he came along. After the initial formal polite talking, my assistant said we had come to seek more information about the topic of Islam's success in Batasan, which the kyai had so kindly taken up in an earlier meeting. The old man placed himself comfortably in the sofa and asked what we wanted to know, and the young man and I both took up notebook and pen. Through the next half hour or so we went through various topics like the hard struggle between various political parties in the 1950s and -60s, the ways Islam could best be spread, various types of Islamic education and so on, and during the whole discussion, which was actually a mono-logue, the young man wrote down what the older told us and supported him strongly with nods and occasional "Alhamdu lillah".

After some time the haji went, with much less grace than would be expected, into the issue of NU's proper place in relation to PPP and stated his opinions clearly. The young man did not change face at all. Instead he said things like: "You know, it is a bit difficult for me, because my family is active in the party," and "I am very grateful for the opportunity to meet you so as to learn more about these things, and you are really one of the most experienced Muslims in this village." Even when the haji started in a very un-Javanese way to blame people on the young man's side for some of the problems the Islamic community in this area faces, he replied: "I understand your points fully. We must seek solutions to these problems and you are the one who has the key." (Neither I or my assistant understood fully what these problems actually were, and sometimes the conversation changed into Javanese and was difficult for me to follow).

The haji agreed that he was the one who had the correct understanding and solutions and went on praising himself. He told us about the new successful techniques of mission he had developed in the village, how he had become one of the most influential persons in NU, how extensive his Islamic knowledge was and so on, the boasting interspersed with "Allahu akbar", "Alhamdu lillah" and "Amen". The young man gave expressions of content on every point with nods, **inggih** (the polite form of "yes" in Javanese) and "Allahu akbar".

I now thought I had misunderstood the young man totally and that he in fact was so active in PPP just because he was trapped by family expectations. I had a feeling that the haji in fact believed so, too, because he smiled heartily and invited the young man back another time, and he again responded with: "Oh yes, we have to continue this." I took the bus back to town while the young man rode on my assistants' motor bike. Here the young man showed his alter ego again fully, blaming the old man for an arrogance and stupidity beyond belief.

4.3. Identity management

The examples given above and numerous other incidents in Batasan everyday life indicate the complexity with which symbolic statements are made. An observer, be it a foreign anthropologist or a local Javanese, cannot simply read public symbolic expressions in religious life in a straight forward way. Ordinary people seem in fact to apply several techniques to complicate the interpretation of their own behavior, and the resulting identity expressions appear to be attempts at identity blurring rather than identity profiling. I will shortly describe these techniques here.

First, there is what I call symbolic complication. The outcome of these attempts is, as in the slametans above, that rituals grow into complex, polysemic appearances that accommodate both old and new interpretations at once. The reason why I treat such ritual forms as an outcome of applied techniques is, of course, that I partly regard ritual appearances as somehow created by human efforts at producing meaning and at solving everyday problems.

Such an approach explains for instance why the recitation part of the ritual through time has come to make up the longest sequence in Batasan slametans. It is a statement of "Islamness" produced by the religious leaders who happened to control this ritual part. The slametan has been "Islamized" also in that offerings to spirits and burning of incense have been cleared away by the religious leaders who claimed that these elements were examples of paganism. This may look like the opposite process of symbolic simplification, but it is worth noting that the ambiguous element, the special food, which is food for man only or for man and the spirits, has remained, and carries, for some people at least, exactly the same animistic meaning as it did before. Such polysomy in ritual occasions is also exemplified in the case above where my neighbor arranged his house initiation slametan during the lunar eclipse.

Symbols and whole ritual sequences can generally be supposed to have the inherent property of polysomy, or multivocality. (Turner 1967, p.50) To understand the existence and the developments of polysomy itself in the Batasan slametan I hold, however, that we additionally need to understand the processes whereby symbols are adopted, discarded or manipulated in given socio-political contexts. I am in fact arguing that multivocality partly is being produced by intended actions on the part of various actors involved in ritual life. The general dynamics is, I think, that ordinary people seek to avoid the very symbols singled out by their leaders as metonyms of paganism. There is for instance general agreement among my informants that to put out sesajen (offerings) is equivalent with being a pagan. And to seek protection from celestial forces is, by some informants at least, regarded as an anti-Islamic practice. The fact that people avoid such explicit signs of paganism does not, however, automatically change their animistic frame of understanding or even stop them from continuing animistic practices. They seem rather to cling to, or even produce, polysemic signs accommodating the conflicting views.

The use of spells is another example. Formerly, people in Batasan uttered Javanese or Islamic phrases when they passed conspicuous trees, stones and the like in nature intending to please the spirits dwelling there. This practice is still frequent, but the spells are now Arabic verses from the Koran, and the Islamic leadership appears to be pleased because "Allah's word is constantly uttered". For ordinary people the verses probably function the same way as before, and, as one informant revealed, you can utter a Javanese phrase in your thoughts when you pass, anyway.

In sum, through the technique of symbolic complication ordinary people seem to formulate religious statements so as to under-communicate conflicting views and opinions through rituals so multi-faceted that they can accommodate different, and even opposing, interpretations at once. They seem to seek the accomplishment of a communal and problem-free religious practice rather than a consensus about interpretations, beliefs and dogmas.

Secondly, there are in Batasan everyday life continuing attempts at staging, in other words attempts at actively concealing or displaying religious or secular elements relative to various audiences. The ritual bath above, taking place inside one's own house is one example of back-staging, the gambling sessions after most slametans another. Such gambling typically take place when, "incidentally", only the appropriate people are present, and it is normally carried out away from public view. Phenomena like ritual baths and gambling (along with dating, cinemas, shadow plays, rock concerts and so on) are problematic for ordinary people in Batasan as they are utilized by the religious leaders as signs of bad religious behavior, and back-staging may be an adequate response in such cases.

Such back-staging has in fact become a characteristic of some of the most crucial parts of religious life in the village. According to most people in Batasan the very criterion for being a true Muslim is to carry out the five daily prayers, but this activity is interestingly back-staged so that public verification is almost impossible. There are certain attempts at publicizing the prayers as the religious leaders try to institutionalize the practice of praying in the prayer houses in the evening, and there are now and then subtle attempts by ordinary people to front-stage the prayer so as to show people that they in fact do pray, by placing a lamp behind them so that the shadow of the prayer falls into the public room in a house for instance, but in general the verification of actual prayer practices is virtually impossible. What appears on the public scene is merely a marking of prayer time by people entering their own homes.

Thirdly, there is the technique of simulation whereby people present a front to give the impression that they are something different, or even opposite, of what they actually are. The meeting between the old haji and the young party official above is an example of this technique whereby the young man buried his contempt for the old haji and presented a positive and pleasing front.

4.4 Religious identities

For Geertz there was a clear connection between animistic beliefs and the slametan rituals. Together with a few other religious features they defined the abangan variety of Javanese Islam, and they constituted the basic criteria for delineating a local and national religious category. From the examples given above it is obvious that this is not the case in Batasan today. It is for several reasons impossible to make clear-cut inferences from public religious practice to individual commitment, and, consequently, one cannot today easily operate with Geertz' distinctions at the level of social identities. We can at most regard certain situations and contexts as more or less "santri" or "abangan", but among ordinary people at least there are very few clear-cut "abangan" or "santri" persons.

First, one should note that the very terms "abangan" and "santri" are not used by the local population in the ways Geertz applied them. Most people associate "abangan" with members of the former PKI (The Communist Party) and "santri" with students at the Islamic **pesantren** schools.

Secondly, to identify subtradition from ritual appearances seems problematic. There is no obvious reason to connect the Batasan slametan merely to spirit beliefs and thus "abanganness". As I have tried to show, animistic interpretations are possible, but as the slametan has grown into a quite complex, ambiguous whole, other interpretations are indeed possible, one of which is purely Islamic and thus a sign of "santriness". A closer look at other defining elements in Geertz' aliran scheme would, I think, reveal the same fact, that there are several frames of interpretation applicable to most of these phenomena.

Thirdly, I have tried to show that there is a clear tendency among ordinary people in Batasan to blur their identity statements through techniques like back-staging, simulation, and the production of ambiguity in symbolic expressions. Due to such strategies, conflicts and even contrasts are under-communicated in ordinary life and inferences from symbolic statements as to personal identity made difficult.

Fourth, if we shift our focus from how people act in single situations to how they combine symbolic statements produced in different situations, we find much of the same ambiguity regarding identity display. Most people would, if they are biased in one situation, try to balance it in another. For instance, many persons do not go to the evening prayer in the prayer houses as the religious leaders want them to do. Some of them do not even attend the Friday prayer in Batasan regularly due to jobs in Salatiga or Semarang. This is, however, symbolically balanced by attending various religious meetings and other Islamic occasions that they find more agreeable.

A good example of this eagerness to balance expressions as to identity is the problem of which type of education to choose for one's children. In Batasan there have been both Islamic and secular primary schools since the 1930s. Prior to 1956 the Islamic school held its classes in the evening, but from this year on both schools started to have classes at the same time in the morning, and people now had to make a choice. The development of these schools indicates that this element of choice is regarded as a statement about identity. Just after the turbulence of 1965 the secular school lost almost all its pupils, and the Muslim school flowered. In the mid 1970s when the power was changed from the Muslim to the GOLKAR (government party) side through a lurah election, the children started to flow back to the state school, and today it is the Islamic **madrasah** that has trouble getting pupils.

This tendency is, however, strongly balanced by an enormous amount of voluntary religious courses for various age groups in the evenings. The education given here seems to be quite extensive, including the mastering of written Arabic, and almost everyone, especially small school children, attend the courses. As a result the work load for a typical school child is quite heavy, and many parents pity their children because of this. Nevertheless, the necessity of balancing the two types of education is overriding their concern for the children, and I suppose this to be yet another example of a tendency to counter balance identity statements made in one context with those made in another.

5. RELIGION AND POLITICS

Above I have tried to describe some signification processes operating in Batasan's religious life anno 1985. My
statements about identity management so far pertain
especially to what I have called "ordinary people", that
is persons who do not control any leading positions in
religious or political fields. It is obvious that these
people cannot be classified on the basis of their religious practice into various aliran-identities as Geertz
did. I do not want to elaborate more on this classification problem here, as I am more interested in discussing
what Batasan villagers continuously seem to be so concerned about, namely the attempt to erase symbolically
any difference as to religious identity at all. First,
how can these strategies of identity blurring best be
explained, and, secondly, what consequences may this
identity management have for the strategies that village
leaders follow?

5.1 The political context

The ardent haji in the last case above illustrates quite
another form of identity management than what is common
among ordinary people in Batasan. His appearance is in
all respects a signalling of his total commitment to
Islam, he wears Arabic styled clothes, he leads religious
courses and the evening prayer in the prayer house nearby,
he states his points of view clearly and with no embar-
rassment, he boasts of his Islamic knowledge and personal
skills ("with God's help"), and he even challenges others
as to their standpoints (as in the case above). There are
a few persons like him in Batasan, that is persons who
tend to act more in accordance with Western concepts of
personality and individual integrity. Most of them belong
to one of the two leadership groups in the village: a
.

group of religious leaders, and a group of village administrators.

In Batasan the term "kyai" denotes highly respected religious leaders, not, as seems to be the case elsewhere on Java, only those religious and charismatic leaders who manage to establish and run private Islamic boarding schools, the pesantren. It seems that the kyais in Batasan centre their efforts on Islamic mission among ordinary people in the village where they are living instead of spending their time with a few ardent students totally isolated from the local community as is often the case with the pesantren kyais. They have frequent contacts with other villagers, but they typically enter such relations in one of their capacities only, namely as religious and moral leaders, be it as a prayer leader, a religious teacher, a funeral specialist or as the conductor of recitation during slametans. For the most active kyais the whole day is filled with religious obligations, and their identity expressions are almost always connected to their chosen role as "fighters for Islam".

Some of the kyais are landowners and manage to survive as religious specialists partly by share-cropping their fields, but they themselves stress the importance of the gifts they receive from people in the village. I have no reliable material about their economy, but I suppose that their income to a great extent stems from such donations from village people. In any case the kyais do not seem to be among the richest. On the other hand, their greatest concern, the building of religious schools, mosques and prayer-houses, is definitely in progress, and along with the frequent religious courses and meetings they manage to arrange, Islam as such seems to be prospering.

Both the "traditional" and the "modern" Muslims are represented in Batasan, but the overwhelming majority of both leaders and followers support Nahdatul Ulama (NU), the traditionalists. A local branch of NU was set up in the village just a short time after NU was established nationwide, and it has since been the dominant religious organization in the village. Formerly it was also the strongest political party.

The other leadership group consists of the lurah, the village secretary and some of the other officials in the village administration. Their explicit aim is to modernize village life by actively promoting the government's various development programs, such as the building of schools, roads and village council houses, the implementation of new agricultural techniques and the use of fertilizers, pesticides and new rice-varieties. They also try to start evening education for illiterates, improve hygiene and health-care, promote medical control of infants and not least implement the family planning program. Also these persons tend to appear with clear-cut identities in everyday life, but their roles in relation to ordinary villagers do not seem to be so specialized as is the case of the kyais. They normally take part in religious life on equal footing with ordinary villagers, and they also spend much time together with neighbors in informal social intercourse. Especially the lurah appeared in many instances as quite an ordinary villager, inviting neighbors in for tea and endless chatting or spending his spare time in the rice-fields.

The material basis for these leaders is partly the right to use communal land while in office. These plots of land are normally share-cropped. Again I have no reliable data about the economic situation of the lurah and his men, but I suppose there are additional provisions and gifts owing to their very positions. The administrative leaders do not seem to be especially rich, however, and according to house standards and overt consumption there are other families in the village which seem to be far better off. These households rely typically on income from work opportunities in Salatiga or Semarang, like petty trade and transport, and I suppose that this adaptation to a modern town and city context has strong implications for the unfolding of local political life.

According to a study carried out by LPIS at "Satya Wacana Christian University" in 1976 as much as 3/4 of all the households in Batasan relied partly on income from non-agricultural activities, and 21% had economic links outside the village. (Pradjarta et.al. 1978) This tendency to depend on off-farm income is probably even stronger today, and consequently I suppose that control of land is a gradually less important factor in political control. The political games played by the two leadership groups to control various key positions in agricultural production and trade did take place in 1985, but these attempts seemed to be somewhat out of place, and finally the lurah gave up his plans to build a rice-mill to compete with the one already established by a son of a kyai. Instead he took interest in house-building and launched a plan to erect 3-4 story apartment houses and commercial facilities on some of the farm land beside the new secondary school. Few villagers could afford moving in there, and if the plan succeeds, the village would virtually be turned into a suburb of Salatiga.

As the importance of land control decreases, the lurah gains power through being the gate to the outside world. He issues the letters of recommendation needed to travel long distances, to apply for jobs, to enter schools, to settle down outside the village and so on, and he grants or refuses licenses to people who want to start businesses based in the village. This important office was transferred from NU activists to an ardent modernizer, a GOLKAR person, in a somewhat rigged lurah election in 1975. All the contestants, 6 persons, had to go through a test in the district office, and only two "sympathetic" persons passed the test, one of whom was later elected. Due to the importance of the lurah position this election set much of the local life on a new course, and the context of local political life was gradually altered.

5.2. Respect vs. Commitment

We have seen that ordinary people in Batasan reacted to this change of leadership by gradually removing their children from the Islamic school. Another response was several new votes for GOLKAR in the 1977 national election. (18.5% of the votes in 1971, 40% in 1977) It is hard to know if this had an influence on peoples' identity management in the religious field, but according to the understanding of Javanese symbolic life I have tried to develop here, I suspect that there was much reformulation in symbolic statements in order to accommodate the new political situation. My hypothesis is that the management of identity described above partly can be understood as responses by ordinary people to a difficult politico-religious situation. (See Slamet 1982 for a discussion of a similar argument).

On one level the stagings and simulations involved in this management can serve as strategic devices for the individual in order to get out of challenging situations or to be able to carry out private inclinations undisturbed. Inversely, and very importantly, he can at the same time pay respect to people in his surroundings by appearing in every instance as it pleases them. Symbolic statements should then, I think, not be taken as the signalling of opinions and commitments, but of respect. This aspect of hypocrisy is very much in accordance with the Javanese' own explanations of the phenomenon. They often referred to the term **hormat**, "respect", to justify lies. (See Hildred Geertz 1961, p.110-114 for a discussion of this term).

Clifford Geertz adopts a somewhat cultural explanation to the simulations he witnessed in Modjokuto indicating that such play is just a life style. (See his discussion of the practice of **etok-etok**, Geertz 1960, p. 245-247). I do not want to turn quickly to the other extreme stating that identity management merely is a matter of strategic adaptations to demanding political leaders as many everyday instances of simulation and staging would not lend itself easily to such an explanation. On the other hand, there are definitely cases where the opportunistic aspect of such play is obvious, and as simulations and stagings seem to be generally accepted as a mode of behavior, they indeed have the <u>potential</u> for strategic utility.

On another level exactly this strong consensus about the practice of identity blurring indicates an influential <u>aggregate</u> response. As the whole community accepts the non-interference in others' whereabouts as such a play requires, the outcome is a life style that constitutes some of the very premises for local political life. So far I have discussed symbolic expressions in religious life as ways to talk about one's own identity, as communicative processes. Now I will argue that these communicative attempts have aggregate implications for more instrumental strategies as well. Both the Islamizers and the modernizers in Batasan have to take into consideration ordinary peoples' identity play in their pursuit to gather followers and gain influence. Particularly, I maintain, they cannot in any simple and straight forward way measure their popularity and support in the arenas of public life. A high frequency of attendance during prayers, for instance, would in this cultural context not automatically be a sign of peoples' commitment to the religious leaders' concerns, be it their Islamization efforts or their wider political or economic games. In short I argue that peoples' identity management is effective in hindering the crystallization of clear cut supporters and opponents in political life and that mobilization efforts by various leaders thus are constrained. I will try to illustrate these propositions through a discussion of some of the characteristics and conditions of the Islamization process in Batasan.

5.3 Islamization

Gustav Thaiss has shown us how Iranian ulamas laboriously reformulated the meaning of Islamic symbols to make powerful and mobilizing statements about Iran's relation to American imperialism prior to the Khomeini revolution. (Thaiss 1978) In the debate about Islamization in Indonesia the same perspective has often been adopted, and the Muslims recent withdrawal from party politics has been understood as a similar mobilizing strategy: By concentrating their efforts on Islamization in a purely religious sense the Islamic activists are seeking to reshape peoples' frames of understanding and true religious commitments in order to secure a strong emotional support in the population. This would then constitute a strong potential for political mobilization on an Islamic ground in a future political confrontation.

With this point of view in mind it is important to try to grasp the characteristics of the Islamization process as it actually unfolds, and Batasan may prove a good case as Islamization appears, from the outside at least, to have come far here.

One implication of identity blurring is, as I have tried to indicate, that Islamization primarily tends to become reformulations of rituals rather than reformulations of meaning. The slametan for instance grows into a highly multivocal ritual with an Islamic face, but with several interpretations as to content and function, some of which are quite unorthodox.

Another interesting attempt at reformulation of ritual form was in progress when I left Batasan. Traditionally there were three ways to relate ritually to the dead: through slametans, **tahlilan** and prayers in the graveyard, but if the Islamic leaders have succeeded in their attempts, this may have changed by now.

On the day of death the family of the deceased arranges, with much assistance from neighbors, a slametan to commemorate the dead, and further slametans are supposed to occur on the two following days thereafter, after seven days, forty days, one hundred days, one year, two years and one thousand days after death. These slametans are normally held in the house of the deceased. There is, however, just a slight difference between such slametans and the tahlilan institution which has been provided by the Islamic leaders. This term refers to a ceremony normally held in the mosque or in the prayer houses, where the Islamic leaders beg Allah to take care of the dead, either specific dead or the dead generally, but the term "tahlilan" is used by many to denote the slametans for the dead held in private houses as well. Additionally, some people do in fact arrange their commemorating slametans in the prayer houses, and we may see here a development leading to the merging of two rituals into one. Presently, however, most people operate with a distinction between the slametans held in private houses and the tahlilan held in religious buildings.

Then there is the practice of visiting the graves of dead relatives. People go to the graveyard, clean the graves, put out flowers (**nyekar**) and pray to the dead. This is carried out every **Kamis-Wage** (a combination of Thursday (Kamis) in the seven-day week and Wage in the five-day week), every 35 days, but some people do this on Thursdays generally. To carry out nyekar is, by those who explicitly make such distinctions, an indication of Javanese influence, and the practices of cleaning the grave and putting out flowers contrast with the simplicity required of a "genuine" Islamic graveyard. What is more, to carry out nyekar is normally accompanied by direct prayers to the dead, prayers about help in difficult times and about magical assistance in personal aspirations. It took me quite some time in the village before I understood that these practices existed at all as people referred to tahlilan and slametans when I inquired about the dead, and I did not feel welcome on the graveyard when I tried to observe what was going on there.

This un-ease about the existence of the very ritual makes sense with regard to another feature of the practice in Batasan. Whereas the people visiting the graves in Modjokuto normally were the closest male relatives of the dead, there is a very strong tendency in Batasan to see either very old men or very young girls visiting the graves, and especially the latter. I interpret this as an attempt at symbolically downgrading the importance of the ritual. By sending young, innocent virgins to the graves, the parents try to state metaphorically something about the innocence of the ritual itself.

Just prior to my departure from the field, there was a new interesting development in this ritual practice. In a neighboring **kampung** (village quarter) some kyais decided to move the tahlilan from the mosque to the graveyard. As a result private prayers to individual dead in Javanese would probably be substituted by collective prayers to the dead in Arabic under the guidance of the Islamic leaders. When I left the field, and I guess for quite some time afterward, this suggestion was put forward for comment in the typical silent, indirect Javanese way, and I do not know if this new ritual practice ever materialized. There is no reason to believe that it did not, however, as several kampungs in the neighboring village a few hundred meters away had their tahlilans in the graveyard for several years already. What is more, I believe that the kyais' new ritual was highly appreciated by ordinary people in that it provided a new area of ambiguity somewhat akin to a slametan with its complexity and considerable potential for interpretations. In this new ritual two significant Javanese features are still intact: The ritual's position in time and in space. The ritual would be held either on Thursday or on the special day of Thursday-Wage as is the case for the nyekar activities, and it would be carried out by the graves.

Secondly, as I have already hypothesized, Islamization generates statements of respect in religious life, not necessarily religious commitment. The ardent haji mentioned above was quite explicit about this. In outlining the Islamization strategies he found most successful, he said the first step was always to get people to act in an Islamic way, then, maybe over time people would become Muslims "in their hearts" (dalam hatinya). As I have indicated above, to be able to uphold an impression of being a true Muslim at the same time as one lives out less appreciated qualities, the techniques of staging and simulation are often adopted.

Batasan was connected to Salatiga with a road in the mid 1970s, and this connection is highly valued by most villagers. I think this enthusiasm partly stems from the immense potential for hiding places which the town and city contexts provide. As far as I have been able to ascertain, many persons traveling from city to village or vice versa do change their identity expressions, and the emerging pattern seems to be that individual inclinations are played out in town, whereas village life grows quite homogeneous. For the Islamic leaders the new connection to town is problematic not primarily, as they themselves say, because the villagers are influenced by the indecency of the towns, but because they loose almost all opportunities to control their followers' actual conduct. The response to this can merely be to try to provide people with religious alternatives in the village, like religious courses Saturday evening for the youths.

Much of the intensification of religious life in Batasan and in many other places on Java during the last decade can probably be understood in this perspective, and we should consequently not take the mushrooming of mosques as an indication of true Islamic revitalization among ordinary people, although conversion may be the religious leaders' intention. The Islamic activists struggle to provide religious alternatives to the modern world, by building prayer houses that serve as informal gathering places for youths in the evening for instance, and by arranging open, religious meetings with a public appeal, but, typically, ordinary people in Batasan respond by attending only enough times to pay the appropriate respect to their religious leaders.

Third, the general acceptance of the values of a peaceful and harmonious community that identity blurring suggests, makes it difficult for the religious leaders to force through statements as to actual commitment in order to measure political support. This is exactly what was attempted by one of the kyais in Batasan just prior to the national election of 1977. (I am grateful to Pradjarta Dirdjosanjoto for this piece of information, personal communication).

The cinemas in Salatiga advertise their films by using a car that travels around to the various villages. It carries large posters, and the films are announced through a rusty loud-speaker. During a public religious meeting in Batasan this car happened to pass, and the kyai immediately ended his speech and launched a veritable verbal attack at the car. He criticized the cinemas for showing pornographic films and for leading the youth astray, and he claimed the "voice of Satan" (the passing car) to be stronger than the sound of the chanting that reminded Muslims of their religious obligations. The moral decay in the village, he said, was stemming from the new road that made such evils enter the village to influence people.

The next day another kyai took up the same theme during the evening prayer in one of the mosques and stated that from now on he would not shake hands with villagers who went to the cinema in Salatiga. As shaking hands is the appropriate Islamic greeting this meant metaphorically that those who visited the cinemas were **kafir**, pagans. As far as it is possible to ascertain this attempt at symbolically dividing the villagers did not succeed at all, and the cinema car continued to come.

Judging from the present situation such attempts at measuring commitments or mobilizing people for an Islamic cause seem to be futile moves in the political game. Not only would it be impossible to determine who in fact went to the three cinemas in Salatiga or numerous cinemas in Semarang and other places; there is in addition a genuine resentment among ordinary people against the appearance of overt political conflict or even discussion, and such attempts at mobilization would be strongly resisted. People would probably pay due respect, but in an ambiguous and pacifying way. This seemed to be the case when PPP, the Islamic party, celebrated its 13.th anniversary in Batasan.

As mentioned above, NU was until recently part of PPP, and the decision to withdraw from politics caused an internal split in the organization. Most of the NU leaders in Batasan support the decision, and this seems to be the case among ordinary people as well. The anniversary started with a "caderization meeting" where some prominent politicians were present, and it was followed by a **pengajian** (a public religious meeting). First of all it is worth noting that a plainclothes policeman was eagerly taking notes during both the cadre meeting and the pengajian in a nearby house. Both meetings were, as is now compulsory in any religious meeting in Batasan, broadcasted through loud-speakers, and all villagers could hear what was being said. The second point to be made about this happening illustrates again the production of ambiguous respect in symbolic expressions. People resented the attempt by PPP to use Batasan as a "baro-meter", as they themselves termed it, in the run-up for the 1987 national election, but they expressed this resentment not by staying away from the pengajian, which would probably be too strong a statement, but by letting only women attend.

6. CONCLUSION

In this paper I have attempted to describe how ordinary people in Batasan handle symbolic expressions concerning their religious identities. Since religious commitment has been taken as indicative of political inclinations, a study of such identity management in the religious field may be an important part of our attempt to understand the operation of local political life. On the part of ordinary people there is a striking unwillingness to appear with profiled identities, and it seems that identity blurring is the preferred strategy in the religious field. Such blurring is achieved through the use of techniques like stagings, simulations and the production of polysomy in ritual performances.

I have hypothesized that these blurring strategies partly can be understood as symbolic attempts at adapta-tion to a problematic religio-political context. Through always appearing in a pleasing way, one is in the Javanese cultural context paying respect to one's superordinates. At the same time there is in such a strategy an immense potential for actually playing out one's inclinations at various back-stages. The emerging identity expressions are thus typically ambiguous, and I believe this ambiguity on the part of single actors partly to be attempts at optimizing safety and peace.

The aggregate outcome of several such individual strategies seem to constitute some of the constraints to the strategies the leaders in Batasan pursue. I have exemplified this with a discussion of the problems which the religious leaders seem to face in their Islamization attempts among ordinary people, and I think the problems facing the "modernizers" of the village could be equally illustrating. I have hypothesized that Islamization primarily leads to changes in ritual forms rather than interpretations, meanings and beliefs, and it also seems to generate expressions of respect rather than statements of religious commitment in public, symbolic life. Hence, from the leaders' point of view, the identification of supporters and followers in the appearance of ordinary, religious life is probably made difficult.

Melford Spiro has warned us about the "invisibility" of factional, political strife in Southeast-Asia, (Spiro 1968), and it would be premature to conclude that because of this drive for identity blurring in Batasan there are in fact no allegiances, alliances, commitments, loyalties or determinations. What I am arguing is that religious life does not portray such factional divisions whereas, according to Geertz, it was exactly in belief and ritual that such divisions found their expressions in the mid 1950s. It should also be emphasized that my fieldwork was carried out in between both local village chief and national parliamentary elections, and that my arguments pertain to such a situation. The mobilization efforts that occur during elections and the local population's responses to them should be studied empirically and in their own right.

For the Islamic leaders in Batasan· the situation seemed difficult in 1985. They were sandwiched between the GOLKAR lurah, who is backed by legal powers on district, regional and national levels, and the local people at large who seemed to be content with this peaceful and stable state of being. The latest developments in Batasan have not only opened up new back-stages and job opportunities for ordinary people in town thereby

93

decreasing the kyais' economic and moral influence, the Islamic leaders are also being restricted on home ground as they have to open up their own influential back-stages (religious meetings) with the compulsory loud-speakers "so that everyone in the village can evaluate what is being said and report to the lurah if they talk politics," as a village official phrased it. This situation seems to make attempts at political mobilization on an Islamic ground futile.

BIBLIOGRAPHY

Bråten, Eldar: Forthcoming cand.polit thesis at Department of Social Anthropology, University of Bergen, Norway.

Geertz, Clifford: "Ritual and Social Change: A Javanese example", **American Anthropologist**, vol. 61, 1959, pp. 991-1012.

Geertz, Clifford: **The Religion of Java** (Illinois: The Free Press of Glencoe, 1960).

Geertz, Hildred: **The Javanese Family** (Illinois: The Free Press of Glencoe, 1961).

Hefner, Robert W: "Islamizing Java? Religion and Politics in Rural East Java", **The Journal of Asian Studies**, vol. 46, 3, 1987, pp. 533-554.

Koentjaraningrat: **Javanese Culture** (Singapore: Oxford University Press, 1985). .

Pradjarta et al.: **Beberapa masalah sosial dan ekonomi penduduk sekitar Rawa Pening** (Salatiga: LPIS, Univ. Kristen Satya Wacana, 1978).

Islamet, Ina E: **Cultural Strategies for Survival: The plight of the Javanese** (Rotterdam: CASP, Erasmus University, 1982).

Spiro, Melford E: "Factionalism and Politics in Village Burma" in Swartz (ed.): **Local Level Politics** (Chicago: Aldine Publishing Co., 1968).

Thaiss, Gustav: "The Conceptualization of Social Change through Metaphor", **Journal of Asian and African Studies**, vol. 13, 1-2, 1978.

Turner, Victor: **The Forest of Symbols: Aspects of Ndembu Ritual** (Ithaca: Cornell University Press, 1967).

DEVELOPMENT IDEOLOGIES, FAMILY SYSTEMS, AND THE CHANGING ROLES OF MALAY VILLAGE WOMEN.

Ingrid Rudie
University of Oslo

Introduction

This is an essay about various kinds of interaction. On one level, I will attempt to throw some light on the articulation between important features of development and planning policies on the one hand, and kinship and local organization on the other.

On another level, and embedded in this problem, I will be concerned with the identity management of Malay village women at the turning point between peasant and industrial society. The paper is thus concerned with the changing lifespace of part of the Malay population in the fast developing, multiethnic Malaysian society.

To be more specific, I wish to discuss how far certain trends in political planning and development ideologies work towards reinforcing some features of traditional family systems and weakening others, and how they affect female identity structures.

This project is fraught with analytical problems belonging, as it were, on each of the two levels suggested above.

One set of problems appears at the level concerned with the impact which environment has on the individual. The individual has to grapple with a society which has rapidly become more complex - or rather, she has to grapple with the new type of complexity that has made its way into village society during the three decades since Independence. Malaysian (or Malayan before Independence) society has been "complex" for centuries in the sense

96

that different ethnic groups and different status groups have coexisted, but there was not necessarily much incentive for each group to take a conscious look at its own position and cultural repertoire. What is new is that particular manifestation of complexity in which the whole world comes to the individual in the shape of widely divergent roles and an additional load of information about alternative role performances and partly conflicting value parameters. All this is brought about through near-universal education and literacy in the younger generation, universal access to mass media, and con- siderable social and geographic mobility. Such changes have taken place in the lifetime of the adult generation. People who are now about 40 years old were born before Independence, and raised in villages which were dominated by a more inert peasant way of life. Some of them went to secondary school and even further during the sixties and seventies, because their parents were hoping for upward mobility. Now they are launched in the midst of a number of societal transformations.

Analytically, it seems convenient to view the individual as an active participant in certain organiza- tional setups, as well as a more or less active processor of information. We then need a comprehensive approach in order to grasp social organizational problems as well as the mass of information which takes place more indepen- dently of interaction proper, and I will suggest the following categories of data as being of special impor- tance for that purpose:

- Live interaction between real people. This can be examined in its task-oriented as well as its symbolic aspects.

- Life histories, which can be studied as histories of adaptation to changing economic and ideological conditions.

- Individuals' explicit or implicit reflections on their own life situation. This can take the form of verbal as well as non-verbal "statements".
- Free-flowing texts which are more or less detached from interaction proper, and which must be "read" and interpreted by the individual.

The interpretive capacity or cultural competence of the individual consists of knowledge of the codes that govern social interaction, as well as her manner of "reading" free-flowing texts. It is shaped through a person's total experience in all kinds of interaction, through formal training, and through all kinds of exposure to impulses. In short, it is a function of the interaction between her socialization history and her present situation.

A method must be found for handling these complex circumstances, in short what I have implicitly conceived of as the individual's environment. This is where the second set of analytical problems presents itself: How far can we allow ourselves to simplify complexity?

First, it is necessary to structure environment in the sense of the individual's fields of action and information. Second, something should be said about politics as part of culture.

As a first device for structuring the field of action and information , I have profited from Grönhaug's concept of social field. (Grönhaug 1978). In the present discussion I simply see my informants as suspended between the local field of neighbour relations and extended family, and the field of modernization politics. My treatment of the two fields will be lopsided, and this lopsidedness reflects what I understand to be important features in my informants' lives. They are immediate participants in the local field, but they are at best indirect participants in the political field. They interact in the family system; they receive and process messages from the political field. For my present purpose I will not, therefore, go into the field of politics as an organizational system, but rather highlight it as a force which creates some organizational strictures on the local field, and circulates some values and fragments of ideology.

Politics are part of culture; politics legitimize and are legitimized by certain themes and values in the wider cultural matrix. There is a blurred line between, for instance, what people think about family morality and what political rhetoric adds to this when it becomes necessary for the politicians to appeal to such feelings. It is tempting to borrow a phrase originally meant to characterize the effects of the TV medium: that culture communicates with itself by cultivating some values and attitudes which are already present in the public (J. Fiske 1982 p.127; ref. G. Gerbner 1970). As much can be said about political rhetoric which, by the way, is well broadcast through mass media in Malaysia. Political decisions and political rhetoric, which are based on well- known problems and shared values, turn to local organization and ideology , and in turn modify these areas. On the micro level, it can be assumed that the individual communicates with herself and her immediate environment in her attempts at identity management, in such a way that some modifications are brought about.

The local field and its transformations

My insights into the local field stem from fieldwork in a Kelantan village community in two periods more than twenty years apart. During the two decades the community changed considerably in economic structure. It used to be a community of small cultivators, where cultivation was often supplemented by other activities, mostly part-time, but where access to land was the ultimate goal and security. In this system women had a firm grip on the means of production and the exchange processes. They were landowners in their own right, they contributed heavily to agricultural production, and they were responsible for the marketing. The responsibilities for marketing and for running the household economy provided them with a basic skill for trading, which some of them cultivated further into a specialized full time occupation. Trading as a female specialty was, and still is, a strong feature of Kelantan society. Women's identity as productive persons was very visible; the notion of women as essentially self-supporting was a central one.

It should be borne in mind that Kelantan has a few demographic, cultural and economic characteristics which may affect gender relations in general and the productive roles of women in particular. The vicinity to Thailand has stimulated border trade, and with improved road connections to the rest of the Federation, the State's importance as thoroughfare for goods has increased in recent years. The overwhelming majority of Malays in the population (93.3% as contrasted to 56.6% in Peninsular Malaysia) has left room for Malay trading enterprise; in fact, Malay traders in other states have often originated from Kelantan. Apart from trading activities, the state has remained less economically developed than the rest of Peninsular Malaysia, which means that production has leaned heavily on the primary sectors of agriculture and fishing until recently. In these sectors the rough division of work in the past leaned towards men being most closely linked with the productive side, and women taking care of the distributive side and networking. All these factors together may have contributed to giving women a strategic position in the economy.

The economic structure of households as late as the 1960s was based on cooperation between productive persons, cooperation through which a number of small resources used to be pooled according to flexible rules about support and mutuality. Aged parents were taken care of by their children, and they usually lived in the same household as one of their children - sometimes they alternated between adult children. As the parents grew older, the relationship between them and their children gradually changed from one of mutuality to one of support. In the extended family, whether co-residing or not, the link between mother and daughter was perhaps the most vital among all the conceivable family dyads. Its vitality and importance was due to its total nature: It represented in the fullest possible sense the continuum of cooperation and support on which the peasant household was founded (Rudie 1971). Elements of cooperation and elements of support shaded almost imperceptibly into each other, as did productive and unproductive phases through a life career. In certain productive situations cooperation between related women was almost as important as that between husband and wife. The divorce rate was high, and the most viable marriages were those in which husband and wife depended on each other in an arrangement of good practical mutuality. It can be argued that the husband-wife dyad contained a strong element of contract, it was conditional and easily dissoluble, while the mother-daughter dyad was flexible, yet unconditional and indissoluble. This state of affairs was maintained and reproduced in a wider socio-religious system which imposed a high degree of gender segregation. Women were economically as important as men, and ritually set apart. All this added up to creating a bond of particularly strong solidarity and mutual emotional dependence between mother and daughter.

Present day village society has changed from this state. More people depend entirely on secondary and tertiary full time occupations, so in many families farming activities have become discontinued. A great deal of land lies idle, some is rented out to other cultivators. Those who do farm, tend to be more specialized cultivators who may or may not supplement their own land with rented land. The generation up to about 45 years of age is the first in which almost everyone has received at least some formal education, and a sizeable number have been educated beyond primary level. Those who are now full time employees have a pure money economy, in the sense that they have mostly given up farming, and buy all necessities. They usually reside separately from their parents. The parent generation hold the land, yet have no physical strength to till it. They depend on their children for economic support - now more definitely in the form of a direct money contribution rather than membership in en extended, multifunctional household. This implies that some differences become very visible. Income differences between the educated and the uneducated employees are considerable, and can be seen in the standard in which they are able to provide for their aged parents. Some may have problems contributing enough money for the bare necessities of life, while others are able to build new houses and send their parents on the pilgrimage. The welfare of the aged thus is highly dependent on the success of their children, and differences that may have been small twenty years ago, have now widened and become very visible. To sum up, the relationship between parents and children has changed from a situation in which there was a mutual dependence which shaded gradually into a relation of support, to a situation in which the necessity of a money contribution is felt more acutely, and often also earlier in life. The duty of support is heavily felt by the productive generation, and perhaps mostly by women, who often now have the lowest incomes at the same time as they have been socialized to a more total sense of responsibility.

Having children is as important as ever, and the children's success is more important than ever, because they will be responsible for one's own welfare later in life. Thus the necessity to invest in the children's education has added to parental responsibilities.

The political field

The transformations of the local level are part of large-scale economic, political and cultural processes. Politics are, among other things, a process of decisions about economic issues. Politics is also, as stated above, a process whereby culture communicates with itself.

Political decisions lead to organizational structures, and political rhetoric adds to the load of texts which flow about in society.

Prominent traits of Malaysian politics are: their centralized structure, a heavy impact of government enterprises combined with a marked anti-socialist philosophy in the political establishment, and the vital necessity of securing peaceful relations between the ethnic groups.

When I characterize politics as centralized, it needs qualifications. For one thing, local government is weakly developed, and the mere idea of it has been subject to considerable doubts and controversies since Independence (M.W. Norris 1980).

Political opposition is partially muted by means of rhetorical techniques and a considerable amount of censorship. The ruling parties probably derive part of their power from personal loyalties of a patron-client type stretching from the top echelons down to the level of the local branches, and this, by the way, takes care of some of the tasks which would otherwise be the responsibility of local authorities. The link between administration and political establishment is a very close one.

Malaysia can be described as an administrative state, and any public agency on District level has its backup on State and Federal levels. In this way all public issues seem to emanate in a very direct way from the Government - let me repeat, the "Government". In everyday speech among the politically unsophisticated, and even some of the more sophisticated, "Government" is a blanket term covering political establishment, administration, and ultimate patron in one.

This structure allows for the heavy government impact in public enterprises. The anti-socialist ideology is visible in a number of issues related to economic policy and public welfare. Announcement of plans to "eradicate poverty" is a recurrent theme in the government's presentation of itself, but there is no belief in advancing this goal by means of redistributive measures with an equalizing effect - on the contrary, it is considered a better strategy to raise the ceiling by "creating millionaires", and the rich enjoy a moderate income tax level. There are no public old age pensions except for those who have been in government service, which means that a worker who retires from private employment becomes dependent on private means, or in reality on his or her children. Welfare for the needy exists, but for one thing this runs to only 30 ringgit a month, and the person applying for it must be proven to be without close relatives who can support him/her. In other words, social policy leans on the family as a redistributive agent.

Malaysian politics is naturally heavily centered on development issues, and a number of grand-scale projects have appeared during the thirty years of independence. These are partly complete government enterprises for land development and community building, like the FELDA (Federal Land Development Agency) and related agencies; partly financing and counselling strategies aimed at building up private Malay entrepreneurship, like the MARA (Majlis Amanah Rakyat - Council of Trust for the Indigenous People); and partly more multifarious strategies for improving established communities. KEMAS (Kemajuan Masyarakat - Community Development Division of the Ministry of National and Rural Development) is an example of the latter. All these particular examples will be briefly characterized below.

Development has to no small extent meant developing enterprise and differential skills among the Malays, and New Economic Policy (NEP) was installed as a direct response to the outburst of ethnic conflict in 1969. Its explicit aim is to upgrade the participation of Malays in all kinds of economic activities - that is, breaking down the ethnic division of work in which Malays were primarily rural and peasants. Some of these initiatives are formally neutral to gender, while others may be detrimental to women's productive roles. The stress put on recruiting Malays to new types of careers implicitly leads to recruitment of a certain number of Malay women even though there are no special measures to secure the participation of women. There are other trends in development ideologies which either subordinate the productive role of women to the reproductive role, or highlight reproductive work to such a degree as to boost up the formation of a specialized housewife identity. For instance on the FELDA schemes, settlers are recruited according to a philosophy which strongly stresses men as primary providers, women as dependent helpers and housewives. It must be stressed that FELDA and related land development agencies do not operate in established villages. However, they recruit people from these villages, and are thus brought into the orbit of the experience of most people. Besides, they are such weighty and prestigious organizations, that their images and ideologies are part of everyone's text repertoire.

KEMAS offers a variety of specific schemes for community development in established villages as well as FELDA settlements. KEMAS also stresses reproductive activities, offering courses in home economics, cooking, sewing and embroidery. Part of the training programs concentrate on income-generating skills, but even here women tend to be confined to a choice within a narrowly defined repertoire of female activities. This tendency has been observed and criticized by the KANITA researchers at the University Sains in Penang, who argue that it would have served the interests of women better, and been more in line with the realities of rural society, to offer agricultural and other work-training courses particularly aimed at women.

Other political issues are less strongly tied to specific agencies or programs. Among these I select Islam, and population philosophy. The Islamic resurgence in Malaysia must be regarded as a political issue for various reasons: It is nurtured by the competition on all levels between the dominant ethnic groups in the country. Islam is the state religion, and at least lip service to Islamic values is an important part of the rhetoric repertoire of the Malay political establishment. The Islamic party (PAS), now in opposition, sees the Islamic State as its aim, and rebukes the establishment for not being truly devout Muslims. On the grassroot level religious activities have been intensified, Islamic idiom has become more visible everywhere, and the younger and more educated part of the population are concerned with purifying Malay traditional customs by throwing away what is seen as un-Islamic elements. It is not easy to assess the effect of this heightened religious awareness on the position of women. On the one hand, the proliferation of occupations and the educational explosion has widened the range of possible activities for women as well as men, and the fear of moving about unaccompanied, so prominent twenty years ago, has now dissolved. But at the same time as women move into public space, they move into more strictly formal Muslim dress, with all its symbolic connotations. In the Muslim moral debate, more orthodox views on the duties of men and women in marriage are expressed, and the primary importance of the husband as provider and spiritual leader is more explicitly stressed. Perhaps we could say that women move from the collective control of the community into the more private control of their husbands.

The population policy such as it has developed over the last few years is another matter which may have complex effects on the women's situation as well as men's and women's views on their own duties and identity hierarchies. In 1984 The National Family Planning Board had its name changed to The National Population and Family Development Board. The issue of family planning is no longer furthered in educational campaigns operating through public meetings, but has been relegated to the relatively closed backstage of the clinic where the individual woman meets the health personnel. Large families have recently had their political blessing on the highest authoritative level - or at least that must be the implicit message in the 70 million population target which was announced in the mid-eighties. Important political issues are there as a given for the ordinary member of village society. They impose some organizational strictures, they send some messages which appeal in different ways to pre-existing values or rules about moral duties in the population. This section can be summed up by means of a brief overview of these two aspects of politics.

Political actions and non-actions as organizational conditioners

Because the political establishment in the form of the government runs large and important public enterprises, especially those aiming at development, it has an enormous power to shape people's lives. FELDA and KEMAS were mentioned above. The former transforms tens of thousands of families from duocentric to unicentric households, because the planning of the settlements rests on the notion that the husband is the provider of the family, while the wife mainly takes care of the reproductive side. The latter concentrates a great deal of its resources on teaching skills which stress the reproductive aspects of women's work. Such policies affect the position of women on two levels. First, their status as landowners in their own right is discontinued if they live in a settlement. Second, they lose their share of relevant productive skills when these are neglected in training programmes. Over and above these direct effects on a limited number of women, such political practices acquire the shape of a meta message which reaches a far greater number, and repeats the notion, which is also presented in numerous other ways, of women as housewives and reproducers.

Political ideologies as free-flowing texts

Both the specific programs mentioned above, and the more principal discussions just touched on, create a mass of information which flows about in society and forms an ideological and cultural reference material. Because of universal access to media and near-universal literacy in the younger population, it flows about more efficiently, and in a form more detached from immediate social relationships than it would have only a couple of decades ago.

The political ideologies which lie behind the action programmes of the political establishment are forcefully announced in advanced rhetorical style. Political opposition is subdued in the media. Differences in party allegiance, and specific criticisms of the ruling alliance, both of which exist on the local level, do not get to the core of the rhetoric, which takes departure in commonly held central values like deference to superordinates, discipline, Islam, and the family. Maximum responsibility is thrown back on the family for the remedy of all kinds of problems. The duty of charity in kin group and community is announced as a Muslim virtue, morally superior to "socialist" notions of a more radical public redistribution. The political rhetoric provides a canopy of near-sacred values which exempts large areas of people's own lives from being politicized. People may regret the lack of pensions, but at the same time they are culturally conditioned to a deep feeling of duty to repay their parents for what they themselves have received, and they are caught, together with their parents, in the growing prestige differentiation, where the differential success of the younger generation is reflected back on the standards which the elderly can enjoy.

The preceding passages give my simplified description of the organizational and ideological world in which modern village women's lives are set. At this point I will anticipate a point which will be further demonstrated in the subsequent discussion: Women may experience a kind of double bind between

1) their traditional upbringing which stresses their productive capacities and expects them to be essentially self-supporting and supporting other family members

2) one side of economic policy which necessitates that women continue to be productive and supporters

3) realities of the general economic development which make it difficult for women to hold the same share in productive life as they did in peasant society

4) explicit and implicit ideological messages which stress women's reproductive roles at the expense of the productive ones.

This is more than role conflict, because it cannot be solved by dramaturgical strategies. I choose the word "double bind" to describe a situation in which the person is told to be a producer and supporter by the same messenger who also makes it difficult for her to fulfill the command.

The identity management of modern village women

The concept of identity is an elusive one referring, in part at least, to a person's self identification. This is not immediately accessible to observation, so issues of identity have to be studied indirectly through discernible bits of information. The rest of the discussion will be such an attempt to explore some features of village women's work situation and comments on their own life.

Village women appear busy. They share their time between house, possible job, religious duties, and ceremonial duties.

It is very common for women with some specific qualifications to want, and hold, a job, but at the same time there is a growing number of women whose most salient identity is "housewife": These are separated from the traditional productive roles, and they have not qualified for, or been able to get, a job in the formal sector. The housewives often look around for a possibility of earning some income of their own, and often try their hand at trade, or at making and selling food, often after having acquired some necessary skills at a KEMAS course. There are still a lot of people involved in trade because it is typically the niche where those who lack other possibilities, are likely to try their luck. I suggested above that there is a double bind between strong incentives to be productive, and growing difficulties to be able to realize this demand. I will now describe the case of a woman who is typical in so far as she is a product of the rapid changes that have taken place during her lifetime. The fact that she is better off than most other village women may mean that she is not the perfect average in every respect, but the kind of reflections that she makes can be found in most others.

Aishah is 38 years old, and with first generation membership in the middle class. Her parents were peasants, not among the poorest, but their resources were still so small that it adversely affected the children's chances for real success in their secondary education. Her father died some years ago, and her mother lives with Aishah's only brother, who is unmarried. Aishah and her two sisters are all married, and well under way in raising their children. Aishah is outwardly the most successful among the siblings. She is married to a professional man, and she herself has a secure job with a public agency. Although her salary is not very high, it alone is above the average family income in the village. Aishah and her husband have a large, modern, and well furnished house. They are greatly concerned with their children's education and so far they have been successful. But Aishah is tormented by feelings of insufficiency. "Ideally", she ought to have had more children, but claims that she has not had the physical strength for it. Sometimes she says that it is better to have few children and give them a good education. "Ideally", she ought to have had a more prestigious job, but was not able to pursue her education far enough. "Ideally", she ought to have kept the house and flower garden in better shape, but does not have enough time. She also compares herself to some of the wives of her husband's colleagues who were born into urban middle class families and socialized to the life-style which she is trying to master as an adult. They have better jobs, are up to date on everything, and know how to give orders to housemaids. Aishah's husband thinks it would be all right for her to quit her job, as she appears constantly overstrained. But she tenaciously sticks to it. One of her explicit reasons for doing so is that she wants to give her mother money which she herself has earned, instead of depending on her husband's good will. Further, none of her siblings are able to contribute as much to their mother as she is; she is the only one who is in full time employment. Aishah's life situation and self concept is shaped and affected by her family back-ground, her life career, and a number of explicit and implicit expectations that confront her in her environ-ment. Into this process of formation and shaping go political ideologies and decisions on a high level, as well as traditional features of the village society, and her own leap from a humble peasant background to a modern middle class existence.

This characterization of village women in general, and Aishah's case in particular, suggests some intriguing similarities with related problems as we see them in Western countries. The problem of being too busy appears familiar, as do the modern woman's account of feeling insufficient in the face of conflicting demands. If we go more deeply into the material, however, differences also become apparent. The content of the demands are partly different. The meaning and purpose of being productive, as well as the meaning and purpose of autonomy may also be tied to other practical problems and other structures of value than their counterparts would be in our own society.

In Aishah's running comments on her own life there is a set of concepts which crop up in various disguises at several occasions, and which are also recognizable in corresponding statements from other women. These notions are:

- -the idea of the self-supporting woman
- -the concept of the good housewife
- -high appreciation of children
- -duty to parents

Some of these notions are doubly or trebly reinforced, and reinforce each other. Some oppose each other, or are adhered to in the face of tremendous counteracting forces. I will now take each point or notion by itself, and suggest how it is nurtured partly by messages from village background and upbringing, partly from the public discourse in which political messages proper blend with messages from other sources.

Notion 1: the idea of the self-supporting woman

The idea of the self-supporting woman is rooted in the peasant society in which Aishah grew up. Women's contributions to the household economy were as important as those of men, even if male and female productive tasks were somehow differentiated. The normal thing for a woman was to be productive and a supporter along with her husband. She had ample role models for this in her own mother and other women in the village.

Instead of being self-supporting through their contribution to the agricultural system of production and exchange, many women now try to be so through seeking jobs, or trying their luck in the already crowded niche of trade. Part of the rationale behind this wish is a wish for a measure of independence of husbands, and obligations felt towards other family members, particularly aged parents. The concept of independence is not a Western individualistic one. It is a notion of being able to support oneself whether or not the husband fulfills his duties, and it is a notion of being free to help other relatives. She is still primarily a family person, just not fully dependent on her husband. The autonomy of women used to be a kind of collective strength in a network of female family members, as an alternative to a fragile marriage tie.

When Aishah grew up, education was becoming available for girls, and she was one of the more lucky, but not lucky enough to go as far as her abilities and ambition could have taken her. This is a fate she shares with many other women of her generation.

Government policy does not give priority to the introduction of public pensions or other economic measures which may ease the situation of the poorer part of the population. On the contrary, economic differences within the Malay population are allowed to grow rather unchecked, and the duty of support is explicitly left to family members.

All the factors mentioned so far work towards making the woman wish to have her own income.

Over the past twenty years the economy even in Kelantan has gone a long way towards higher industrialization and monetization, and people's productive roles must be transformed accordingly.

Some areas of planning in which the political establishment has invested great resources and prestige, tend to favour "nuclearfamilism" and stress women's reproductive roles while overlooking or even counteracting their productive roles.

Outside these realms of detailed planning, clerical

and industrial jobs open to women tend to be poorly paid and hard to get.

All these forces make participation in the workforce difficult.

The notion of the self-supporting female, then, is fraught with dilemmas of a double bind nature: there are strong incentives towards prolonging it, and strong obstacles to realize it.

Notion 2. The idea of the perfect housewife

When I came back to the field in 1987, I learned a new word: suri rumah, "queen of the house", or housewife. It may be one of my shortcomings that I did not learn the concept in 1965, but it is also certain that it was not part of most village people's active vocabulary at that time. In 1965 I also spent a good part of my time talking to women about their work, and those who did not take an active part in farming or other things that could be unambiguously classified as "productive" chose other terms to describe their activities. Most commonly, they would describe themselves as "sitting only" or as "looking after house and children" - and probably add "only". Even today many will choose these phrasings, but suri rumah is commonly gaining ground, particularly among the young. This indicates that a housewife identity akin to the Western one is rapidly being formed.

There are many incentives to ambitious housekeeping in Malay culture. Even in traditional peasant village society the standards in cooking and clothing were high seen against the background of the resources available. It was also always important for women to take care of ceremonial duties, and offer hospitality up to the standards one could afford. This is still important, but new demands are arising out of the higher material standard in most houses. There are simply more material

115

things about, more furniture, more utensils, more "frills and decorations" - which take time to keep in order. The better the economic resources of the household, the more work to be done.

When I have expressed the opinion that some important government-sponsored programmes favour reproductive activities, this is another way of saying that they favour a housewife identity.

Beside the political leads, there is a mass of public discourse in magazines and TV which pulls in the same direction, applying symbols which strongly appeal to such ambitions in women. A housewife can be kept busy doing housework. Staying at home with the children is a frequent adaptation. It may be involuntary - either because there are no jobs around, or because her husband does not allow her to work. It may also be voluntary in some cases if she feels that she would not be able to cope, or there is no strong need for the money. In these cases being a housewife is an alternative identity to being gainfully occupied. But the expectations to good housekeeping are felt by all. For those who are gainfully occupied, it has become an additional burden.

Notion 3 and 4 - appreciation of children and duty to parents

The high appreciation of children is a very strong and very basic trait in Malay society, it is given both emotional and practical rationale. People "love children", "enjoy having many children around", the house is "empty and desolate" when the children are away, not "quiet and peaceful" as the same situation tends to be construed in Western society. And children are a great help when grown up - they contribute with all kinds of practical assistance, and ultimately it is their duty to take care of parents in their old age. This is part of the unconditional tie between parents and children. Because of the strength and sentimental intensity of this tie, any person - man or woman - will feel more direct responsibility for his or her own parents than the spouse's parents. The dominance and totality of the mother-daughter bond probably adds to the women's demands on themselves regarding the quality of support that they feel obliged to give: it should be both financial, and direct practical care. The ideal child is probably a daughter who earns her own income, and is married to a man who takes the main economic responsibility for the family of procreation. Aishah should thus be an ideal child for her mother. She herself feels that she is less than that because she does not have the time and strength to give her mother as much practical assistance as she would like.

Family ties are becoming more asymmetric, but no less strong. Twenty years ago most rural families existed in a precarious balance where a multitude of petty resources were pooled to make a living, and the borderline between being productive and being dependent was a fuzzy one. Now this borderline has become more clear cut. The pooling strategies are greatly reduced, and the burdens of support lie heavily on the wage-earners. The further the children have advanced from their family of origin in economic success and lifestyle, the more the pooling has broken down, and the greater the expectation and assumed obligation for support. Family ties which used to be strong and symmetric, have now become strong and asymmetric. This development is a logical one in a situation where the conditions are: strong family solidarity at the outset, rapid social mobility and economic differentiation, and a development ideology where poverty is fought by a carte blanche for individual profit-seeking rather than by measures for redistributing resources. This policy can then to a certain degree be seen as depending on a certain cultural feature, and at the same time reinforcing it.

Those who are raising families in the 1980s expect to be taken care of by their children in old age, just as they feel the obligation of taking care of their own parents now.

Having many children adds to the workload in a certain phase, but also increases the chances of reaping help later, or does it? Some are beginning to doubt it. Having many children also increases the problem of investing satisfactorily in each, as far as education is concerned. This uncertainty becomes visible in Aishah's inconsistent views on family size.

In the public, political sphere there are some seemingly contradictory messages. The family planning services of the health clinics coexist with a newly forged urge to increase the population. The third pole is religion - many interpretations of which ban family planning.

So, both in the "private" and the "public" fora of discussion there are arguments favouring both large and small families, and in any case, the number of children is something which is given a great deal of thought.

Concluding remarks

The last couple of pages already contain a number of specific partial conclusions directly geared to the questions which were asked initially. Moreover, this brief discussion has been concerned with very complex interdependencies between different levels of socio-cultural integration. In this complexity there are many possible ways of "reading" connections which have not been touched on at all, and even with reference to the connections that have been made, many shortcuts have been necessary. I will therefore finish with a few more general reflections which, in different ways, seem to point to further analysis instead of underlining definite answers.

One such set of reflections is concerned with change and continuity. New issues are introduced in the political field, and organizational changes occur in the local field. Family morality is retained, but the distribution of resources as well as the distribution of events of support and cooperation within families have changed. Political rhetoric creates a holy alliance between government strategies and people's own understanding of religion and custom, so that a simile of continuity is created. I have, however, not gone more deeply into the problem of how meaning is re-created on the local level. To widen the understanding of people's own perception of sameness and change, we should need to expand the analysis of the kinds of information processing that take place in public as well as private local fora.

Analytical problems on the level of identity management are related to the ambition of simultaneously seeing the person as participant in organizational setups and a receiver and processor of texts. A more refined analysis is needed to decide how far information processing depends on the kinds of face to face interaction in which the person takes part. For instance, as has been indicated above, the concept of autonomy does not seem to be primarily individualistic, but more a question of alternative interdependencies within an extended family. In other words, the choice seems very much to be a choice between ways of being a family person, not between being a family person on the one hand and a self-sufficient individual on the other. A deepened understanding of the problem of identity management would have to take account of such givens. One promising project could be to go into the processes of role modelling which are governed by such widely different fields as family, school, and media

119

communication. The aim of this would be to compare similarities and differences in the identity structures that result from different socialization histories, and this could result in a further refinement of the understanding of the articulation between different levels of socio-cultural integration.

BIBLIOGRAPHY

Fiske, John: **Introduction to Communication Studies** (London and New York: Methuen & Co Ltd., 1982).

Gale, Bruce: **Politics and Public Enterprise in Malaysia** (Singapore: Eastern Universities Press Sdn. Bhd., 1981).

Grönhaug, Reidar: "Scale as a Variable in the Analysis: Fields in Social Organization in Herat, Northwest Afghanistan"; in Frederik Barth (ed.): **Scale and Social Organization** (Oslo: Universitetsforlaget, 1978).

Hutheesing, Otome: **Pros and Cons of a Government Programme for Women** (KANITA publ., undated stencil).

Lochhead, James and Vasanthi Ramachandran: **Income generating activities for women: A case study of Malaysia** (Preliminary draft, Nov. 1982. KANITA report).

Maaruf, Shaharuddin: **Concept of a Hero in Malay Society** (Singapore: Eastern Universities Press Sdn. Bhd., 1984).

Mohamad, Mahathir: **The Malay Dilemma. The Challenge** (Petaling Jaya: Pelanduk Publications, 1986).

Muzaffar, Chandra: **Freedom in Fetters. An analysis of the state of democracy in Malaysia** (Penang: Aliran Kesedaran Negara, 1986).

Islamic Resurgence in Malaysia (Petaling Jaya: Penerbit Fajar Bakti Sdn. Bhd., 1987).

Norris, Malcolm W: **Local Government in Peninsular Malaysia** (Westmead, Farnborough, Hants.: Gower ·Publishing Company Ltd., 1980).

Rudie, Ingrid: **Market and Neighbourhood** (Unpublished manuscript, 1971).

ZERO AS COMMUNICATION.
THE CHINESE MUSLIM DILEMMA IN MALAYSIA.

Long Litt Woon
The Ethnographic Museum, Oslo

INTRODUCTION

I am interested in exploring some of the social implications of subscribing to two socially irreconcilable identities. I approach this task by studying the Chinese Muslim converts in Malaysia.

In the flow of private and public events there is a vast complex of social differentiations that Malaysians find relevant in their interactions with each other. These differentiations are imperative when it comes to the structuring of peoples' self awareness and their judgement of others. In Malaysia such differentiations are represented by cultural categories like ethnicity, religion, wealth, education, occupation and social position. Social interest in these categories is seen as "normal". An example of this is the Malaysian interest in specifying ethnic identity: "Was the traffic accident victim Malay, Indian or Chinese?" is not an irrelevant question for Malaysians to ask. One common feature of cultural categories is that events are often viewed and explanations are sought from their angle. They point the directions for questions but are not questioned themselves. These cultural categories make up some of the main "pillars" in the Malaysian world view.

Some cultural categories are regularly associated with others to the extent that they become familiar clusters of categories. The ethnic and religious categories in Malaysia are so closely associated that ethnic memberships have corresponding religious affiliations and vice versa. The main ethnic groups that make up the Malaysian population are the Malays (55%), the Indians (10%) and the Chinese (34%)[1]. The religions subscribed by the above ethnic groups are Islam, Hinduism and the polytheistic blend of Taoism, Buddhism and Confucianism respectively.[2] In the case of Malaysia, we can refer to the ethnic and the religious categories together as a **cultural cluster**.

A cultural cluster implies standard norms. A standard norm arising from the ethno-religious cluster is that Islam is the religion associated with the Malays. Since we are dealing with an ethnically bipolar state[3] where the two main ethnic blocs are the Malays and the Chinese, this also implies that Islam is not associated with the Chinese. What are some of the social implications for a group that **defies** the standard norm arising from the ethno-religious cluster?

---

[1] These are figures for Peninsula Malaysia where Malays number 6.3 million, Chinese 3.9 million and Indians 1.2 million. The total population of Peninsula and East Malaysia is 13,745,000. 1980 Population and Housing Census of Malaysia. Volume One. Dept. of Statistics. Kuala Lumpur.

[2] The distribution of the major religions in Peninsula Malaysia: Muslim: 56% of population in Peninsula Malaysia; Hindu: 8%; Buddhism: 19%; Confucianism/Taoism: 13%/32%; Christianity; 2%. 1980 Population and Housing Census of Malaysia. Volume One. Dept. of Statistics. Kuala Lumpur.

[3] Milne describes the ethnically bipolar state as one that is constituted of two major ethnic blocs, both making up eighty per cent or more of the population. He also suggests that the "uncertainty over ultimate strength of power" (Milne 1981:8) between two more or less equal blocs in terms of numbers and in political influence is more likely to produce competition and confrontation than in ethnically divided societies which are not bipolar.

The **Chinese Muslim converts** represent such a group. They are thought to use conversion to Islam as a means toward non-religious ends and they are ascribed religiously insincere motives by Malaysians. It is difficult to obtain exact figures of the total number of Chinese Muslims and the rate of their conversion. However, PERKIM[4] usually sets the total number of converts around 100,000. Since the trend has been that more than half of all conversions at PERKIM are Chinese, we are led to the figure of 50,000 Chinese Muslims though this could still be an inflated figure.[5]

The limited scope of this paper does not allow me to describe how Chinese Muslims actually handle the implied limitations and possibilities connected to the unusual combination that their ethno-religious identity presents, nor why they convert to Islam in the first place. That is

---

[4] Pertubuhan Kebajikan Islam Malaysia. (Muslim Welfare League) Started in August 1960 and is headed by Tunku Abdul Rahman, the former Prime Minister of Malaysia. Its total membership today is over 80,000. This volunteer organization has branches and affiliate offices in all the thirteen states of the country. Its activities include welfare work, the training of missionaries and the spreading of the word of Islam. This is reflected in its public image as a major "convert association".

[5] According to the 1980 Population and Housing Census of Malaysia, Volume Two (pg.230, table 2.8), there are 7428 Chinese Muslims in Peninsula Malaysia. However, officials at PERKIM insist that the figure in the states of Selangor and Wilayah Persekutuan alone exceeds this. Technically, one may convert to Islam in the presence of two Muslim witnesses and the person performing the conversion. Whether the conversion is registered at all or where it may be registered is not a clear cut matter, hence the difficulty in obtaining complete records. The administration of Islam in Malaysia, characterized by the split in final authority with the Sultan (or the King, in states without Sultans) as the Head of Islam in his state on one hand and the Prime Minister's Dept. on the other accentuates this problem.

the subject of my thesis.[6] Here I shall only try to sketch the social framework which Chinese Muslims find themselves using as a reference point for their lives today.

I shall use the ethno-religious cluster as an analytical axis. The ethno-religious cluster has spatial and temporal dimensions. The geographical scope of this paper is restricted to Peninsula Malaysia. The historical processes that are of particular interest here are the Islamic resurgence in Malaysia from the end of the sixties till today and the relationship between the Chinese and the Malays during this same period. In this paper I will try to explore some of the main social implications of these changing historical processes for Chinese Muslim lives.

ONE: THE ETHNO-RELIGIOUS CLUSTER

Ethnicity

Among Malaysians, ethnicity is often employed as explanation for events and as reason for action. As such ethnicity is part of the Malaysian world view and is thought of as a "natural" category of social differentiation. Ethnicity is a category of cultural diversity in Malaysia on both the grassroot level and on the level of officialdom which tends to see social and economic problems and their solutions in "ethnic" terms.(Nagata 75:6)

The salience of ethnicity today should not be seen separate from history: the different ethnic groups have concentrated in different niches of livelihood. Colonial policy supported their separation from each other. The

---

[6] **Alone with my halal chicken. The Chinese Muslim converts and ethnic bipolarization in Malaysia** (Mag.art. thesis in Social Anthropology, Univ. of Oslo, Norway, Spring 1988).

Chinese kept themselves to mining and to commercial services in the urban areas and were not seen in the public administration and agriculture which were the Malay dominated fields, whilst the Indians were recruited as indentured labour to the rural lying plantations. Among the various ethnic groups that make up Malaysian society the Malays and the Chinese tend to be the most visible because of their size and more important, because of the place they command in national power negotiations.

The Chinese and the Malays hold negative ethnic stereotypes of each other. In Chinese eyes, the Malays are "religiously prejudiced, more backwards than themselves, more apt to be lazy, not willing to work for what they want...."(Winzeler 1985:118). On the other hand, the Malays view the Chinese as "hardworking, materialistic, economically sophisticated, crafty and ambitious" and worry that they will "end up owning the entire country". (Winzeler 1985:117) On the level of daily interaction however, these broad and generalized stereotypes have not prevented Chinese and Malays from forming personal friendships with each other. This suggests that Malaysians might use broad (and negative) ethnic stereotypes "to think with" on the level of public role expectations of each other but that thinking in this way does not necessarily dictate their behavior in one direction or the other.

Religion

Religion is another category into which people divide themselves. Any casual description of the relationship between ethnicity and religion in Malaysia would state that the majority of Hindus are Indian; the syncretic blend of Confucianism, Taoism and Buddhism practiced by the Chinese remains theirs alone and as mentioned, the majority of the Muslims are Malays. This description is also true if turned around: Indians are almost exclusively Hindu, the majority of the Chinese practice the particular polytheistic blend mentioned and almost all Malays are Muslim.[7] In other words, ethnic boundaries can easily be translated into religious boundaries and vice versa and we can think of religion as an important indicator of ethnic identity.

The negative ethnic stereotypes that the Malays and the Chinese hold of each other are echoed here in the mutually unflattering image they hold of each other's religion. The Malay idea of Chinese religion is that the Chinese are idol worshippers overconcerned with ritualistic practices. The ceremonial paraphernalia are seen as unnecessary expenses. The lack of a single Godgiven relevation, an organized written scripture and common theological knowledge among the Chinese only confirms Malay suspicions that Chinese religion "has no logic". In fact, many Malays wonder if it can be classified as a religion at all.

To the Chinese, Islam has always been associated in a limited way to the prohibition of the eating of pork, the possibility of marrying four wives, the practice of male circumcision, praying five times a day and the obligatory annual fasting month. Whilst some men might appreciate the rules for polygamy as they are commonly

---

[7] 1980 Population and Housing Census of Malaysia. Volume Two (pg.230, table 2.8) Dept. of Statistics. Kuala Lumpur.

6035985	Malay Muslims
909912	Indian Hindus
3425220	Chinese Buddhists/Confucianists/Taoists

This is to say that 95% Malays in Peninsula Malaysia are Muslim, 75% of Indians are Hindu and 87% of Chinese practice a syncretic blend of Confucianism, Buddhism and Taoism. There are 82061 Indian Christians (6% of Indians) and 120231 Chinese Christians (3% of Chinese).

interpreted by Muslims in Malaysia, to most Chinese, Islam is usually "a religion full of restrictions".

The ethno-religious cluster: Its changing display and significance

It is easy to describe the regular association of ethnicity and religion but the meaning of this cluster eludes us if we do not look at how it has been reproduced and how its meaning has evolved in social life. In colonial times, ethno-religious division of the population also coincided with cultural expression, geographical concentration, political participation and economic specializations. The ethno-religious cluster was socially relevant within the context of **local** residential and market communities and no further. Upon Independence (1957), communal differences were fought in the **national** political arena in the form of political bargaining though racial clashes and open violence between the Malays and the Chinese also took place. The ethno-religious cluster had expanded its social relevance from the local to the national level.

Following these historical and political processes, though display of ethnic identity among the Chinese today does not appear to be dramatically different in form from colonial times, it has acquired new political significance.

Turning to the Malays we see that there has been a change in the display and in the political significance of Malay markers too. Islam provides us with an example of this. The Islamic revival that started haltingly as a grassroot movement in the sixties has grown in momentum. It convinced some Malays that there are parts of their traditional culture as well as parts of Western culture that they have adopted like dress, greetings and social interaction between the sexes that are in conflict with the proper practice of Islam. They are committed to a "re-Islamization" of their whole way of life.

The one outstanding characteristic of the dominant trend is its fervent belief that society should be organized on the basis of the Quran and the Sunnah. ...New ideas and institutions are acceptable as long as this supreme principle is not compromised in any manner. (Muzaffar 1984:9)

In fact, part of the force of the Islamic revival has spread from grassroot level and is now accommodated and become part of government policies.[8] The policy to inculcate Islamic values like "efficiency, discipline, loyalty, diligence and trustworthiness" ("New Straits Times" 5 Feb 1986) into the government administration is another move in this direction. In the competitive, ethnically bipolar situation in Malaysia the way the ideas connected to the Islamic revival have manifested themselves in official policies has lead to the situation where Islam has new political **significance** as a marker of Malay identity and as a negating marker of Chinese identity.

There have also been other historical processes that have given Islam new political significance. Immediately after the race riots in 1969, Chinese converts to Islam were the objects of abuses from the Chinese community. They were regarded as "traitors" to the community. One Chinese convert was threatened by his business associates that "the next time there was trouble in town it would be his head that they would be carrying".

It was at this time that the bumiputra/non-bumiputra distinction became an important issue in government

---

[8] S. Siddique describes the new administrative programmes in the seventies onwards that were designed to contain and to control Islamic revival forces coming from the grassroot level and to build up an Islamic infrastructure of within the government administration.

policy. Bumiputra[9] is an administrative term coined to distinguish individuals that are to benefit from government programmes "to correct imbalances" and "to restructure Malaysian society". All Malays (who are Muslims) are classified as bumiputra. Though this category also includes non-Muslims like the indigenous peoples, descendants of Portuguese and of Thai settlers, this is an unknown or insignificant fact for most Malaysians for whom bumiputra is equated with Malay. As a result of this the term has an Islamic connotation. In Chinese eyes therefore, Islam is seen as one of the factors that handicaps them in what they perceive as an unfair policy of opportunity and wealth distribution.

The **display** of Islamic identity has changed with the coming of the Islamic revival.

> "At a more specific level, this outlook on Islam has expressed itself in a number of ways. It is perhaps most obvious in the rejection of old habits such as gambling or consuming alcohol or frequenting night clubs and in the acquisition of new attitudes which could stretch from faithful observance of daily prayers to dressing in proper Islamic attire....more subtle changes in conduct and behavior (like a) more restrained attitude towards the opposite sex is, for instance, one of the transformation which accompanies this new outlook." (Muzaffar 1984:10)

We shall look closer at the changing display of Islamic identity and some of its implications later in this paper.

---

[9] Bumiputra is usually translated as "son of the soil". When Malaysia was formed in 1963, the indigenous peoples of Sarawak and Sabah were given similar rights as the Malays (Articles 153 and 161A of the Constitution). This new administrative category created a unified bloc vis a vis the "immigrants" (the Chinese and the Indians).

TWO: THE CHINESE MUSLIM DILEMMA

Ambiguity

The current obsession with ethnic membership in Malaysia
puts the Chinese Muslims in an awkward position; the man
on the street is unable to decide whether they are still
Chinese or whether they have become Malay. The identity
of the Chinese Muslims is, therefore, ambiguous. Furthermore, because of the Islamic connotation of the term
bumiputra, many also wonder if they can qualify for
bumiputra privileges by virtue of their conversion.

The Chinese Muslim stereotype

Upon confrontation with the fact of Chinese conversion to
Islam, the nagging question that springs to the public
mind is "Why have they converted?". When I expressed my
interest in finding out more about Chinese Muslim converts
in Malaysia to Malaysians of various ethnicity I repeated-
ly met similar responses. Reactions like "Oh, they are
just opportunists. Trying to get bumi (colloquial for
bumiputra) privileges you know" or "I know a Chinese
Muslim. Converted because of marriage. Dooon't practice
the religion at all" were the usual fare. Some responses
might have been more hesitant and less outspoken but
generally they had the same pattern of focusing on the
motives of conversion. In the same breath, stories might
be told to illustrate and to prove the dubious religious
motives of the Chinese Muslims. Their choice of a religion, looked upon as strange, becomes socially intelligible
when they are pigeonholed with popularly ascribed motives.
Dismissal of the Chinese Muslims in this manner makes
"sense" of the social ambiguity of their identity.

The Chinese Muslim stereotype is public judgement of their character which supposedly is evident in the two ascribed categories of motives: convenience and opportunism. The converts of convenience are the ones who convert for the sake of wanting to marry a Malay/Muslim spouse. The opportunists are those trying to sneak into the privileged category of bumiputra. Some might of course straddle these two categories by marrying a Malay spouse **in order to** gain bumiputra privileges. Empirically, the ascribing of these motives could be justified but it is striking that sincere faith is not an acknowledged motive. It would seem that Chinese Muslim converts have no legitimate social claims to the religion that sets them outside the ethno-religious cluster.

Changing political processes have continued to reproduce the idea that Chinese Muslims are weak in their Islamic faith and that they first and foremost are opportunists. This fits the stereotype of the Chinese ("greedy and religiously pragmatic") in Malaysia that also has also endured. The Islamic revival has not closed the cleft between the Malays and the Chinese. In fact, the forms in which the recent Islamic revival has expressed itself are so difficult for most Chinese to accept that their distance from the religion is emphasized.

Before Malay nationalism broadly translated itself politically through the bumiputra policy, Chinese conversion to Islam was not seen as threatening to the interests belonging to **whole** ethnic groups. They were just odd individuals, usually poor, who saw a chance to improve their material standing through conversion. As we have seen the idea of 'rice bowl Muslims' with opportunistic motives is still very much alive today but they no longer can be dismissed as the odd handful of individuals. In the context of present Chinese-Malay relations, increasing ethnic polarization and the awareness of ethnic group interests makes Chinese conversion to Islam a concern of the whole groups who reject or who claim them.

Social demands

To start with, Chinese would check to see if Chinese Muslims "have become Malay" and if they still qualify as Chinese. Muslims would do likewise to see if they "still live as Chinese" and if they can be classified as true Muslims. This situation brings us to exploring the intricate **social demands** of Chinese identity and of Muslim identity in Malaysia.

There are a multitude of markers that can be identified as Chinese or as Islamic. Obviously, the ambiguity of Chinese Muslim identity suggests that Malaysians do not depend on the long lists of 'typical' Chinese or Muslim markers alone. Furthermore, readily identified markers of Chineseness or of Muslim identity are not automatically socially demanded and displayed. For example, though personal names can be identified as Chinese or Muslim, it is not uncommon for Chinese to preferably use names like "Christina" or "Elvis" or for Muslims to call themselves "Zed" or "Bob", depending on changing fashions.

This might suggest that though markers like personal names are recognizable in origin they need not be crucial for identity marking among the Chinese and the Muslims. This implies that there may be other features that form decisive criteria for identity marking and therefore function as socially crucial markers of Muslim and or Chinese identity. We need, therefore, to examine the ways that these identities are interpreted and translated to behavior and meaning.

Are they true Muslims? or, The social codification of Islam

The concept of universal brotherhood obliges Muslims to welcome non-Muslim converts into their social circle. In a climate of ethnic bipolarization, this is easier said than done. The Malays say they dislike the idea that Chinese Muslims might just embrace Islam and renounce it at a whim and thus "make a mockery of Islam". This is why they are concerned, they say, about whether the Chinese Muslims really make efforts to learn about their new religion. They want to know if the Chinese Muslims are doing their best to practice the Muslim way of life.

The Chinese Muslim converts are always closely observed and tested in order to determine the extent of their interest and knowledge of Islam. They are checked if they still follow their previous lifestyle or if they have adopted a Muslim lifestyle. For example, children of Chinese Muslims are sometimes drawn aside by neighbours or by the Islamic Knowledge teachers at school and asked if their (convert) parent "still eats Chinese food" or prays five times a day at the prescribed time. Chinese food is commonly equated with haram[10] food. Sometimes, Chinese Muslims are asked these questions straight to their face by colleagues and friends. During a Hari Raya celebration[11] at a Chinese Muslim home, Malay women guests pointed to the cakes and asked "Boleh makan kah?" (lit. "Can the cakes be eaten?", meaning "Have they been prepared in accordance with Muslim dietary laws?") As these were cakes she offered her Muslim guests during a

---

[10] Unlawful according to Islam. In this case, Islamic dietary laws have been disregarded.

[11] The Malay term for the festival marking the end of the fasting month for Muslims. The Arabic term is Id-al-Fitr.

Muslim celebration, the convert felt insulted by the inquiry.

The (born) Muslim Malays are not tested in the same way. Nobody asks the Malays if they know how to pray, if they pray at the prescribed time at all, or if they eat pork. In other words, it is more easily accepted that some Malays are slack Muslims and that other Malays are pious Muslims. The converts are subjected to a more thorough scrutiny. They have to work harder to prove that they are 'true Muslims'.

What exactly is 'true Muslimness'? How is it socially codified and signalled? What are some of the issues that have been and are socially perceived as important in public identification of Muslim behaviour? These questions are inter-related. Since we are dealing with a context of ethnic bipolarization, another way of putting these inter-related questions would be: what does Muslim identity **not** imply socially, and how is it **not** signalled? In this way, we may discover the **boundaries** which encompass **variations** in the social codification of Islam in Malaysia.

By observing the Muslim community in Malaysia, what meets the eye is a whole **range** of behaviour that all claim, using appropriate quotations from the Koran, to be Islamic and at the same time dismissing others as too liberal or too fanatic. This can be illustrated by looking at some issues the general Malaysian public connect with the Muslim identity.

The issue of eating pork in Malaysia has a position among the Malays that perhaps is extraordinary in the Muslim world.[12] Though the Koran forbids the consumption of other food as well, we could perhaps say that in Malaysia, special attention is given to the non-consump-

---

[12] See Muzaffar, C. **The Islamic Resurgence** (Kuala Lumpur: Fajar Bakti, 1987:7).

tion of pork among the Muslims as a marker of Muslim identity. With the coming of the Islamic resurgence, many Muslims are following stricter rules of dietary observance. For example, they would now refuse to eat food prepared in non-Muslim kitchens for fear of it having been contaminated with kitchen utensils that have been in contact with pork. More extreme, some Muslims also refuse to share refrigerators with non-Muslims. The pork issue causes Malay unease when they suspect Chinese converts of taking advantage of an opportunity to consume it secretly. In Muslim eyes, an example of such an opportunity is when Chinese Muslims return to their Chinese families for a social visit. Malay unease increases considerably if these Chinese Muslims are married to Malays and are accompanied by their children on the visit. "Did you eat with your family?" is asked in a casual manner by Muslims, but its probing of possible contact with pork is clear. One Chinese Muslim always visited her parents' home in-between mealtimes, and always made the time of her visit known to the curious, so that they would "understand that she had not eaten there".

This issue cannot be fully understood by referring to Koranic scripture alone. In the social context of ethnic bipolarization between the Malays and the Chinese, pork is a **positive** marker of Chinese identity. It has a singular position in the Chinese diet. One convert was sarcastically asked by some Chinese if he had converted "because the price of pork had gone up".

In the Chinese diet, pork is an important ingredient in a number of dishes from common snacks to festive delicacies. To refrain from pork is unthinkable for most Chinese. For example, on being told that a Chinese colleague was trying to stop eating pork, following his conversion to Islam, the reaction among his Chinese friends was "whatever for?".

Lard is also frequently used for Chinese cooking in general. Even vegetarian dishes in Chinese religious cuisine include many cellulose surrogates called 'roast pork', 'barbecued pork' etc. So it is not surprising that both Muslims and non-Muslims wonder about the practical observance by the Chinese Muslims of the prohibition of pork in their diet.

Though Chinese vegetarian food should meet the criteria set by Islamic dietary laws, it is looked upon with suspicion by Malays because of its **Chinese origin** and because it is prepared in Chinese kitchens. Another Chinese Muslim complained, "I cannot even sit in a Chinese coffee shop with my (Chinese) friends because they (the Malays) will think I am eating Chinese food, even though I might be just sip a drink out of a carton with. a pre-packed straw." What seems to be important for acceptance as Muslims in Malaysia is, in a way, not only avoidance of pork but **the avoidance of Chinese food** in general.

The issue of dogs is another one that arouses Muslim reaction. One European convert married to a Malay girl recounted the episode of how he found a stray puppy which he brought home to be fed. When the Malay grandmother saw him carrying the dog she screamed loudly and dashed into the house. The Malays point to the Koran to explain their attitude towards dogs. Some say that, in general, Muslims cannot rear dogs. Others are more specific and say that Muslims cannot be licked by a dog or come in contact with a wet dog. Should a Muslim be so unlucky as to have this happen to him, he would have to wash and to rinse the contaminated part of his body seven times whilst reciting appropriate Koranic verses. Malay children are taught from an early age to avoid the situation getting so far.

Though the rest of the Muslim world might have other

attitudes[13], for the Chinese Muslims, the Malay attitude means that Chinese Muslims have to avoid dogs the way Malays in Malaysia do. Otherwise, they risk being stamped as 'insincere' Muslims. It needs to be mentioned that it is not uncommon for Chinese to rear dogs in their homes, treating them as watch dogs. The Chinese seldom keep dogs as pets in the Western manner where the animals might be pampered as special members of the household. In fact, dog meat is something a Chinese food stall dealing with special menus[14] might serve. However, this is not to say that dogs represent a positive marker of Chinese identity as in the case of pork. The case of dogs here illustrates how social codification of Islam in Malaysia is tied up with **Malay interpretation** of the Koran.

Another obvious way of communicating identity is in the style of clothing. On one occasion some Malays were telling me about a convert who lived in the neighbourhood. They didn't think she was a practicing Muslim because, amongst other things, she "wore Chinese clothes all the time". Whether Chinese clothes for women pass Islamic requirements is, of course, an important part of this matter, but I would suggest that what is at issue here is also the disapproval of the continued use of Chinese clothes by the convert. A Chinese Muslim male told me that he used a pair of traditional Chinese trousers and jacket suit, complete with Chinese cloth buttons and

---

[13] For example, among Egyptian and Moroccan Muslims, it is not uncommon for households to keep dogs and also "spoil them" (personal communication from various Egyptians and Moroccans).

[14] Usually these are in the back lanes of Chinese business areas. These stalls serve herbal teas steamed with meat from pythons, monitor lizards, monkeys, tortoises, crocodiles and sometime also meat from other protected and wild animals.

skull cap, when he went for Friday prayers "just to show the Malays that Chinese clothes can also be Islamic".[15]

The growing popularity of so-called Muslim attire is often seen as an indicator of the growing momentum of the Islamic resurgence. To wear the tudung[16] or not to wear the tudung is a pressing question for Muslim women today because it is given emphasis as "evidence of a return to Islamic living" (Muzaffar 1986:10). In the sixties and the early seventies, the women wearing the tudung were referred to as 'fanatics' by the non-Muslims and by many Muslims themselves. Today the tudung is a much more common sight.[17] This trend affects judgement of convert behaviour. One Chinese Muslim complained that when she did gardening these days she could not wear shorts, as she used to because "now you have to 'cover up', you know, or else the neighbours will talk."

It is important to note that Islam holds a very wide range of meaning for Muslims in Malaysia. This is to say that though I have only concentrated on issues with **emblematic** function i.e. popular issues which serve to **differentiate** Islam from other religions in Malaysia, we have to remember that Muslims themselves have varying opinions on these issues. Taking the example of pork again, I have met (Malay) Muslims who pick out and leave aside pieces of barbecued pork from a bowl of noodles

---

[15] Chinese men in Malaysia normally do not dress in this way. Being metonymic for Chinese culture, such apparel can most often be observed in Chinese films and comics. Therefore, the above example is an over-communication of Chinese identity on the part of the Chinese Muslim.

[16] Muslim headgear for women.

[17] Muzaffar suggests that today, about "60-70 percent of all adult Muslim females wear such apparel." **The Islamic Resurgence in Malaysia** (Kuala Lumpur: Fajar Bakti, 1987).

before eating the noodles heartily and, as mentioned earlier, I have also met Muslim students who refuse to eat their own food if <u>haram</u> food has been placed in the same refrigerator.

Though the above cases do not cover the full range of issues that are locally important in the identification of Islamic behaviour, they do suggest that the display and judgement of Islamic behaviour in Malaysia is tied up with the common **Malay interpretation** of Islam and also with the communication of **negative markers of Chinese identity.**

Since ethnicity and religion tend to merge in the daily lives of Malaysians, and since the equation of Muslim identity with Malay identity is a most persistent one, the codification of Islam is at the same time a question about the social codification of Malayness. <u>Masuk Islam</u> (to convert to Islam) is often used interchangeably with <u>masuk Melayu</u> (lit. to become Malay) by both Muslims and non-Muslims. For example, it is not uncommon for converts to be asked "<u>masuk Melayu dah berapa tahun?</u>" (lit. how long have you been a Malay?) when the question really is how long they have been Muslim. Malays have identified themselves and have been identified by others as Muslims all their lives, and many Malays think that their way of life is essentially the Muslim lifestyle. Therefore, many Malays reason, if someone wants to convert to Islam, he or she has to be ready to adopt the Malay way of life.

Malays who do not even know the 'ABC's' of Islam will proudly say "I am a Muslim" when asked about their faith. (S.H.Ali 1981:42) It is not realized by many Malays that there are elements of Malay culture that were of Hindu or animistic origins[18] and that the way these are practiced may be contradictory to Islam.[19] The interchangeability of markers of Malay ethnicity with those of the Islamic faith and lifestyle means that very often, in Malay eyes, converts are expected to prove their ethnic solidarity with the Malays as proof of their sincerity in the Islamic faith.

This is to say that, when Chinese Muslims are subjected to Malay inspection of their religious observances of Islam, they feel that what seems to be an important issue to Malays is whether or not their behaviour is acceptable **Malay** behaviour. As long as something can be identified as 'typically Chinese', it is classified as unMalay, and, thus, unIslamic. It is difficult for some Malays to accept that there are elements in the Chinese culture that are **not** contradictory to Islamic values. For example, some think that eating with chopsticks is Chinese and therefore unacceptable for Muslims. For them, it is unthinkable that a Chinese who only speaks a Chinese dialect, reads the Chinese newspapers and who lives in a Chinese neighbourhood can also be a practicing Muslim "because he is so unMalay".

One highly educated convert related the story of how he was given "a Hang Tuah[20] costume" when he dropped in to visit his Malay friend on the way to the mosque for prayers one Hari Raya, the most important festival for

---

[18] For example, it is now often debated if the Malay marriage rite of bersanding is in accordance with Islam. Critics say that it is unIslamic to allow a public viewing of the bride who usually is wearing a tight fitting outfit.

[19] These sorts of issues have gained importance with the Islamic resurgence.

[20] A historical figure and a legendary hero among the Malays.

the Malays. He had worn new and clean trousers and a long sleeved shirt for the occasion. He felt very hurt that his Malay Muslim friends, who were wearing the traditional Malay costume, wanted him to wear the same style of clothes as they. Their reason was that he would "look better" ("lebih elok") if he wore Malay clothes. Not wanting to reject their gift, he changed his clothes. Thus, he pointed out, "it is not enough to be Muslim, you also have to be Malay".

Displaying Muslim behaviour alone in a context of ethnic bipolarization without trying to activate Malay ethnic idioms is controversial because of the merging of Malay ethnicity and Islamic religious practice. To be acceptable to Malays, Chinese Muslims have to communicate that they are 'true Muslims' and 'good Malays'. While many elements that are unMalay or unIslamic in origin are sported by Muslims, the **critical qualifier** of Muslim identity in Malaysia is that these elements are **not associated with the Chinese**. This brings us to the social codifications of Chineseness.

Are they still Chinese? or, The social codification of Chineseness

When we observe Malaysians who identify themselves and who are identified by others as Chinese we see that they employ a very wide range of behaviour and of markers. Some of these do not have clear cut Chinese overtones at all but displaying them do not **disqualify** the person as Chinese. Use of the English language among Chinese[21] in private spheres is an example of this. Behaviour and markers like language behaviour, free time activities,

---

[21] Many English educated Chinese are unable to read or write Chinese even though they might speak several Chinese dialects.

food, preferred personal name and style of clothing could therefore very well be thoroughly 'modern' (read Western) and un-Chinese in origin, but could still not be a valid cause to question the Chineseness of the bearer. He or she would still be recognised as Chinese, along with more 'traditional' Chinese who only speaks Chinese, carries a Chinese personal name, socializes only with Chinese people and wears typically Chinese clothes. A 'modern and free-thinking' Chinese is considered as Chinese as a 'traditional and religiously- minded' one who consults temple divinations for oracular answers to daily problems. In other words, merely not using a Chinese name, eating Chinese food, observing Chinese religious and traditional rituals, speaking the Chinese language etc. might be mildly frowned upon, but certainly not give reason to doubt one's Chineseness.

How, then, is Chineseness socially codified? Put inversely, what are the **critical disqualifiers** of Chinese identity?

Names are important markers of identity in Malaysia. A look at a name will reveal ethnic backgrounds and along with this, extended assumptions about religious affiliations and so on. The Chinese practice patronymity very strictly.[22] Therefore, it becomes important for Chinese to avoid the family name 'dying out'. In order to prevent this happening, strategies like the adoption of male children or the marrying of a second wife, may provide practical solutions. It can be suggested that the use of fashionable personal names is acceptable when the surnames remain clearly Chinese. Hence in Malaysia we meet Chinese who prefer to be called Christina, Elvis or Ricardo whose Western personal names are acceptable since they still are followed by Chinese surnames. However, we see that Chinese women who marry non-Malaysians and who replace

---

[22] The passing of surnames through the male line.

their Chinese surnames with foreign surnames are still socially accepted as Chinese. The critical issue is, therefore, not whether one bears a Chinese surname or not but rather, what one **replaces** it with. When the Chinese surname is replaced by 'Abdullah', as is common with converts, it makes the bearer's Chineseness questionable in a way that is unmatched by Chinese women taking on the surnames of their foreign (and non-Malay) husbands.[23]

Another cultural factor of relevance to Chinese identity is food. Food is a great passion of the Chinese, and they can discuss the subject for hours. The preparation of a dish, the combination of ingredients, the particular technique of cooking are some different aspects that might be discussed by Chinese young and old, poor and rich, male or female. The rich might also travel on 'eating holidays', for example, to Hong Kong, to sample delicacies not available locally. Though a Chinese might eat a Malay breakfast, an American lunch, enjoy an English tea and an Italian dinner, he still is 'loyal' to Chinese food. A Malay, being Muslim, would be able to consume such exotic meals only if they are <u>halal</u>.[24] This is to say that the ingredients, the kitchen and the manner in which these meals were prepared in have to be in accordance with Muslim standards or, as we have seen, with varying Malay interpretations of Muslim standards. In other words, a Chinese puts his Chinese identity at

---

[23] The problem of replacing the Chinese name with a Muslim one is an old one for Chinese converts. In 1954, a reader wrote to the press asking if "it would be unIslamic for a Chinese to retain his/her Chinese name after embracing the Muslim faith"...and pointing to the fact that "Malays do not also have Muslim names nowadays (and that) surely this doesn't make them non-Muslims?" (ST 26 October 1954).

[24] Lawful according to Islam. Fit for Muslim consumption because the Muslim dietary rules have been followed.

stake only when he **replaces** Chinese food **altogether** with Malay halal food.

Chinese festivals connected to special dates on the Chinese lunar calendar are celebrated with different degrees of observance of ritual and detail by both 'modern' and 'traditional' Chinese. The most central of these is the Chinese New Year. Rites de passage connected to events like birth, marriage and death are also occasions which are observed as ethnic events, again to different degrees of ritual observance. Lesser degrees of ritual observance do not make one's Chineseness more questionable. In fact, some 'modern' and rich Chinese take advantage of the long vacation to go abroad on holiday, when the traditionalists are gathered for the annual Chinese New Year family reunion. Therefore it is futile to try to 'measure the Chineseness' of a Chinese Muslim convert by counting the number of festivals he celebrates[25] and the manner in which this is done.

From the Chinese point of view the number and the degree of ritual detail observed alone are not sufficient criteria to decide on Chineseness. For example, it is because of this that Chinese Christians who refuse to observe funeral rites[26] the way the rest of the family does are usually given disapproving looks, without any more serious consequences for their ethnic membership. Therefore, the critical line is not drawn at **refusal** to

---

[25] This is an example of imposing stereotypical and static definitions of Chineseness to see how well or how badly Chinese Muslims 'fit' into them.

[26] The conversion to Christianity also means the weeding out of heathen, superstitious Chinese practices that are 'against Christianity'. Chinese Muslim converts too have to do this, in relation to Islam. The problem for both these groups of converts arise when it comes to the definition of what exactly is 'traditional and cultural' and what is 'religious', since Chinese religion and culture are closely intertwined.

participate in Chinese rites but at the **replacement** of these with Malay or Muslim rites. The **critical disqualifier** of Chineseness is, therefore, not only negative marking of Chineseness alone but, to be more precise, the bearing of any element that is identified as 'Malay'.

The Hokkien (a Chinese dialect) term for conversion to Islam reflects the general Chinese attitude towards the religion and the Malays. <u>Jeep huan</u> literally means "to become a native" in the negative sense of the word. Perhaps this is a reflection of the attitude of the Chinese who pride themselves with a long history of 'superior' civilization; anything unChinese must be second-rate. To renounce the religion of their forefathers for another faith is seen as a move rejecting an illustrious heritage for something that must categorically be inferior. When the new religion is Islam, its close association with the Malays (the <u>huan</u>, the natives) makes the choice totally devoid of wisdom in the eyes of the Chinese. By converting to Islam, the Chinese Muslims are thought, in the words of a convert, "to renounce race, culture, everything!" Therefore, having converted to Islam, their Chineseness becomes questionable. To be acceptable to other Chinese, Chinese Muslims have to demonstrate their ethnic loyalty to the Chinese, and this means to show that they have **nothing to do with the Malays.** The fact that the Chinese too equate Islam with Malay is a matter that complicates the situation for Chinese Muslims. Ali Tan, a Chinese Muslim, was told by his Chinese friends that they were relieved he didn't start wearing a songkok[27] after his conversion. In other words, they had expected him to signal Malay identity because of his conversion to Islam.

---

[27] Malay male headgear made of cloth or velvet. The Malay <u>songkok</u> looks like the Turkish fez without the tassel.

Zero as communication

From our exploration of the social codifications of Islam and of Chineseness in Malaysia, we see how ethno-religious identities in Malaysia are bound up in clusters.

We have seen how the social codifications of Muslimness and of Chineseness in Malaysia cannot be seen separately, but should rather be seen in **relation** to each other. In a context of ethnic bipolarization, we observe how the **mutual exclusiveness** of the Muslim and Chinese identities gives rise to the inter-relation of the marking of these identities. This is the root of the **social ambiguity** of the Chinese Muslims.

When trying to pinpoint the social codification and the critical disqualifiers of Chineseness and of Muslimness, I have spoken about **positive** and **negative marking**. For example, as avoiding pork is a positive marker of Muslimness, it is a negative marker of Chineseness. Following this line of thought, a Chinese who does **not** eat pork can be suspected of being Muslim.

In the world of communication, that which is **not** can be perceived as information because "because **zero** is different from one." (Bateson 1972:452) Therefore, by making it known that he does **not** eat pork, a Chinese will also be perceived to be communicating something else besides his dietary preferences i.e. he could perhaps be Muslim. This is because of the rule of **zero as communication**.

It has been suggested that the Muslim reaction to pork in Malaysia is unmatched in the Muslim world. Thus, it is logical to assume that there are contextual reasons for this. In the world of communication, 'zero' is **contextual** and not absolute.

In a study of social process and change, we cannot ignore the context of **changing circumstances**. On one hand, we observe the competitive and divisive nature of ethnic bipolarization in Malaysia. Here the qualification or the disqualification of ethnic and religious identity is a more overriding social issue than the empirical examination of religious motives. On the other hand, we observe some effects of forces like nation building and modernization which contribute towards homogenizing trends in the population. The social implications of bearing the Chinese Muslim identity are as complex as its context of changing circumstances. However, the current Chinese Muslim dilemma can be understood better by grasping the rule of zero as communication.

BIBLIOGRAPHY

Ali, S.H: The Malays. **Their Problems and their Future** (Kuala Lumpur: Heineman Asia, 2 ed., 1982).

Milne, R.S: **Politics in Ethnically Bipolar States. Guyana, Malaysia, Fiji** (Vancouver: University of British Columbia Press, 1981).

Muzaffar, C: "Islamic Resurgence: A Global Perspective", **The New Straits Times**, 14 August, 1984.

Muzaffar, C: **The Islamic resurgence** (Kuala Lumpur: Fajar Bakti, 1987).

Nagata, J.A: "Introduction"; in J.A. Nagata (ed.), **Pluralism in Malaysia : Myth and Reality (Contributions to Asian Studies,** vol.7) (1975).

Siddique, S: "Dakwah's Role in Malaysia", **The New Straits Times**, 2 December, 1978.

Winzeler,R.L: **Ethnic relations in Kelantan** (Singapore: Oxford Univ. Press, 1985).

SOCIO-CULTURAL ASPECTS OF WORKING CLASS FORMATION
A study of industrial and labour relations in Malaysian manufacturing enterprises

Peter Wad
University of Copenhagen

1. ETHNIC HARMONY AT THE FACTORY LEVEL?

On a field trip to West Malaysia in early 1984, I visited 34 manufacturing enterprises with around 18.000 employees altogether. The plants (except for one) were selected on the basis of union information, and they were (except for the same one) unionized factories. 32 were studied through systematic interviewing, both of the management about production, economy, labour force and labour conditions, and the shop stewards about industrial and socio-cultural relations.

Questioned about the most pressing problems to be tackled in 1984, nobody mentioned ethnic tensions or open conflicts. The shop stewards addressed problems like economic problems at the company and reduced employment, direct retrenchment or unjust dismissal, renewal of collective agreement, inflation, safety and health issues, or deteriorated industrial relations between management and employees in general. In three cases, no serious problems faced the work committee, according to their own opinion.

Asked about ethnic conflict in the factory, only 3 answered that this had occurred, while 26 said this had not occurred and 3 did not answer at all. Later I was told that in one of the 'no-conflict' factories ethnic tension had in fact been serious.

Gender relations were the triggering factor of the problems in 2 of these cases, I was told by the male shop

stewards. At one plant, only Malay men not Chinese or
Indian or Eurasian were allowed to speak to Malay women.
If non-Malay men addressed Malay women, the Malay men
would get very angry. Discriminating promotion practice
and ethnic divide-and-rule tactics by the foreman and
personnel manager caused the other conflicts.

Asked about social interaction between ethnic groups
in or outside the factory, again the overwhelming majority
(28) told me, that they mixed in one way or another.
Nowhere did I hear about complete social segregation
between ethnic groups in their daily life. 4 did not
answer.

The main result is that shop stewards did not
experience grave ethnic conflicts at their unionized work
sites in 1984. But can this finding be generalized, so we
might cautiously indicate that ethnic tensions were non-
existing in Malaysian manufacturing enterprises? If so,
how can we interpreted the changes from 1984 to 1987,
where ethnic tensions were used by the government as an
explanation for mass arrests of oppositional groups?

In the following I will discuss ethnic, gender and
class relations at Malaysian manufacturing enterprises.
The purpose is to explore how socio-cultural aspects
interfere with the processes of labour organization and
activities in the working life of Malaysian factories in
the 1980s. Finally, I will consider the political struggles in 1987 in the perspective of the investigation 3
years earlier.

2. THEORETICAL-METHODOLOGICAL CONSIDERATIONS

The field trip was set up to address the question of how
socio-cultural relations condition the integration of
Malays into the manufacturing work force in West Malaysia.

Since 1970, the Malaysian development policy has
been carried out within the guidelines of the New Economic

Policy and the 5-years plans. The ultimate goal of the NEP was, in combination with other measures, to reunite the nation after the outbreak of inter-ethnic violence in 1969 and secure political stability. The specific target of the NEP was double: 1) to eliminate ethno-economic inequalities between the ethnic communities, and 2) to reduce or eradicate poverty. Rapid economic growth and industrialization was seen as one important measure to fulfill these goals, and the Malaysianization of foreign companies was another important means. Later, direct job-quotation for Malays was used at industry or company level to secure the transfer of Malays from the tradition-al (primary) to the modern (secondary and tertiary) sectors.

The NEP was conceptualized in the ethno-economic perspective and preconditioned Malay job expansion. Yet, the most conspicuous Malay job expansion were gender-biased and took place in 'female industries' like textiles and electronics, the so-called world market or run-away industries, related to the drive of export-industrializa-tion in Malaysia and the whole region of East Asia.

In the NEP planning and assessment, the majority of the new female workers did not count as women, but as Malays. Very late -in the Fifth Malaysia Plan 1986-1990 - the problems of women were introduced into the objectives of the NEP.

The opposite situation prevailed in social research. Here female workers and 'female industries' were the main objects for research about women internationally. This was related to the international debate of the NEW INTERNATIONAL DIVISION OF LABOUR and its basis in sweat-shop industries and exploitation of women in the Newly Industrializing Countries (NICs).

My study was directed to the 'male industries', which have had as big an increase of employment as the female industries. But they were overlooked by the researchers just as was the dynamics of the home market manufacturing sector (Wad 1984).

This study is a part of a larger research program on the conditions and prospects of the trade union movement in industrializing Third World Countries using Malaysia as a case. The program includes four interrelated areas:

1) the political economy of Malaysian development, conceptualized in a Marxist structural-historical perspective (mode of production, social classes, state, foreign sector, production & exchange) with economic growth and distribution as criteria for development,

2) the Malaysian trade union movement in general and specifically the unions in the manufacturing in- dustries (Wad 1988)

3) the Malaysian local unionism at the factory level: the work (or area) committees (shop stewards com- mittees), workers' collectives, collective resis- tance and sub/counter-culture.

4) the everyday life and local community of rank-and- file industrial workers within and outside the work place.

While the Danish Research Council of Development Research rejected a research proposal on Malaysian trade unionism, the council accepted the study of the socio-cultural aspects of industrial relations in Malaysian manufacturing industries.

The change of priorities about development theories in the 1980s has not outdated the topic. On the contrary, the socio-cultural and anthropological approaches have had a renaissance, for example conceptualized around the catch-word 'everyday life studies' (see Stepputat 1987). In my view, the concept is appropriately defined as the individuals' ways of reproducing themselves (see Nautrup 1987). Hence, the life-approach focus at the spheres of

153

local production and reproduction, of sex, gender, family and kinship and of cultural traditions, symbolic interpretations and cultural innovation.

Studying local level unionism in the perspective of socio-cultural structures and dynamics, the very question of class formation is whether wage workers (employees without the power of the employer) become socialized as workers or other social categories, and whether class contradiction becomes the main (hegemonic) contradiction among all social contradictions, organizing everyday life and struggles of working people.

The hegemonic principle (working class struggle) and the hegemonic agency (autonomous labour organization) are human constructions, not just the results of structural contradictions and determinations (Laclau and Mouffe 1985). Unionists compete with other organizers for the hegemony at the local level, where everyday life is a complex of economic, political, social and cultural contradictions. Furthermore, unions may compete or cooperate at the intermediate level of social formations for the hegemony among a variety of organizations and movements. Finally, unions may be part of class/social forces at the societal level in the national struggle for development and social transformation (the international level is left out in this context).

The focus of the article is on everyday factory life in the perspective of union organization. This more narrow study, then, has to take into account both the structuring of everyday life and the more encompassing structuring to prevent short cut explanations - structuring as conceptualized by Giddens (1984 p. 25) as "conditions governing the continuity or transmutation of structures and therefore the reproduction of social systems".

3. RESEARCH DESIGN AND 'POPULATION'

At first, the study was intended to be 'explorative', searching the qualitative dimensions and problems of class formation in Malaysia with her heterogeneous population. A later second research phase could be used for a more representative, systematic and quantitative study or more in-depth anthropological case studies of selected enterprises and workers' collectives.

For various practical reasons, I decided to combine the two stages into systematic stratification and selection of the sample of manufacturing enterprises, according to the two NEP-criteria: 1) national and ethnic ownership and 2) the ethnic composition of the workforce (the percentage of Malays, using the ethnic composition of the total population as the yardstick as it is used in the development policy of the NEP (Table 1).

Table 1: Manufacturing enterprises, according to ownership (share capital) and ethnic composition of work force (bumi = Malay), Peninsular Malaysia 1984

Workforce Ownership	Bumi > 58%	Bumi 58-48%	Bumi < 48%	Total
Private bumi	1	2	0	3
Private Chinese	1	2	4	7
Private foreign	7	4	4	15
State owned	3	0	1	4
Joint venture	1	1	1	3
Total	13	9	10	32

155

The selection of enterprises took place, based on the knowledge of the industrial unions about their local membership and ownership of the factories. Table 1 is nevertheless constructed on the data from the visits to the companies. Inconsistencies appeared in a few cases, caused by misunderstandings, misinformation or recent changes.

This sampling procedure was in addition differentiated according to gender-composition of the workforces. At least one factory of each type (defined by ownership) was a 'female' industry. The majority of the enterprises were 'male' industries, because I wanted to rectify the research bias towards female industrial workers in Southeast- and East Asia.

Finally, the sampling was geared to cover several branches (automobile, electronics, drink production) in order to be able to minimize branch specific factors. The majority of the selected enterprises would be classified as 'metal industry' in European terminology, while the Registrar of the Trade Unions (RTU) artificially splits this branch in a number minor branches to prevent the formation of one big metal employees union.

The pivot of the whole sampling was the industrial unions. A key topic of the study was the start and development of local union organization and activity, i.e. the work committees and the shop stewards. But studying these affairs should unveil problems and obstacles to unionization and class formation, especially related to Malay workers in the manufacturing sector. Thereby, the research should be a stepping stone to an industrial anthropological study of the rank-and-file and their everyday life, producing more insight into the complexes of workers' creation, mobilization, participation or evasion of labour organizations and other social movements.

4. THE ETHNIC QUESTION RECONSIDERED

The ethnic antagonism in Malaysia between the two big ethnic communities (Malays (Bumis) and Chinese) have constituted the basis of and reproduced the ethno-political system of political parties (UMNO, MCA, PAS, Gerakan, DAP etc.), the multi-coalition politics and the whole political structure with special rights for Malays. The goal of NEP was intended to eradicate the causes of ethnic conflicts, namely ethno-economic inequalities and poverty. But would it also transform the whole ethno-political system, or would the politically determined restructuring and modernization process strengthen this system?

Finally, is ethnic antagonism produced and reproduced at the societal, the local or the organizational level of Malaysia?

In short, the problem is one of explaining the interrelationship between class, politics and ethno-culture: Are ethnicity and politics determined by class structure? Or is it the other way around? Or are there some indeterminate interplay between these fields? Should the fundamental approach to the problem be from the perspective of essentialism (economism, 'classism', culturalism etc.) of agnosticism or something else?

In our study, the problem is very concrete: How do we interpreted our little enterprise survey? Does it indicate that the NEP works or does it reveal counterproductive effects or quite unexpected results?

First, we should stress that the sample is not statistically representative of the ethnic relations at Malaysian manufacturing work places or of the total labour force in 1984. Still, the result of my investigation shows that the ownership of the enterprises is heterogeneous in terms of nationality and ethnicity, that the ethnic distribution among the factories are varied (from 30% to 80% Malay in the work force), and that the Malays and non-Malays are mixed at the plant level. This variation is contrary to the more homogeneous pattern found in the World Bank study in the early 1970s among locally owned factories (Mazumdar 1981), and it should theoretically increase the opportunities for controversies, tensions and open conflicts in the working life. Yet, these problems are only rarely reported. The conclusion could be straightforward: Ethnic conflicts disappear when the ethnic communities are mixed in productive life.

These findings can be supported at the societal level by the fact that no serious outbreak of violence between Malay and Chinese has taken place since the NEP started.

The NEP looks indeed like a success, judging from the improvement in ethnic relationships.

When I visited Malaysia in 1987, people were very concerned and afraid about the rising ethnic tensions and in October 1987 the government clamped down on opponents within and outside the ruling parties and non-party organizations. Had the situation changed dramatically, had it been misjudged in 1984 or both?

These questions open up for the second qualification of the study: it is a synchronic, not a diachronic study. We have not followed the same people and enterprises through years and cannot know the changes which have taken place in one work place or for one group of people. We can only speculate about the more general impressions of ethnic tensions and cooperations.

Third, the ethnic relations might differ according to social levels. At the local level in personal, daily relations, people may get along well with each other, despite different ethnic backgrounds and different ways of life. The ethnic tensions may be produced at the public or national level, contrary to the inter-ethnic acceptance in everyday life. Tensions may be created in relations to state politics to secure the reproduction of ethno-political organizations, especially in a conjuncture of rising intra-ethnic tensions among the Malays and Chinese. The problem may be created in the Malaysian political economy, not at the level of everyday life.

Such an interpretation would be more in line with a class analysis where one should expect the class contradictions to be more impressive and dominating in private and public life as the ethno-economic boundaries vanish. The tensions should be rising between Malays especially, because the Malay community undergoes a class transformation. And indeed, we have seen such tensions explode in open protest and violent struggles. Yet, these outbreaks of violence do not necessarily disclose class contradictions. They may as well follow political-cultural tensions, caused for example by the intensifying religious-secular struggle parallelling the 'modernization' of Malaysian society.

Fourth, a class interpretation may follow a more structuralist or a more actionist perspective. The class formation may be determined by the class structure and its logic, or it may be acted out be the class actors, creating a class cultural model for a class movement. The national or local unionists may so to speak shy away from ethnic classifications and define the reality in a class terminology.

There are strong indications for this way of reasoning. The survey took place in the 'closed' (unionized) manufacturing sector. The union movement propagates (and produces in fact) a social and not an ethno-cultural outlook among its members. They deliberately resist ethnic registration. When they record information about their members' ethnicity, it is because they are forced to do so by the Registrar. They made critical comments about my interest in getting the data.

159

The unions' anti-ethnic and pro-class ideology impede outright ethnic thinking, but thereby we get a new, fifth problem of interpretation: Have the shop stewards told only the public union opinion and hidden the private and incorrect, deviating attitudes and behaviour, especially in the presence of the national union leaders?

In one case, a union officer corrected the version of shop stewards when they had told me there were no ethnic conflicts! But the pressure to forget the ethnic problems have indeed been great, both because of the union officer's presence and because of the mixed ethnic composition of the work committee. I felt also more and more uncomfortable during the visits and interviewing due to the fact that the question created tensions in the room and maybe was interpreted as an unkind or even hostile question. Furthermore, I got the feeling that I was asking a stupid question, for which I already knew the answer and has wasted time - and yet I might through this question receive some unexpected news.

The few cases of reported ethnic conflicts indicated interesting relationships. The conflicts stem from partly ethnic-gender relations, partly ethnic-class relations.

Inter-ethnic interaction between the sexes was seen as a deviance by the Malay males in the female Malay group, and they reacted against the violation of the ethnic-gender boundary (for example when a Chinese boy talked to a Malay girls, the Malay boys told him to keep away or fight it out). In relation to gender, the ethnic community was seen as a closed community by the Malay men at least. In general, they too were in a disadvantaged position because they were less skilled than the Chinese.

While the ethnic closure seems to be legitimate in gender and family affairs by the Malays, it is more dubious in cases of favoritism and outright ethnic discriminations by the management towards the workers.

The discriminated feel very insulted, and the union officials react generally strongly against it. In practice, the discrimination may work both ways, for or against Malays depending of the ethnic ownership of the company, while NEP broadly speaking makes a 'positive' discrimination to the Malays.

So far, one may conclude that the reproduction of ethnic boundaries at the work place is related to the 'reproductive' sphere of gender and family, and their 'deproduction' is related to the class relations of the enterprise, but in both cases the boundaries are contested and the disadvantaged community uses 'ethnic closure' to uphold or widen its position in everyday life.

5. ISLAM AT THE WORK PLACE

Ethnic problems are most outspoken in relation to religion and in particular Islam. Islam is the official state religion and the Malays are all Muslims, but Malaysia does have freedom of religion. Religious affairs are now a central demarcation line between the ethnic communities after the implementation of Malay as the medium of education from start to finish.

At the work places visited, every Muslim was allowed to carry out his religious activities as he wanted: daily prayers, and attendance of the Friday prayer. The routine and work rules were not reported to impede the Islamic 'musts'.

And still, the freedom for the Muslims was not without problems. In 9 cases, the religious activities took place without pay, either these activities took place during the breaks or you worked longer to make up time lost due to participation in the Friday prayer. Several of these companies were owned by Chinese, and the religious relations were very sensitive. In one case, the

Muslim workers had no adequate prayer room so they had to spend time walking to the Mosque.

Even Islam-conscious managements did not necessarily escape religious problems, despite the fact that they might pay for the prayer time. In some cases, the non-Muslim had to work while the Muslims were praying. This happened in some foreign-owned companies. The non-Muslims felt discriminated against.

The most tolerant attitude and practice in religious questions were found in Bumi-controlled (private or state) companies, or in firms, where the problem was less important because the workforce had few Muslims, the women dominated, or because the employees were rather secularized.

The religious question was very much a question of the Malays' Islam. The other religious communities did not matter, except in relation to the public (federal or state) holidays. And the Malaysians had a lot indeed, thanks to the cultural plurality of the population (in 1987, 14 national holidays, plus state holidays, in Selangor 3).

6. UNIONS AND RELIGION

Among the union officers and shops stewards, three attitudes to religion prevail:

1) The union/work committee disclaims the responsibility for religious issues. It is not regarded as a union matter.

2) The union/work committee intervenes actively in religious questions, and organizes the religious activities.

3) The union/work committee tries to solve the religious problems in a pragmatic way as they turn up in a

pragmatic way, according to the seriousness of the case.

The response of the union/work committee seems to be conditioned by the estimation of danger of the religious conflicts in relation to the union activities and goals. They might be seen as dangerous, harmless or even useful in furthering the union cause. In one case, I was told that the management tried to use the prayer room for negotiating industrial relation problems and even to turn the workers against the shop steward. In another, a church area was used as a meeting place for the discussions leading to the unionization of a factory.

Religious institutions can, thus, be used by both management and workers individually or collectively in either a defensive or offensive way. And the Muslims have a special right or advantage due to the political power of the Muslim community and Malay parties. The Malaysian Employers Federation (MEF) is concerned about the handling of religious matters among the member companies and has made a survey. The daily praying caused some disciplinary problems. The management was often powerless, because praying is a 'must' for muslim males (Muslim women do not have the same legitimate claim to do their prayer; they are expected to do it when it fits into their other duties).

Religion can not only become a field of domination and resistance in class struggles at the local level. It can split up the employees, too, despite religious tolerance among colleges. Too many prayer breaks may increase the work load on non-Muslims, and in assembly line production, it must be regulated because the whole flow of production may be brought to a standstill.

Ethnic organizations are widespread in Peninsular Malaysia. Even some unions started as outright ethnical unions. Today, unions and ethnic organizations may cooperate. For example, a union might borrow a hall form an ethnic association for a meeting. But neither the union, nor the ethnic or religious associations take care of the social reproduction of marginalized, unemployed people. This is still the prerogative of the household, the family and kin, and not least the women.

7. GENDER CONTRADICTIONS AT THE SHOP FLOOR LEVEL

Within the issue of the sexual division at work, I will focus on the male's problems facing female workers at the 'male factory'. Three aspects may be outlined:

1) the substitution of male workers with female workers in traditional male jobs,
2) the female passivity in collective labour and union activities,
3) the sexual relationships and sexual abuses.

A case story:

At an car assembly factory in the Kuala Lumpur area, the management experienced continued labour shortages, despite the fact that the enterprise has paying above the local average wage level. The management wanted to remedy the situation by hiring female workers to the all male production section. At first, the men protested against the new recruitment policy because they feared that their section would end up as a 'sweatshop' with increase management control of the labour process. After a while, they accepted the situation as an experiment on the condition of equal pay for equal work.

When I visited the factory, the recruitment of both sexes for production work had become permanent to the satisfaction of everybody. Several factors may explain why.

The management solved its labour supply problem and could show a higher productivity level than in other car assembly factories in Malaysia. The high productivity level was explained by the personnel manager by reference to six variables:

- A new factory with a production system devised on the basis of experience.
- A conveyor assembly line.
- Higher wages.
- Picnics for the employees.
- Subsidized canteen.
- Good industrial relations procedures.

He did not include the gender-mixed work force as a productivity raising factor. He only mentioned that women were a more stable work force than men, and that they returned after maternity leave. Maybe the management had not noted any productivity increase since the introduction of female production line workers. The hiring of women was done as a response to a labour supply problem, not a disciplinary problem. Management might of course regard this as a secret social technique, but they had little reason to withhold such information as we talked without the presence of union representatives.

Visiting another transport equipment enterprise (motorcycle assembling) on my own and without the union representative, the junior personnel manager proudly told me, that the management deliberately employed some women as production line workers, to work alongside the men. This increased productivity considerably, because the female workers worked faster than the men and the men did not want to fall behind. The management thus exploited the typical male competitive behaviour of their employees to increase productivity. The composition of the work force at the motorcycle factory was 84 percent male and 16 percent female. The junior manager explained that 10-15 percent female workers worked wonders.

At the above mentioned auto assembly factory with the high level of productivity, women formed 25 percent of the workforce, much higher than in other similar factories where the women made up about 10 percent with almost no women in production.

The high productivity level at this factory could then be related to the presence of the female workers, too. But the problem in this connection is that the assembly conveyor was automated at the car factory and manual at the motorcycle factory. Everybody had to work at the same speed in the car factory, while the women could raise the productivity in the motorcycle production line through a manipulated gender competition game.

In any case, the management might be satisfied that the productivity did not decrease with the employment of female production workers.

The female workers felt they were given equal rights through this opportunity to work in male jobs. In the words of a female committee members in this car assembly factory (translated by the male union officers in the presence of other committee members):

"We feel proud to be employed and are proud that the jobs of men can be done by women. If a job is done by men, women should also have a try. Women workers have been recognized and unity has been created".

Women also see no formal obstacles to female activity in the factory, but the activity level is low compared to the male workers. The same girl explains why:

"There is a little fear among women. They fear their supervisors. The male workers can leave early for football. The women don't dare to ask for leave even though they have the right. They have never been given time off for netball. There are no female supervisors".

This fear may be caused by the continued pressures from male supervisors to get sexual favors in exchange for work privileges. Only one case of sexual abuse by a male supervisor had been reported at the factory some years ago, but this may be only the tip of the iceberg. This supervisor was fired following union pressure.

The gender relations are structured like a patriarchy where men dominate women, and the women are submissive by socialization. The union officer interpreted this as a remnant of the rural values which still prevail among the migrant workers.

The male workers at the car factory were very anxious to get a chance to work next to women. Now they seem to enjoy the relationship, which may develop into courtship and marriage. The atmosphere has improved.

This improvement is related to the personnel policy too. Women are not being used by management in 'sweat-shops' and women are not useful tools in the management's attempts to increase labour control.

8. LOCAL UNIONISM AND FEMALE WORKERS

At the car assembly factory, female workers were repre-sented in the work committee. This was not an exceptional case. In the enterprises visited, 14 out of 28 reportedly had female committee members (5 enterprises has a majority of female employees). Each committee had only one or two female members though.

The female participation at the work committee level is indeed much higher than at the regional and/or national union level, despite attempts to recruit female workers and female shop stewards to higher positions. In 'female industries' like textiles, there may be quite a few women at the local level of the union, but above this level they disappear or become shadowy. At the headquarters, women union members may even enter a male chauvinist world where they encounter women as sex object on posters in the office of the male general secretary.

In the unionized factories, women are union members and even shop stewards, but they are seldom very active unionists. Union work seems to be psychologically and socially demanding and culturally alien to female workers, generally speaking. The unions are dominated by male values, norms and work habits. At the management level, the same male world dominates.

Union member activities, like study circles, take place outside working hours, and even if women do not have children or family responsibilities commuting may impede longer hours at the work place. The company may provide a bus which leaves shortly after the shifts and disperses the workers in the region.

But the factory patriarchy is not the only patriarchy to overcome in the activation of female union members. The domestic patriarchy, a father, husband or brother, may be very suspicious to public activity, which is not necessary for work and family life, especially if it takes place outside working hours away from the work place and in the evening.

In an effort to counter the arguments of the family (including other women), one union rotated the meetings among the homes of the committee members. Rotation principles, including the residences of the unionists, may, too, be a wise devise to display union work for the family and thus integrate the family into the daily life of union struggles.

Active and courageous female unionists do indeed exist. In a 'female industry', a female executive committee member told me how she was participating in the unionization of 'open shops' (non-unionized factories) to the extent of relocation in the target place of unionization.

In the 'male industries' and the 'male unions', female workers may nevertheless be involved in labour struggles under the hegemony of men. The experience of

168

self confidence of these women may pave the way for equalizing the gender relations among workers in the 'male industries' and furthermore generate a pool of female activists who might be able and willing to enter the 'open female industries' (especially electronics) and successfully unionize these black holes on the union map.

The unionization of the electronic industry in Malaysia may therefore start in the unionized 'male industries'. The 'fifth column' of women unionists might be educated there.

The question of unionization and mobilization of female workers is only a part of the whole question of class formation and struggles in the everyday life of working people. But it stresses the strategic connection between the productive and reproductive sphere of human life.

9. SOCIO-CULTURAL CONTRADICTIONS, WORKING CLASS FORMATION AND THE POLITICAL EVENTS OF 1987

Ethno-cultural antagonism seems to be banned among workers and shop stewards in the class constructed social reality of the work place. Ethnic differences are clearly subordinated to class considerations.

Ethnic boundaries are nevertheless upheld in the domain of gender relations and religion, which again are interconnected. The intersection between the world of production and reproduction, family and ethno-culture manifests itself around the norms of sex-interactions among workers, and the reactions to this indicate that class and gender relations are two separate domains, regulated by different norms and values.

This separation of the class and gender world is difficult to uphold, especially when the economic trends are changing from rapid growth to stagnation and employment reduction. The female workers may be the first to be fired, despite the fact that they are often Malay. Gender contradictions seem stronger than ethnic contradictions in relation to women. Patriarchal and male values regulate implicitly the gender-discrimination in retrenchment. The bread-winner status of men is heavily propagated.

The mass retrenchment had not yet started in 1984. In 1987, I was told that the female workers were among the first to be retrenched. In 1984, the reduction of employees was carried out more smoothly, taking advantage of the continuous flow of employees, local flexibility or the internal markets of bigger companies.

The retrenchment of female workers may not continue unopposed, and the result may be a dispersal of more radicalized and/or experienced union activists to non-unionized enterprises. The men will come to realize that the women's wages are important in the reproduction of the family and that women have become more self-reliant and self-confident through their work in factory production

Male values dominate the factory, and the ethnic contradictions seem very much related to male culture. Ethnic boundaries are reproduced by the men as in the case of religious activity, where women did not count or were seen as creating problems. Men control the sexual relations of 'their' women. Men and not women seem to be the problem in the elimination of ethnic antagonism among malaysians.

For men far more than for women in the 1980s Malaysia, class identities are an alternative to ethnic identities. But in order for class identity to become a hegemonic identity, working class organizations needs to develop a working class culture.

One important collaborator for the ('old') labour movement in such a project could be and has been so-called ('new') social movements (non-class grass root movements oriented toward a specific objective and with a decentralized power structure) (see for example Tornquist 1986).

Although these movements are often dominated by the middle layers (academics and intellectuals), they are very conscious of the labour aspects of anti-consumerism and environmental protection. Besides, they are not constituted on ethnic issues like the dominant political parties. They are also not anti-ethnic in the sense that they want to eradicate ethnic inequalities. Finally, a cooperative relationship developed between some of these 'new' movements and some of the 'old' labour organizations (unions like Transport Equipment and Allied Industries Employees Union). Labour education and occupational health and safety are issues on which they cooperate.

The 'new' social movements have gained some strength in Malaysia since the early 1970s, particularly the consumer movement (Consumer Association of Penang, CAP) and later the environmental movement (Friends of the Earth, SAM; Environmental Protection Society of Malaysia; Perak Anti-Radioactive Committee, PARC), the academic organizations (Institute for Social Analysis, INSAN) and the women's movement (Women's Development Collective, WDC).

The mass arrests of opponents to the Mahathir faction of the ruling Malays party (UMNO) and the government in October 1987 only partly affected the Malaysian union movement, while the 'new' social movements were hard hit, and specially by the following 2-year detention orders for at least 35 people and 2-year restriction orders for 10 people, which were served in late December of the same year (see for example ECHRIM 18.1.1988).

This attack on the alternative, non-ethnic social movements can be seen as an attempt by the government (or by the Special Branch, see Jome 1988) to suppress or eliminate the social forces which are able to promote the cause of a non-ethnic public opinion, based on the widespread inter-ethnic and trans-ethnic patterns of urban and industrial daily life in Malaysia of the 1980s. While the 'old' labour movement had been severely controlled and pacified during the 1980s, the 'new' social movements made spectacular inroads into public debate and political influence. This position could even have been strengthened if a broader cooperation and alliance between the 'new' and the 'old' grass root organizations had evolved.

But besides the 'new' movements, the 'grand old' movements of religious organizations operate in Malaysia both in working class neighborhoods and work places. The antagonism between the religious movements themselves have been more prominent than between the religious and non-religious movements. The Islamic revival and state support for Islam caused the cooperation of the non-muslim religious organizations for the first time in 1983 (Lee 1985). Yet, the Islamic revival has a strong fundamentalist streak, which is perceived as a danger to the government policy of modernization. Both Islamic fundamentalists and Christian activist were imprisoned under the ISA in October 1987.

The political events of 1987 were created by and even consolidated the ethno-political system of Malaysia. The price of this has been an increased stress on Islam in modernization, a dramatic split within the dominant Malays Party (UMNO) and a weakening of the governing Chinese party (MCA). So far, the inter-ethnic movements have not succeeded on the political scene, but they are still rooted in everyday life despite the repression of activists, organizations and media.

BIBLIOGRAPHY

Emergency Committee for Human Rights in Malaysia (ECHRIM):
Update no. 4 Malaysian ISA Detention Alert (mimeo
18.1.1988).

Giddens, A: The Constitution of Society (Cambridge 1984).

Jomo K.S: Malaysian Detains caught in Tangled Web (mimeo
1988).

Laclau, E. & C. Mouffe: Hegemony & Socialist Strategy.
Towards a Radical Democratic Politics (London:
Verso, 1985).

Lee, R.L.M: "The Ethnic Implications of Contemporary
Religious Movements and Organizations in Malaysia",
Contemporary Southeast Asia, vol. 8, 1, 1985.

Mazumdar, D: The Urban Labour Market and Income Distribution (Oxford: Oxford University Press, 1981).

Nautrup, B.L: "Hverdagsliv og udviklingsdynamik"; in C.
Bloch et al. (eds.): Hverdagsliv, kultur og subjek-
tivitet (Copenhagen: Akademisk Forlag, Kultursocio-
logiske skrifter nr. 25, 1987).

Stepputat, F. (ed): Hverdagslivsstudier i Den tredje
Verden (Copenhagen: Institut for Kultursociologi
Reproserie 1987 nr. 4).

Tornquist, O: "Socialistisk strategi på prøve. Om behovet
for demokratisk kamp i Asien", Grus (Copenhagen), 7.
årg., 20, 1986.

Wad, P: "Malaysian Industrializations and the Dilemmas
of the Trade Union Movements"; in I. Nørlund et al.
(eds.): Industrialization and the Labour Process in
Southeast Asia (Copenhagen: Institute of Cultural
Sociology Reproserie 1984, nr. 6).

Wad, P: "The Japanization of the Malaysian Trade Union
Movement"; in R. Southall (ed.): Trade Unions and

the New Industrialization of the Third World (London:
Zed Books, 1988).

MRS. AQUINO'S NEW SET OF CRONIES
INTERVIEW WITH JOSE MARIA SISON

Viggo Brun
University of Copenhagen

Question: Judging from the number of strikes, protests etc. lately there has been a decline in the popularity of Aquino. But when it comes to elections she still has considerable popularity. How would you explain this apparent contradiction?

Answer: The kind of popularity that Aquino has had is of the anti-Marcos and at best anti-fascist type. This is a shallow and fleeting kind of popularity. It is not one based on arousing, organizing and mobilizing the people along the anti-imperialist and anti-feudal line. What I mean to say is that Aquino has not been attending to the most fundamental problems.

The drop in her popularity is due to non-solution of the fundamental problems of the Philippine people, such as US dominance and the continuing feudal exploitation and you may add, corruption, which has gone on unabated. A new set of cronies headed by the brother of mrs. Aquino has been taking over the recoverable assets of the old set of cronies. So there is this widespread perception that Aquino is not fulfilling previous expectations. A few people might say that too much is being expected of Aquino in so short a time, but they should be told that even if mrs. Aquino had all the time or even eternity she would never solve the problems. Because in the first place she does not have the orientation to solve them. She has not expressed anything that would bring her out of the framework of US domination, feudal exploitation and bureaucratic corruption. And she has been bringing the more dramatic problems upon herself. Even as she was able to maintain her anti-Marcos popularity for some time by restoring the formal bourgeois democratic rights and processes, she has failed to reorganize and reorient the Armed Forces of the Philippines, and remove the fascists within this military organization.

The so-called voting results in the legislative elections last May or even the plebiscite, cannot be used as a measure of the popularity of Aquino, because the registration and voting records have been rigged in the same way as Marcos used to rig voting. Jose Cojuangco has been the master operator in the rigging operations, and he has been as masterly as Marcos. Following the plebiscite on the Aquino constitution last February there has been no exposure of the rigging of registration and voters' records, although fantastic figures were being claimed. It is completely unbelievable that 95% of eligible voters registered, and more than 90% of the registered voters actually voted. We must recall that normal registration and voting patterns were established in the 50s and 60s, before Marcos started to rig the registration and voting records in the 70s and onwards. The normal registration pattern was for eligible voters to register to the extent of 60-70%, and of the registered voters 60-70% would actually vote. It cannot be said that Aquino is different, in the sense that she has been so popular especially in contrast to Marcos. But we must recall that there was also a US-type hero, in the person of Magsaysay, who fought the hated president Quirino. And then Quirino was effectively prevented from misusing the military and rigging the elections because the US saw to it that registration and voting would be relatively honest compared to the 1949, elections which were clearly dishonest and unclean. I am referring to the 1953 election of Magsaysay when the registration peaked to the level of 70% and voting also peaked to the level of 70%. It is only after the May 1987 legislative elections that any direct evidence has surfaced, that there was a rigging of the registration and voting records. Diskettes of the computerized cheating have been uncovered by the Enrile faction. But one does not even have to rely completely on the evidence that has been obtained by Enrile. In so many areas the Aquino slate of candidates got more than 100% of the total number of voters! The popularity of Aquino can be more reliably gauged by the size of mass action that she has been able to get in connection with non-electoral threats from the Enrile and Marcos factions, as well as in the election-related rallies. Soon after the Honasan coup attempt the August 28. movement or ATOM headed by Butz Aquino, called for mass action to support Aquino against Enrile. Only 200 people showed up in that rally.

If we step back a little in time, let us consider the election rallies of mrs. Aquino, where before she could easily get 100.000 people, she would now get only 5-10.000. So there is nothing more of the big mass actions spontaneously joined by so many people, starting with the Aquino funeral in August 1983 up to the March 1986 rally in which mrs. Aquino restored the privilege of the right of habeas corpus. Even where mrs. Aquino could practically order the government employees to participate in her rallies, just as Marcos did, there has been a drastic drop from the level of the mass actions in the past.

The most effective method for effecting bogus landslides for the Aquino slate, would be the rigging and manipulation of the registration and voters' records. But there were more special measures adopted by the Aquino regime to wipe out the hopes of Partido ng Bayan in getting 20-30% of the seats in the lower house. 695 towns and cities were declared "trouble spots" and this is a sizeable number because there are only 1500 towns and cities in the Philippines. These were located all over the country in areas suspected as bailiwicks of the progressive movement, including the revolutionary movement. Military operations were also intensified in this area. Anyhow, in these towns and cities considered as trouble spots, voting was done in the town centres and the military surrounded these voting centres, so people were discouraged from going there. So the personnel of the Aquino regime fabricated the results of the elections.

Q: Just before the Honasan coup-attempt in August 1987 there was a nationwide strike. Why?

A: There was a nationwide strike because Mrs Aquino raised the price of oil, and she was doing so at a time that world oil prices are going down, and this is regarded as betrayal by the people. The nationwide strike was participated in by people from the basic toiling masses of workers and peasants, and by the middle social strata. And even the pro-government Trade Union Confederation of the Philippines (TUCP) had to go along with KMU. So, this was an action taken to protest Aquino's betrayal of the people's trust. It has been said that Honasan tried to take advantage of the nationwide strike while the troops were being preoccupied with the mass actions. The strike, you see, paralyzed transport in the majority of the 13 regions.

Q: How would you describe the situation during and just after she got into power? The impression we get here in Europe is that she has an organized mass basis, the so-called 'yellow forces'. What are actually these forces in more concrete terms and how have they developed?

A: Before I answer directly the main thrust of your question, regarding the organized following of Aquino, I would like to discuss first the illusion that prevailed before - both inside the Philippines and abroad - that Aquino was going to stabilize and democratize the Philippine situation completely. The non-solution of the basic problems has led to the worsening of the social, economic and political crisis, and of course the most dramatic thing about the socio-economic crisis is fact that the country is being pinned down by a huge foreign debt , and Aquino continuously submits to the imposition of the US and other multinational firms and the foreign creditors. With regard to the political crisis there has been an increasingly violent conflict among the factions, and this internecine war - this internal strife among the factions - serves to demonstrate that the Aquino regime is a weak, unstable, corrupt and pro-US regime. Now, continuing my answer to the previous question serves to link up with the main thrust of your question. Aquino does not really have a big, solid, organized following. The yellow organizations which are strictly Aquino's are PDP-Laban, which has some 200.000 members, and Bandila which does not go beyond 5000 members. This Bandila, which is a copy-cat of Bayan, is nothing but an agglomeration of small groups, even paper organizations, basically cooked up by such ultra-rightist Jesuits like Father Blanco and Nebres. Aquino has had to go into a coalition in the last elections to make the so-called Lakas Bangsat. So somehow Aquino has to go into a combine and the other important members of the combine, aside from PDP-Laban, are the Liberal Party (LP) of Salonga, and UNIDO of Laurel.

Q: What are the actual sizes of LP and UNIDO? What is their mass following? Could you quantify them somehow?

A: The LP of Salonga has a high potential organizationally. For some time it has remained small, but the potential for making that party bigger lies in the revivability of the LP loyalties on the local officials of the eve of the declaration of martial law. But you see, these were converted by Marcos into Marcos loyalists. At the moment however, LP is quite small. The UNIDO is a somewhat bigger organization than LP-Salonga. UNIDO used to fight for even half of the pro-Aquino campaign machinery; as in the snap-election and the last legislative election. UNIDO is an organization comparable to PDP-Laban, and because it is not getting at least half of the slates of candidates it has been a great discomfort in the combine. UNIDO does not get the seats at every level which it thinks it deserves, and so things have come to a head with Laurel breaking off from the alliance with Aquino. Now, you asked me about the organized strength of the yellow organizations: we should not miss the armed following of Aquino, which is important in this period when the internal strife of the reactionary classes involves armed followings. The direct and organized Aquino following in the AFP (Armed Forces of the Philippines) is still small. Of course by her power to appoint, assign and promote military officers, Aquino has somehow developed some military support from scratch. Then there is the Illeto floating following, which is largely unorganized. There is also the augmentatory support given by Ramos since his break-up with Enrile, or the split within what was previously the RAM. Aquino has to maintain a posture of following the regular system of promotions. In the newly reinstituted Philippine Congress her ability to manipulate promotions is restrained. In other words, she does not have as much lee-way as the outright fascist dictator Marcos, upon whom the promotion and appointments depended exclusively. But Aquino has been relying on an armed following outside of the AFP. Only to a limited extent, however, has she been able to promote officers of the hacienda Lucita guards (Hacienda Lucita is Cory Aquino's 6000 hectare plantation. Ed.), and enlist these men into the regular armed forces. So far what she has done is to make sure that hacienda Lucita guards compose her close-in security. That could be one or two companies. In turn, these trusted armed personnel are surrounded by the long-time regular troops. Outside the AFP, the armed following of Aquino is even more impressive. The yellow army is composed of three sub-armies. under Jose 'Piping' Cojuangco, Len Oreta and Butz Aquino. So, Piping Cojuangco has put into the security force of several government corporations men loyal to him, private corporations beholden to state banks, corporations and plantations that have recently been taken over from the old set of cronies and the like. So there has been an expansion of the scope of Piping Cojuangco who used to have the security force of the old companies and plantations. Len Oreta, who is the brother-in-law of Aquino and husband of These Aquino, has been engaged in the private security business for quite some time, and he has been quick at expanding his company, and getting some share of the security force for the government corporations, and private corporations beholden to the government, but he has been favoured as the man to get security men from by so wide a range of private companies. Butz Aquino has the smallest armed force, and he distributes in the style of the old politician, maintaining the loyalty of war leaders by giving them arms. The more solid part of this armed following would be acting like as his body-guards. But the value of Butz Aquino in the so-called yellow army is that men close to him, who hold high positions in tho customs, have been facilitating the importation of fire-arms for the benefit of the yellow army as a whole. And one report is that they get the arms mainly from Israel. So there is a proliferation now of Israeli firearms.

Q: Could you give any kind of indication of the size or quantify this yellow armed force in the security business? Can it be mobilized rapidly? Is it just scat-tered units or what?

A: A conservative estimate would be that the yellow army has 10.000 men now outside the AFP, but they are not as solid as the manoeuvre battalions of the AFP. They are somewhat scattered and they are guarding hotels, offices, warehouses and plantations. The big gain made by the private security agencies under the control of Jose Cojuangco and Len Oreta is that they were able to take over the security business of General Ver, and probably the yellow armies are already taking over the security business of Enrile in a big way. You should recall from the newspapers that a security agency of Enrile was raided under the suspicion of storing firearms taken from the arsenal for the AFP. This raid was conducted soon after the Honasan coup attempt.

Q: Before we go further into this, couldn't you briefly review the other two factions within the AFP?

A: The two other major factions are of course those of Marcos and Enrile. I suppose that the biggest faction of officers in the AFP still belongs to Marcos, but the weakening of this faction has been due to the removal of the generals and the colonels identified as Marcos loyalists. And so, for quite some time, there has been no rallying point, be it an organization or some commanding figure. The Marcos faction can be activated, and this activation becomes more probable after the Honasan coup attempt. You see, Marcos was in power for so long that certainly many officers owe their positions to him. And then there is this traditional character of the AFP as being more than 60% Illocano. The officers and men are Illocano, soldiers coming from Northern Luzon, to the extent of more than 60%. So there is what I might call the 'Illocano factor' which has not acted up yet.

Q: So there is some kind of regional loyalty that keeps the Marcos faction together?

A: It is there dormant, ready to be activated. And its activation is now more probable because of the encouraging effect of the Honasan coup-attempt. The Enrile faction is the main part of the RAM. You see, this clique of officers consisted of two parts: one part is the one led by Honasan, and the other part is led by colonel Victor Bata. But then there was a falling out between these two cliques of officers, so as of June 1987 many people of the Philippines had an idea that there was a RAM-MND-Enrile faction, and a so-called RAM-AFP-Ramos faction. Now, of course, these labels should not be understood to mean that Enrile had the entire RAM-MND and Ramos had the entire RAM-AFP. Those labels were used mainly to distinguish the two factions. This faction was number one in the AFP up to some time in July 1986, and the Aquino faction was only number three, but then as the Enrile-Ramos tandem held, and as it combined with the Aquino faction, the AFP seemed to hold up Mrs Aquino and the combination then served to put under restraint the Marcos faction. I think the biggest manifestation of the strength of the Enrile faction so far was the Honasan coup attempt. Reports are that 2000 men were moved by Honasan against the Aquino faction. In terms of firearms that are supposed to be in this faction, Honasan is supposed to have obtained 8000 rifles before he was removed as the chief of the Ministry of National Defence Security Battalion in November 1986, at the same time as Enrile was removed as Defence Minister. In the coup-attempt last August 28. 2000 men were utilized, but only 800 men were apprehended, which means that 1200 weapons cannot be accounted for, and there are supposed to be anywhere between 5000 and 10000 of rifles missing from the arsenals after the August 28. coup attempt.

Q: You have given an overview over the major political and military forces at play in the Philippines right now. There is another concept - people's power - which is used to give the impression that Mrs Aquino has a large unorganized following on grass-root level. What is actually this concept of people's power, and how does Aquino herself relate to this concept?

A: The concept of people's power as espoused by Bayan means that the fundamental national and democratic rights and interests of the people are upheld, promoted and realized, and that the people need to be empowered or that power should belong to the people. And there is a clear idea of 'the people': it includes all patriotic and progressive forces, including classes, parties, organizations and individuals, and if we go by class terms, the term people refers to the working class, peasantry and the middle social strata, which are the urban petty bourgeoisie and the middle bourgeoisie. The concept of people's power means that these people must have the power and share the power. The Aquino concept of 'people power' simply means that the people can be manipulated to serve the interest of the upper classes - the compradore big bourgeoisie and the landlord class - to which mrs Aquino belongs. The expression 'people power' as used by Aquino and her kind is like 'horse power' or 'main power'. The expression reveals the class bias of the yellow forces. After Mrs Aquino had taken advantage of that broad popular movement against Marcos, and after putting on some democratic facade in a formal way, or specifically in the bourgeois democratic way, Aquino does not care any more about arousing, organizing and mobilizing the people around their own national democratic rights and interests.

Q: Somehow one could say that in Bayan's definition of people's power the people is the acting subject, while in the Aquino expression 'people power' the people is reduced to an object.

A: Yes, an object to be used and manipulated. So there is a big difference between the concept of 'people's power' and the concept of 'people power'.

Q: What are the relative strengths of the various organized political forces in the Philippines?

A: The multi-sectoral alliance Bayan is still the largest political organization in the Philippines. Bayan grew in size and strength in the course of the struggle against the US-Marcos regime. It has more than 2 million members, in more that 2000 organizations, and the principal components of this multi-sectoral alliance are the sectoral alliances like KMU (The First of May Movement, a labour organization with 600.000 members), KMP (a farmers' organization with 800.000 members) League of Philippino Students (100.000), the comprehensive youth organization Kadena (200.000), Alliance of Concerned Teachers (70-80.000), Gabriela, the women's alliance (30.000, excluding the women's organizations for working class and peasant women). These are the major organizations of Bayan. I have already referred to the strength of the yellow organizations. The Marcos and Enrile factions may include the traditional political leaders and their retinues, mostly former or current officials at lower levels and war-leaders. And I would say that these factions have smaller organizations than the Aquino faction. This is because the traditional politicians at every level always have the tendency to seek membership in the structure of those currently in power. The organizational strength of Bayan, however, does not mean the automatic realization of people's power. This is because the big campaign money and the arms belong to the upper class factions of Aquino, Marcos and Enrile. Furthermore, the reactionary factions benefit from ownership of the means of production, control of the mass media and the catholic church, and they can use the civil bureaucracy, and most important of all: the military and police forces of the state.

Q: You mentioned the church as one of the organizations supporting the ruling class. Could you explain in more detail about the position of the church as an institution?

A: As an institution the catholic church is conservative or reactionary. It is a big comprador, landlord institution,- if we consider it in terms of its class affiliation. The church has become a far bigger big-comprador or mercantile bourgeois institution, more than ever before, because it was able to make use of the funds paid for the friar estates to invest in big comprador operations, such as the commercial banks and the import-export firms. That is the reason why there is a big tie-up between the church and the old super-rich, involving the Rojas, Ayalas and Sorianos. But the church has also persisted as a feudal institution. It retains large land holdings despite the expropriation of the friar estates during the first decade of the century. Part of the compensation the church got for this expropriation was remitted to Rome, and another big part was invested in the modern corporations. Historically the church has been involved in commercial operations. It was involved in the galleon trade between Manila and Acapulco (Mexico) and in the export of agricultural crops in the 19th century on the basis of its possession of the friar estates. But the scale of its big compradore involvement would become bigger in the semi-feudal society developed by the US monopoly capitalism. So there is a socio-economic connection between the catholic church and the US. And of course the church retains its old material feudal base. The material and class character of the church influences its ideology, that is, its theology. The church, as you go up the hierarchy, and horizontally too, the priests and nuns tend to be conservative and reactionary. The sacredness of the ownership of the means of production is still a principle upheld by the church, and it is so close to the upper classes in large as well as small social terms. A typical priest does not become progressive, but is usually a ritualist for the upper class, and he does certain chores for the upper class, such as gracing their parties or delivering them to the airport. So that is the character of priests who are less concerned about what has been termed as the church becoming that of the oppressed, the poor and disadvantaged. At the same time, since the early 70s, there has been the emergence and growth of the progressive religious, including priests, nuns and the laity. They try to relate the church to the oppressed people. They see the church as a defender of the people and promoter of the interests of the people. They consider their mission not simply spiritual, but also social. In other words, while they keep to the First Great Commandment, they also live and act according to the Second Great Commandment. The most progressive group of these religious people is the Christians for National Liberation (CNL). It is a member organization of the National Democratic Front (NDF). It is for the national democratic revolution and it approves of armed struggle as a just and necessary form of struggle, in view of the prior violence and prior possession and monopoly of the instruments of violence by the upper classes, and the present big comprador-landlord state. There are of course so many organizations above ground, which take a progressive line, and in the course of the struggle against the US-Marcos regime, there have been so many defending the human rights of the people. The most prominent among those is the Task Force Detainee, The Ecumenical Movement for Justice and Peace, and so on. The priests and nuns have been given much lee-way in social action under the guidance of Vatican Council the

Second. Specifically 'Gaudium et Spes', which was issued or proclaimed by the Vatican Council the Second. This is an adaptation of the church to the modern world.

Q: Does it not create tension within the church when the leadership is largely conservative, while the rank and file priests and nuns are being radicalized through their social involvement?

A: Yes, of course there is tension. First after hard work the progressive religious had an impact on the high clergy or the bishops. The Catholic Bishops' Conference of the Philippines (CBCP) blessed the Marcos declaration of martial law in 1972. And it said that Marcos should be given the chance to undertake social reforms including land reform. The CBCP at that time was under the leadership of an ultra-conservative: Ruffino Cardinal Santos. But later on, in 1974, there was a new cardinal who received the impact of the progressive religious. I am referring to cardinal Sin. But the line of cardinal Sin and the CBCP was that of 'critical collaboration', that is, occasional criticism of the Marcos regime on the grossest human rights violations, but consistent collaboration on the fundament of the oppressive and exploitative society. That was the line of the church until February 14. 1986, when it issued the pastoral letter which condemned the Marcos regime to its very roots. It described the Marcos regime as immoral and illegitimate to its very foundation. The Christians for National Liberation started with a few members in 1971, - you could count on the fingers their number. Then they became scores in 1974. Before the end of the decade of the 70s they had become hundreds. In the 80s they have become a few thousands, including priests, nuns and church workers. So the number of the progressive religious is now considerable.

Q: How do you consider the reaction of the church to the Aquino take-over? What has happened in the church after her coming to power in February 1986?

A: The CBCP pastoral letter in February 1986 helped a lot to bring down Marcos and push Mrs Aquino to the presidency. And there was a wide ranging combination of causes: the right, middle and left of the church converged against the Marcos regime. Each wing of the church had its own motivation: the right and the middle had the reactionary motivation that Marcos had to go because he would destroy the system, - because he would bring down the system with himself if he stayed in power any longer. So it was out of fear of the revolutionary movement that they pushed Marcos to fall, and Aquino was the one in sight to be supported, to be the successor of Marcos. In the case of the left, those who belonged to CNL as well as the above ground human rights and more progressive organizations within the church, they were simply being consistent in their desire to overthrow the Marcos regime. The religious within the church are so progressive that they make fundamental criticism of the social system. There are of course those who are progressive only to the extent of being for human rights, but then by being for human rights their eyes tended to be opened to the roots of the oppressive and exploitative system and they would be sympathetic to and supportive of the people's struggle. Now, going back to Aquino's standing within the church, well, cardinal Sin and his following, which I suppose would cover the right and the middle, have been supportive of the Aquino regime. As a matter of fact, this trend in the catholic church has been boasting for some time that a pre-emptive revolution had occurred. The ultra-rightist jesuits have been the most vocal about boasting about this, up to May 1986 when progressive forces thoroughly exposed the continuing weakness of the system. At a certain point cardinal Sin observed and criticized the back-sliding in the Aquino regime, referring to the corruption which was already very obvious, but he remained supportive of the sugary figure of Cory Aquino. But during the last coup attempt by Honasan, cardinal Sin and the rest of the catholic high clergy seemed to be dumfounded: they could not issue any statement while the crisis was going on. They just asked the people: stay at home and pray for the government! That was the most they could pronounce!

Q: So neither Aquino nor the church tried to mobilize the people to support her at this critical moment?

A: Probably the catholic church leadership agreed that the best move was to stay home and pray, because those making the coup attempt had already killed quite a number of civilians, and there could also be a distrust of the masses.

Q: You mentioned the sugary figure of Aquino. How would you evaluate the personality of Aquino? I am asking this, because in the news we get here, it is her person which is focused upon. Now, how important is she as a person in Philippine politics, and how would you describe her personality?

A: Aquino has always been a firm adherent to her own class: the big comprador-landlord class. But she has been quite flexible in riding on the broad popular movement against Marcos. She knew how to make use of populist slogans, and she knew how to make sure what concession she could give to the broad popular movement without departing radically from her big comprador-landlord adherence. So I am relating Cory Aquino's personality to her class standing. Previously, soon after she came to power, I used to describe her mental processes, and I said Aquino's brain had a certain number of parts in relation to political affairs. Number one was that she had a sentimental resentment against the US military bases. That was because despite the fact that her husband Ninoy Aquino was a CIA asset - a fact mentioned in the book of Nick Joaquin: The Aquinos of Tarlac (1983), which has been approved by the Aquino family - he stayed in prison for so long, and the Aquino family used to say that the US allowed Marcos to do what he pleased simply because the US wanted to keep the military bases. So there was some bitter resentment about that. That is the reason why Aquino in 1984 signed the document uniting the presidential hopefuls, containing a program binding all the opposition presidential hopefuls: whoever would be chosen would be bound by that document. It was framed under the so-called Convenor Group. Among the progressive provisions in that document was one stating that the US military bases must be dismantled not later than 1991. At the time she assumed the presidency and for quite some time Aquino has been a champion of human rights because she and her family suffered so much under the Marcos regime in connection with the detention of her husband by Marcos. And so she shared the feelings and thoughts and conditions of persons and families victimized by the fascist regime. It is with regard to this second part of her personality, her strong adherence to human rights, that Aquino has been able to link herself up with the popular movement and it would be along this line that human rights lawyers would be given positions in her cabinet and other levels of her government. The third part of Aquinos personality involves her inheriting what may be called Ninoy Aquino's political instinct. You see, Ninoi Aquino developed his political skills in Tarlac province, and he knew how to speak populist phrases which would impress the middle and the left, without offending the right. And he remained a big landlord even as he was someone appreciated as a populist figure. Mrs Aquino has

191

acquired the same political skills and instincts as her husband had. The fourth part of Aquino's personality involves her low level of knowledge about economics. She does not know much about economics beyond what she learned in an American catholic convent school at the height of the cold war. Therefore she has been impressed very much with the technocrats like Jolo Fernandes and Jimmy Ongpin. After all, her basic faith economically is in the US and in her own class, so she has retained practically the same type of technocrats that Marcos had, in so far as the economic ministries of the government are concerned. The Aquino government has been pursuing the same economic policies as Marcos pursued. The fifth part of mrs Aquino's personality involves her being religious. She is religious in the way that a political leader was religious during the renaissance. Her religiosity has brought the influence of the Jesuit mafia and the Opus Dei into the government. Even as these two groups compete with each other, they definitely are for US and reactionary interests in the Philippines, only their phraseology and style are different. It is Mrs Aquino's religiosity that has brought into the cabinet US-line technocrats who are at the same time close to religious organizations, groups like the Jesuit mafia and the Opus Dei. Because Mrs Aquino had these five tendencies in her personality for a long time when she took power, there is nothing surprising in the fact that she has succumbed so easily to US pressures and has acted to preserve the semi-colonial and semi-feudal system, dominated directly by the big bourgeoisie and the landlord class. The first three tendencies have made mrs Aquino look open to social reforms, but the two last tendencies have also thrown her wide open to the pressures of the US and the most reactionary interests in the Philippines. Before November 1986 Mrs Aquino as well as her cabinet had a real liberal democratic tendency, but as of that month, when she conceded in a big way to the demands of the US, she was definitely and consciously using what was previously a real liberal-democratic tendency as a facade for the most imperialist and reactionary policies.

Q: You have mentioned the security forces of Jose Cojuanco, Len Oreta and Butz Aquino. You have mentioned corruption of 'the new set of cronies', as you call them. Could you elaborate on this concept of 'new set of cronies'?

A: Well, the new set of cronies is headed by the innermost group of men behind mrs Aquino. This includes Pedro Cojuangco who is the eldest brother of mrs Aquino and reputed to be the financial wizard. Jose Cojuangco who is the more obvious personality, because he acts as the direct negotiator with the former cronies in cases of asset transfer. There is also Ricardo Lopa who is the brother-in-law of Mrs Aquino. Then there are the two cousins, Igmidio Tanjuatco and Johny Sumulong. So these are the finance men behind Mrs Aquino, and then there are the heads of the three sections of what has been called the yellow army.

Q: What has happened to the assets of Marcos and his cronies?

A: The recoverable assets of Marcos and his cronies have been transferred to the new set of cronies, whose most important leaders I have already enumerated. The most notorious transfers of assets have been in the gambling corporation - in control of 'jai alai' (pelota game) and the hotel casinos - , the Meralco, San Miguel Brewery Corporation, Philippine Long Distance and Telephone Company, Philippine National Oil Corporation, United Coconut Planters' Bank, the Manila Port Services Corporation, and so on. The plantations owned by Marcos in Negros and Palawan have been taken over. The big banana plantation Tagung Agricultural Development Corporation has also been taken over. The new set of cronies are so greedy that even the gambling in central Luzon, including the gambling in the two cities attached to the Subic Naval Base and the Alongapo City, and the numbers' game in the entire region, have been taken over. And this has offended the military very much, because the gambling in central Luzon used to be conceded to the military based in Camp Olivas, but Jose Cojuangco has been so greedy as to take over this. So it is not surprising that the most active military opponents of Mrs Aquino spring from Camp Olivas and Fort Magsaysay. The method used in the take-over goes this way: the Presidential Commission on Good Government (PCGG) is used to investigate and identify the Marcos and crony corporations. The front man of Marcos would be told behind the scenes: 'Tell us how much Marcos really owns. And if you do, you get a reasonable share. We can give you as much as Marcos could give you.' So the real figure is arrived at. Then the world would be told subsequently that negotiations have taken place between PCGG and the Marcos front man, and that such and such is the value of the Marcos assets. Of course, officially the assets of Marcos are understated, and a check is made to pay for the assets to PCGG, but the rest of the Marcos assets would be taken over by Jose Cojuangco and his group. Let's take TADECO-Tagum Agricultural Development Corporation. That corporation is worth billions of pesos, and the share of Marcos runs into billions of pesos. Behind the scenes the negotiations transpired, and so the news would come out later that the front man of Marcos, Antonio Florendo, paid only 200 billion pesos to the PCGG, but the rest of the Marcos assets would go to Jose Cojuangco's group, using a new dummy, Cito Ayala. That is one example of a take-over. In the case of some other enterprises the PCGG is not even in the picture. For instance, with regard to the several haciendas of the pro-Marcos cousin of Mrs Aquino, Eduardo Cojuangco, amounting to more than 9000 hectares in Negros, these never came within the jurisdiction of the PCGG. There was simply a take-over as a result of the negotiations between the cousins Jose and Eduardo. And even the entire CHDF - Civilian and Home Defence Forces - was completely turned over to Jose Cojuangco. These plantation guards had taken the cover of CHDF, - the paramilitary force of the government.

Q: So some Marcos assets have been recovered by the government, while a sizeable share has been taken over by the new set of cronies.

A: Yes, and the most recoverable assets are those left behind in the Philippines. As regards the assets abroad there are great difficulties. We suppose that hardly 10% of the total still held by Marcos can be recovered. The assets stacked away abroad are so great in magnitude, but it is the assets in the US which stand to be most easily recovered, and it is most likely the Philippine state taking over.

Q: How do the other groups within the compradore bourgeoisie and the middle class react to these illegal take-overs?

A: The best of the big bourgeoisie, excluding the inner circles of mrs Aquino, and not sharing in the loot, is of course repelled by the scandalous transfer of assets from the old set to the new set of cronies. There is resentment especially because there is not much loot to go around and divide. And so when greedy men cannot get as much loot as they want, because those in power now are in a better position to satisfy their greed, they are more resentful. Whereas before during the hay-day of Marcos in the 70s, the cronies of Marcos got the lion's share, the foreign borrowing was so large and so easy that the spin-off could still satisfy the sections of the big bourgeoisie outside the circle of Marcos cronies. But since 1981 there has been a conspicuous constriction of opportunities for the big bourgeoisie as a whole. With regard to the middle class they are repelled - the leading economic lights of this stratum have been repelled by the pro-imperialist economic policies of the Aquino regime. I refer to such policies as import liberalization, conversion of the foreign debt into equity, privatization by the foreign multinational firms and so on.

Q: Do you consider that the magnitude of the spoil after Marcos acquired by the new cronies is of such a magnitude that it has disturbed the balance within the compradore bourgeoisie and the landlord class?

A: Because the loot now is relatively smaller than before, the proportion of the loot that is taken by the Cory Aquino cronies is much bigger than that taken by the Marcos cronies, because the size of the loot was much bigger during the times of Marcos due to the heavy foreign borrowing. So the looting now is more noticeable. The big bourgeoisie expresses its resentment towards Aquino by pointing to the supposed impotence of the Aquino regime in dealing with the revolutionary movement, and therefore it seems as failing to create the stable conditions and the favorable conditions for foreign investments.

Q: What is the relationship between the progressive and revolutionary organizations and the Aquino government?

A: Since the breakdown in the negotiations between the NDF and the Aquino government in early February 1987, and the subsequent declaration by Mrs Aquino of total war against the revolutionary movement, there has been a clear line dividing the Aquino government and the broad ND movement. The two sides became diametrically opposed. It is Mrs Aquino's own responsibility, because she, together with other high civilian and military officials, has been celebrating as effective tools against 'communism' : the death squads and vigilante groups, like the Alsa Masa and so on. But in certain areas some vestiges of the old relationship of Bayan and PDP-Laban are still there. And so some progressive elements not clearly identified as particularly objectionable to the Aquino regime would still be elected. But these would compose a minor part of the Aquino slate.

Q: What do you think are the conditions on which the NDF would consider it possible to re-open negotiations with the Aquino government?

A: I think that the NDF would be reasonable to agree to a re-opening of negotiations with the Aquino government if this government would also be willing to negotiate the substantive issues, such as US dominance, feudal exploitation, and the removal of the fascist and bureaucratic corruption. The NDF would be willing to negotiate with and come to an agreement with the Aquino government if only the peoples' demands for national liberation and democracy can be fulfilled.

Jose Maria (Joema) Sison is a prominent political figure on the Philippine left. He was born in 1938 and studied for a Master of Arts (English) at the University of Philippines. Imprisoned in 1977 on suspicion of being a founding leader of the Communist Party of the Philippines, and of being the author of 'Philippine Society and Revolution', still considered the main analytical text of the Philippine left. Released from prison in March 1986 just after the Aquino take-over.

Copenhagen, October 5, 1987.

SOUTH KOREA AND TAIWAN - PROSPECTS FOR DEMOCRACY

Thorkil Casse and Laurids S.Lauridsen
Rambøll & Hannemann and Roskilde University Center

Introduction

South Korea and Taiwan have faced an outspoken demand for democracy during the past several years. Their governments have tried to counter the struggle for democracy which is on the rise in the two countries, but they are, at least to some degree, pledged to a process of democratization. The violence has escalated following confrontations between students and riot police, but there is little doubt that an element of compromise is about to enter the political scene. The days are over when these demonstrations could just be run down by the police and the military.

In the face of changes in the world economy, development strategies in the two countries have relied on purely economic modifications; it is striking how little has changed in political terms until recently. This fact gives explosive power to one crucial question: Whether capitalism will make room for a democratization process as an incontestable historical stage in its own development. This paper explores the character of the struggle for democracy in South Korea and Taiwan and the chances for a western style democracy in the future in the two countries. It should, however, be emphasized that the scope of the paper will be confined to a discussion of the formal democratic structure and not to the question of whether a democratization process really will lead to power sharing and decentralization (see Peter Wad, 1987).

Whether capitalism and democracy will, in the long run, go hand in hand is still a theoretical question, particularly when we are dealing with Third World countries. Some people argue that a parliamentary system is inevitably linked to the development of capitalism. Others regard the emergence of democracy in conjunction with the strengthening of the national bourgeoisie, while other observers defend the position that the interest for democracy in the embryonic capitalist class will diminish as the capitalist development becomes more profound. Finally, there are those who support the view that the process of democratization springs from specific circumstances; they are more likely to presume that other classes, for example the working class, through class actions will determine the fate and shape of a bourgeois democracy.

Development strategies in South Korea and Taiwan

South Korea and Taiwan have been the subjects of much interest from the outside world. How did they manage to build up their presumably sustained economies and is it possible to emulate their strategies?

For several years, a comprehensive understanding of the development strategies adopted in South Korea and Taiwan has been blurred by the flow of studies undertaken by neoclassical economists on the one hand, and on the other hand, studies which conclude that the economic development of these two countries is the mere reflection of the fact that foreign multinationals companies have delocalized their production in free-trade zones. Today, most people are convinced that the economic success in South Korea and Taiwan has involved a high degree of state intervention and rests on a self-sustained development which imposes restrictive regulations on the activities of foreign firms.

Neither of the two countries is endowed with natural resources of any importance, and they were both under Japanese colonial rule from the beginning of the century to the end of World War II. Whatever humiliations and oppressions the two countries suffered during the Japanese occupation, the economic heritage was an important trump in the hands of the new national regimes. In contrast to the attitude of European colonists, the Japanese regarded their colonies as provinces and devoted much energy to mobilize their proper development. The Confucian education which raises people to establish and obey a strong state power is yet another characteristic of the development strategies of the two countries.

For a developing country aiming at high-speed industrialization, an efficient agricultural sector is somehow a precondition. The United States, in cooperation with the first national governments, introduced a land reform which provided the countries with the means to become self-sufficient with regard to food. One of the main differences between South Korea and Taiwan is marked by the deviation in the efficiency of their agricultural policy. In Taiwan, state intervention was far more outreaching. The state extracted a large volume of resources from agriculture (finance, food, labour and exports) so support industrialization through obligatory rice deliveries and monopoly control over fertilizer supply etc., while at the same time it introduced a green revolution and raised productivity. While Taiwan has achieved a food surplus, South Korea remains with a food deficit.

In the fifties, both countries were recipients of American aid and assistance. The Korean government at that time was highly corrupt and depended on aid for speculation purposes. In Taiwan, however, the growth in the economy was much higher, a growth based on import substitution financed by the extraction of surplus from the agricultural sector. Export promotion was started already in the fifties, contrary to the Korean experience. South Korea did not enter the export promotion phase until the sixties. In both countries, the involvement of the state was maintained throughout the development process, in Taiwan mainly relying on production of industrial inputs in public enterprises and price control of industrial goods. South Korea conducted a selective approach, through allocation of underpriced credit to priority sectors. The result was a substantial difference in industrial structure. In South Korea, the ten largest conglomerates account for 25% of GDP, whereas the industrial structure in Taiwan is based on small family companies.

As Menzel and Senghass (1985) point out, South Korea and Taiwan distinguish themselves from other developing countries in the fact that their development has been linked to **an homogeneous and egalitarian strategy.** The spill-over effects of economic growth benefitted even workers and peasants, even if the statistics in the Korean case seem biased. Only urban inequalities are provided.

Differences in the pattern of economic transformation in Taiwan and South Korea are also illustrated in table 1.

Table 1. Development indicators - South Korea and Taiwan

	Year	South Korea	Taiwan
GNP US$b			
	1961	2.3	2.8
	1986	95.0	73.3
Per capita income US$b			
	1961	87	254
	1986	2,296	3,468
Manufacturing as % of GDP			
	1961/62	14	18
	1985	28	36
Heavy industry as % total manufact.			
	1961/62	29	28
	1980/81	53	65
Share of workforce in manufacturing			
	1986	25	34
Share of workforce in agriculture			
	1986	24	17
Total foreign trade as of GNP			
	1986	70	97
Export of manufactures as % of total merchandise exports			
	1986	92	98
Current account balance US$b			
	1985	-887	9,195
	1986	4,017	16,217
Foreign reserves US$b			
	1986	8,114	71,000
Debt-service ratio (%)			
	1986	14	4.6

Sources: Ulrich Menzel: **In der Nachfolge Europas. Autozentrierte Entwicklung in den ostasiatischen Swellenländern Südkorea und Taiwan** (München 1985). **Asia Yearbook 1988**, Far Eastern Economic Review. **World Development Report 1987**, World Bank 1987.

GDP per capita is substantially higher in Taiwan, and due to its favourable current account balance, financing of industrial development has been unproblematic. As a result of a still larger surplus in trade particularly with the US, foreign exchange surplus has grown to 75 billion US $. During the 1980s, however, the local capitalists have been more interested in squeezing profits out of current goods than developing and investing in new goods and production processes. Due to substantial deficits in its current account balance during the 1970s, and early 1980s, South Korea has appeared as one of the most indebted nations in the Third World. Instead of using surplus resources coming from agriculture and local savings, South Korea has been forced to finance its industrial development by means of foreign loans (direct foreign investments being of minor importance). On the other hand, the high level of concentration in industrial capital has made it possible for South Korea to advance further than Taiwan in the transformation process towards higher technology of industry.

In both countries, foreign technology and foreign investment have been strictly scrutinized and directed towards these economic sectors in which the local capacity is missing.

The centralist form of capitalist development in South Korea and Taiwan reflects the existence of **strong social categories having their basis in the state apparatus**. In both countries, they have successfully been able to insulate themselves from particular class interests and minimized their commitment to existing social groups. Autonomously organized economic and political groups have had no effective access to the strategic decision-making centres and the state has effectively controlled the channels of interest articulation.

The national capitalist development has been founded on a tacit alliance between the political leadership and big capital. The state has not simply protected individual capital interests but intervened economically and politically in order to support the long term interests of the capitalist class and especially the upper part of it.

If we thus classify the state as very strong and very autonomous, it still has to be explained, why this has been the case. The question falls into two parts. First, how has it been possible for the state to function in such an autonomous manner? Second, why has it been necessary for the governing elite to use its autonomy to follow an aggressive capitalist industrialization strategy?

The first question can be answered by pointing at a set of particular circumstances:

a) The Japanese colonial "direct" rule implied that the local power elite - the landlords - at an early stage lost its political power.

b) When the Japanese withdrew, their monopoly of power was transferred to civil and military bureaucracies.

c) Decolonization eliminated any influence of foreign capital. Until the late 1960s, the American interest in the two countries was political and military rather than economic. Therefore, pressure from this powerful ally was not primarily guided by the need to protect American monopoly interests but the need to "modernize" these economies. The American pressure, therefore, became instrumental in capitalist accumulation in the two countries.

d) Civil and military bureaucracies inherited a substantial part of the industry already in existence, and got firm control of the financial institutions leading to a state-centered accumulation process.

e) Due to land reforms in the 1950s, the landed aristocracy also lost its economic power and was eliminated.

f) At an early stage, opposition forces and especially left wing elements were either eliminated or driven into exile.

g) Further, the general militarization of society in the two countries contributed to a centralization of political power and a consensus in relation to defence of sovereignty.

h) Finally, bureaucratic rule and state control over trade and business have very deep roots in both Chinese and Korean history and culture.

In addition, as far as **South Korea** is concerned, it must be stressed that the processes of primitive capitalist accumulation and transformation of commercial into industrial capital were as much political as economic. During the Syngman Rhee period, the essential source of accumulation was close links with the state apparatus. Access to foreign exchange, to American aid (in form of commodities), to military contracts, to former state-owned enterprises and to state loans with low interest became the basis of prosperous business activities in the sphere of circulation. During the Park period, these resources were invested in productive activities but the tight cooperation between state and big capital continued under state leadership.

In **Taiwan**, the political elite became a "foreign" elite. The local Taiwanese looked upon the Nationalists as another elite coming from "outside". The Nationalists situated themselves in certain areas of the major cities and this separation developed further due to ethnic and language differences between the two groups of the population.

This brings us to **the second question**: why has the elite been following an aggressive industrialization strategy. We think that the basic point is that the state has forced industrial development for political reasons.

Internally, the elites needed legitimacy, and economic growth benefitting a majority of the population has been instrumental for that purpose. Externally, pressure from the big ally in the west and confrontation with China and North Korea have made quick economic success necessary, partly in order to compete with the system of communism and partly in order to build up the necessary industrial basis for military strength. Aggressive industrial development, therefore, has been closely linked to national security and anti-communism.

Type of Government

Within the framework of political systems, Peter Wad (1987) distinguishes between four different concepts from the ultimate state of dictatorship to the western style of representative democracy.

1) Bureaucratic autocracy:
   Repressive dictatorship.
2) Parliamentary autocracy:
   The state power reigns within one class and elections, when schedules, leave no room for surprises.
3) Parliamentary oligarchy:
   The state power can change between groups within the elite but limits are narrow in regard to parties that are authorized to run for elections. Restrictions on freedom of speech and freedom to organize are imposed as well.
4) Parliamentary democracy:
   Western style representative democracy.

We name 4) as the most democratic form of Government (we assume that direct democracy of some socialist configuration is not put on the agenda). In order to make it operational, we define parliamentary democracy as based on four principles:

- free, fair and normal elections
- civil rights are stipulated in the constitution
- freedom to organize
- independent courts.

How do the two countries, South Korea and Taiwan, adjust to these provisions?

South Korea

The rapid industrialization encountered economic difficulties in 1979/80 due to the rise in oil prices and a bad harvest. Workers and farmers became more outspoken about their grievances and a number of people were arrested and sentenced to long terms of imprisonment. On 26 October 1979, the former President Park Chung-Hee was assassinated by Kum Tae-Kyu, the Director of the Korean Central Intelligence Agency (KCIA).

Partial martial law was declared and Prime Minister Choi Kyu-Hah was elected President in December 1979. He tried to conduct a revision of the Constitution, pushing ahead for a democratization of the society. But students were impatient and anti-government opinion grew, demanding the abolition of martial law, adoption of a new constitution, an end to press censorship and, not least, the resignation of General Chun Doo-Hwan, new Director of KCIA. Martial law was extended in May 1980, after which date all political activity was banned. A student-peasant led liberation of a major town, Kwangju, in the south-western province ended in extreme violence, when paratroopers killed between 1200 and 2000 persons in order to reinstate 'normal law and order'. Ever since this event, anti-American feelings have emerged among opponents to the regime, who accused the American troops of complicity in the Kwangju-massacre. The paratroopers had come from the border of the demilitarized zone between North and South Korea, where all forces are under the control of an American general.

Following the insurrections in the Spring of 1980, President Choi resigned and General Chun took over office in August 1980 following another coup-d'etat. A new constitution was passed in the Assembly limiting the presidential period to a single seven-year term of office. The 1980 Constitution was in force until October 1987. Martial law was eased in October 1980.

Until 1971, South Korea was governed by President Park, who came to power after a coup-d'etat in 1961. For the first time in the history of South Korea, the new president was to be elected by direct vote by all the people in the country. President Park was re-elected only by means of substantial **election** fraud. In response to the nationwide protest, the president proclaimed a state of emergency. A new constitution was amended and gave the president almost unlimited power. A presidential college was established to elect any new president. Since then, only the elections to the Assembly in 1985, when the opposition party won 30% of the vote, could be characterized as somewhat fair.

According to the 1980 Constitution, all citizens shall enjoy **freedom of speech and of assembly**. But in reality, many opponents and critics have been arrested on charges of endangering national security. It has been common practice for many years to consider opponents to the regime as pro-communist and thus liable to prosecution under very hard condition, which in fact were unconstitutional. Many persons have been detained for weeks without an arrest warrant, during which period they have been tortured. In general, criticism of the government's economic policy has been allowed, but political criticism has been seen as a criminal offence against the regime. The alleged criminal acts which opponents had supposedly executed in favour of North Korea have served to justify the brutality of the regime. Because of the widespread fear of a North Korean invasion, many South Koreans accept these unfair trials.

The **freedom to organize** is also stipulated in the constitution. However, the right to collective action must be exercised in accordance to the law. Persons other than the workers at a local work place are not allowed to engage in collective bargaining. The Federation of Unions (controlled by the government) has the power to negotiate a collective agreement only with the approval of the Ministry of Labour. Changes in the labour laws in 1980 led to a shift from a system of industrial unions to company unions. Unions can at present only cover a single work place. Any labour dispute has to be reported to the Labour Relations Commission, consisting of representatives from workers, employers and the state. This commission has the right to dismiss the dispute. Under this law from 1980, strikes are formally authorized, but since workers dispose over only one-third of the members of the Commission, few strikes are approved.

According to Amnesty International, the right of defendants to a **fair trial** was undermined in many cases under the Anti-Communist Law. These 'irregularities' included illegal detention without an arrest warrant, denial of access to lawyers until the opening of the trial and verdicts not being made public or even known in detail by the defendants.

This short description of the Korean political system suggests that normal civil rights, as we know them from western capitalist countries, even though stipulated in the constitution, are seldom respected when applied to concrete cases. Until recently, the capitalist class, represented by the large firms - the chaebols - together with the political leadership, have retained their monopoly of state power. However, signs of less repression of criticism of the government's economic policy and of the right to form other political parties than the leading party, put South Korea in the second category: parliamentary autocracy.

Taiwan

Taiwan is regarded as an indivisible part of China by both the government in Taipei and in Peking. The Kuomintang party that dominates the government of Taiwan thus also claims to be the legitimate ruler of Mainland China, which it calls the Republic of China (ROC). The KMT looks on the communist rule on the mainland as a continuing rebellion from the republic, which was founded in 1911. This configuration has had and still has a significant influence on the whole question of regime development in Taiwan.

The power structure has been extremely centralized around Chiang Kai-shek and later his son Chiang Ching-kuo. As chairman of the party (KMT), president and commander-in-chief both leaders were almost **dictators**. The autocratic rule was enforced by means of three institutional structures - the party, the security forces and the governmental institutions.

The party is a Leninist-style party and constitutes the core of the three institutional structures. The party exercises ideological-political control through the party itself, which has more than 2 million members, equal to one-third of all adult men (the majority of the members are men), but also through a variety of mass organizations such as the youth league and the women's organizations. Further the party controls mass communication channels, educational institutions, trade unions and Peasant Associations.

The external and domestic **security forces** do not have the same degree of independence as in South Korea. The armed forces are not allowed any consolidating influence. Alongside each combat unit commander the KMT has placed political warfare officers, and few general-class officers receive more than a single two-year term of duty on any given post. The intelligence service consists of ten individual units all subject to a central coordinating bureau which again is placed under the president/the chairman of KMT.

There have been no national **elections** since 1947-48. Under the "Temporary Provisions During the Period of Communist Rebellion" legislation of 1948 and based on the theory that constituencies remain under communist control, the originally KMT deputies have been "frozen" in office without having to face elections, or vacancies have been filled from among those, who unsuccessfully ran for office for the KMT on the mainland. Starting in 1969, however, there has been a series of supplementary elections in Taiwan itself in order to replenish the dwindling number of legislators. These elections have given Taiwan a greater share of the seats than the proportion of its population in China plus Taiwan. The strategically important National Assembly which elects the president and the vicepresident, and which makes amendments to the constitution has also had a few new members added. In Taiwan, therefore, you find universal and equal suffrage but elections have not determined the composition of the national representatives. Further, these elections have been dominated by one party - the KMT - and until recently, opposition candidates have not been allowed to enter as a political group or party. Elections, therefore, have not been part of some kind of representative democracy but a pillar for authoritanism.

Based on the official assumption that Taiwan is still at war with the People's Republic of China, the population on Taiwan has lived under martial law until recently. The provision of the martial law has abrogated all guaranties of **civil liberties** in the constitution. They proscribed public meetings, strikes and demonstrations and banned opposition political parties. Further all trials concerning internal or external security were held in military courts and basic legal safeguards were absent. In addition, special laws and statutes adopted later have circumscribed the civil liberties by giving arbitrary power to the military and police to ban meetings to screen and confiscate publications, to confiscate property, to retain defendants for infinite periods etc. According to Amnesty International, psychological and physical pressure during interrogations has been reported continuously, although the number of political prisoners has decreased in recent years. Finally, all organizations are required to seek official sanction in advance and all organizations are tightly controlled by the KMT and the security forces.

Summing up, there seems to be good reasons for characterizing the traditional political regime on Taiwan as a **bureaucratic autocracy**. In fact, the political regime has many similarities with the political structure in the so-called socialist countries. The crucial decisions take place in the Central Committee of the party in which the chairman has a powerful role, and the population is tightly controlled by a network of security forces and other organizational structures.

Social classes and the struggle for democracy

In order to obtain a more distinct understanding of the process of democratization, it is useful to relate this transformation process to the social classes and their articulation of interests.

One of the very few observers, Asche (1985), has conducted a genuine class analysis of the Korean society and compared it to the class structure of Taiwan. He concludes that:

1) The existence of a rather small capitalist class in conjunction with an important marginalized fraction of the population seems to indicate that South Korea must be labelled a transition country ("Schwellen-land") and that the economic stage of Taiwan, where the capitalist development is much more advanced, has reached a level similar to an industrialized country.

2) The poor development of the capitalist mode of production in South Korea requires a repressive political system which can disengage social unrest and keep the major part of the population in deep distress.

What is striking about this analysis is Asche's insistence on the small number of capitalists in South Korea, a fact which seems to be the cornerstone of his argument. But with a high degree of concentration in regard to industrial capital, it follows automatically that the capitalist class will be small in number.

This observation, however, does not provide crucial evidence for the conclusion that the capitalist mode of production has been less penetrating in South Korea than in Taiwan. In 1961, the military regime confiscated all capital, but the 'illicitly earned profit' (capital accumulated during the Rhee period of corruption when fortunes were created by illegal sale on the local market of import restricted consumer goods) had already returned to the few wealthy families in 1964. By this act, the military government in South Korea proved its commitment to growth coupled with the belief that the actual accomplishment of that goal should be carried out by the wealthy families. Economic growth has been generated ever since through investment of family fortunes in big enterprises. The families had their fortunes, but under the strict condition that the capital should be invested in industrial production. The banks remained in the hands of the military regime, which by this remedy could guide industrial development. The concentration of capital, therefore, was the result of the economic heritage from Rhee and cannot be used as proof of the quasi non-existence of a capitalist mode of production in South Korea.

Partial, mutuality should, in this case, be seen as a concept which underlines the common interest shared by the government and the capitalists. Thus, the capitalist has displayed little enthusiasm for political changes. Only recently, with Chun's approach of giving priority to small company projects, has the "Federation of Korean Industries" manifested any discontent with the Chun regime. To a certain extent, the Federation, which represents big business, is an advocate of a more regulated labour market system which includes minimum wages and central wage bargaining, but the capitalist class does not support a democratization of the political rules.

The strongest call for democratization has its origin in the **middle class** and its mass movement organizations. Peasants, students and small businessmen have not enjoyed the fruits of the rapid development of South Korea in the same way as the capitalist class and the workers. Throughout the history of South Korea, the student movements have gained experience in challenging the different regimes. Violent demonstrations in 1960 forced Rhee to resign from his position as president, and Chun declared martial law in 1980 as a reaction to the Kwangju uprising. The struggle for autonomy of the universities and protests against US pressure to liberalize the Korean import regulations are other issues which have helped to strengthen the determination to fight for democracy. The students constitute the only leftist opposition of any importance in the country.

The establishment of farmers association, regardless of how much they are controlled by the state as in the case of Taiwan, has no parallel in South Korea. Farmers have suffered from the gradual removal of subsidized producer prices effectuated by Chun in the eighties in order to reduce the deficit in the state budget. The farmers' manifestations are less outspoken, but they have in great numbers supported the first non-conformist opposition party, NKDP, when it was formed in January 1985.

NKPD was a rather conservative party with support ranging from student groups to small businessmen, and with this construction obviously a weak party. The democratic struggle in Korea distinguishes itself from the one in the Philippines, where right wing opposition movements have not united with left wing oppositionists.

In the absence of a genuine national structure, the government controlled FKTU (Federation of Korean Trade Unions) being little more than an agency for technical training and statistical information, several church-based and other social organizations have played the part expected of independent unions. But even the activities of FKTU have been suspended and then re-established on several occasions when supporting the weak governments of transition in 1961 and 1980. In the eighties, the Chun regime restricted its status even further through the shift from industrial unionism to company unionism.

But admitting the important role of the **working class** during the short periods of transition towards democracy and the unofficial labour movement's concern for working conditions, can not blur the picture that democracy has not been the most urgent issue for the working class.

During the seventies, only about 100 labour disputes were reported on average per year. And most of these disputes were initiated to get higher wages or following non-payments from the employer. The main explanation for the separation of strikes from the call for democracy seems to be the development in real wages. With one exception, in 1979/80, real wages have shown a positive tendency since the beginning of the seventies, and in periods even outpaced the evolution in productivity. In 1980/81, the increase in real wages lagged behind productivity increases by about 36%. From 1982 to 1986 the gap was about 16%. While many keep in mind what they perceive to be a worker-taming Confucian ethic, according to which members of the society submit to the guidance of one leader (cf. Peter Wad (1987)), the economic benefits which workers have enjoyed provide a better explanation for the passive-support attitude of the workers toward the Park and Chun regimes. Minimum wages and a social security system are the topics on the agenda which the working class addresses to the government. It was not until the start of the students' anti-government campaign in the Spring of 1987 in response to the death of a student under police torture that workers were inspired to make the move for nationwide industrial action.

At this stage, we can thus conclude the following:

1) The difference in economic development between South Korea and Taiwan is an incontestable fact, but there are no grounds to presume that the capitalist mode of production is less advanced in Korea. The model of accumulation does not represent an impediment for democracy, neither in South Korea nor in Taiwan.

2) The struggle for democracy is rooted in the discontent of the middle class. The political party, NKPD, formed in 1985, has served as a mouthpiece for the opposition, but some of the groups are even involved

in mass movements (a double-organizing participation). The capitalist class does not support the struggle for democracy and the working class has been reluctant to join the movement. Both classes are more in favour of a institution-based reform of the labour market (fordism).

Taiwan

Compared with South Korea, the capitalist class in Taiwan is made up of a large number of small family-owned enterprises. Generally, their capital basis is weak, they have a low technological level, they lack management knowledge and produce with a very short horizon of profit and they finally show high flexibility and diversify into new lines of business when these appear more profitable. Besides this majority of small and medium scale enterprises there are a few giants, most locally owned and controlled.

The capitalist class seems to articulate its interests in an individual manner, utilizing their numerous contacts within the political-administrative system. The leaders of the largest corporations often have special access to the state apparatus.

As regards the question of democratic development, the capitalist class and especially big capital have not shown any interest in supporting a democratic transformation. To them, democracy imply an opening for the independence forces and thus a threat to capitalist accumulation on Taiwan because peoples Republic of China considers a move towards independence as an unacceptable development. Furthermore, the interests of this class and particularly the big capital have been taken care of through the tacit alliance mentioned above between the economic and political elite. As in South Korea, it is among the

middle classes we find the social forces behind the struggle for democracy.

Among the independent middle-class, **the peasants** have a more unobtrusive role. The peasants are organized in and subordinated to the Peasant's Associations. They collect land tax and other taxes, they deliver inputs and supply credits, they take care of a comprehensive extension service and are in charge of storage, reselling etc. By means of these associations KMT has a firm grip on the agrarian sector. The leaders of the individual associations are elected through local elections but the candidates have to bé approved by special KMT-controlled committees. So far, the opposition has only obtained a modest influence among the peasants.

Concerning the remainder of the independent middle class, the call for democracy and self-determination has obtained some popularity both in the more **traditional petty bourgeoisie** and among **professionals** such as lawyers and doctors. However, it is primarily in the **state-based new middle class** and among **students** that we find the core of the opposition movement.

During the 1970s and encouraged by the growing isolation of Taiwan, an opposition movement began to emerge. The participants were recruited from two main sources. On the one hand from the radical student movement that appeared with an anti-imperialist attitude and a socially oriented consciousness in spite of the strong control by the KMT at the universities. On the other hand, the localist monopoly of power by the Mainlanders in the central parts of the political sphere.

Since 1977, the opposition movement has run for elections first as the so-called Dangwai movement and since 1986 as a party - the Democratic Progressive Party (DPP). The party is rather heterogeneous. Basicly it is divided into two main fractions - the moderates who follow a parliamentary road to political reform and who cooperate with the liberals in KMT (the "Young Turks"), and the radicals, who try to mobilize a countervailing social force and therefore favour street demonstrations and other types of mass actions and who finally are influenced by leftist ideas. Both fractions support the ultimate goal of an independent Taiwan.

The labour class is organized in or more precisely by the trade unions. These unions are first and foremost to be regarded as a part of the KMT machinery. The unions play no role in wage determination but enter into discussions with management on such issues as social welfare. The labour class has only to a limited degree manifested itself as a class in itself ("Klasse für sich"). Besides state intervention in order to control and repress the labour class, such passivity is to be explained by three circumstances: First, the labour class is very fragmented and segmented. Second, the class structure, and thereby the class identity is very blurred as major decision-making takes place in extended families which obtain their income from various sources - from various class positions. Finally, and third, the Chinese moral and mentality combined with a period of rapid growing real wages - 5.6 per cent during the 1952-80 period - have had a pacifying influence.

Various polls among workers show that they are fairly satisfied with their share of Taiwan's economic miracle. These polls also reveal that the working class generally is dissatisfied with the working conditions and the social security system.

Labour class resistance and protest has mainly taken individual forms. The most common mode of protest has been to leave the job and find employment elsewhere. Such reactions may be found in smaller enterprises but is very common in large companies in which the workers normally are recruited outside the normal family networks and where the level of social responsibility therefore is limited.

During the period of martial law which was lifted in mid-1987, strikes were prohibited and no national strikes have occurred since 1949. Although the possibilities of launching strikes still are severely restricted signs of a more militant position against union officials have appeared during the last six months. At the political level, a DPP legislator in December 1987 formed Taiwan's first Labour Party in opposition to DPP's ignorance of labour issues. The new party is still limited to a circle of labour activists and intellectuals. Among other things the party calls for free unions, tighter enforcement of laws governing industrial health and hazards, and a more balanced way of sharing the nation's wealth. However, the party still has to show that it can get support among Taiwan's more than five million labourers. A major hurdle, besides the weak class identification already mentioned, is the anchoring of the party intellectuals in the one-China policy of reunification with the mainland.

In sum, as in South Korea the middle classes must be looked upon as the main social force in the struggle for democracy. The capitalist class, particularly the big capital, scarcely support any significant change of status quo and the working class still plays a limited role in the struggle for democracy.

Towards democracy?

South Korea

It is difficult to ascertain the real background for the Chun regime's fall and the succession of power. But, in the first place, it is desirable to note that the constitution, which was adopted after Chun seized power, stated that the presidential term was restricted to seven years. In Chun's own understanding, the nomination of his successor was to be assumed by a presidential college issuing from the National Assembly in which Chun's party, the Democratic Justice Party, holds the majority.

The first step towards democracy was taken in the beginning of 1985, when the first non-conventional opposition party was authorized to nominate candidates for the National Assembly elections in February 1985. Despite the minor role of the parliament in policy-making, the capture of nearly 40% of the vote demonstrated a popular support for initiating a democratization process. The seats in the Assembly were also used as a platform for proclamations on numerous economic and political issues. In 1984, a Council for the Promotion of Democracy was formed with the two opposition politicians, Kim Dae-Jung and Kim Young Sam, leading the group. The Council became the core of the New Korea Democratic Party (NKDP) which until 1987 was the leading opposition party in the Assembly.

In 1986, the NKDP together with other groups pressed for a constitutional reform which would allow the next president to be elected by direct election. At first, Chun denounced the constitutional debate as illegal and a threat to national security, but later the same year he suggested a reconciliation with the opposition which implied that the opposition would join the government to maintain law and order until the post-olympic period. The idea was rejected by the opposition.

As movements for constitutional revision mobilized thousands of demonstrators in the Spring of 1986, and the US pressed for some sort of compromise, the Chun regime responded by proposing instead a cabinet system, in which the president would be a figurehead and the prime minister elected by parliament. This seemed the only way for the leading party, DJP, to win the elections. But there was one major obstacle left: this constitutional revision needed more votes in the Assembly than could be secured by DJP's members of parliament.

Once more KNDP refused to compromise and the party managed also to convince the smaller "opposition" parties in parliament to reject the Chun plan. In June 1986, however, an agreement was reached between the DJP leader Roh Tae Woo and the KNDP leader Lee Min Woo. The agreement called for a special session of the Assembly to begin revising the constitutional provisions for presidential elections.

The compromise was strongly condemned by the different popular movements for democracy, and a long period of internal debate within KNDP began about whether to refuse the compromise or join it. In any respect, meetings between DJP and NKDP were begun. Then, in March 1987, it was clear that the two parties could not agree on how the rules for the presidential election should be designed. The two Kims now opposed any compromise with the government, and Chun took the opportunity to cancel the constitutional debate since it was obvious that no compromise could be reached. Chun would nominate his own successor in February 1988 when his term was to expire. On May 1, the two Kims formed a new party, the Reunification Democratic Party (RDP).

The following months of 1987 were decisive for the final outcome of several years of struggle for constitutional reform. When Chun, in June, appointed the DJP leader, Roh, as his successor, he triggered disturbances of a magnitude not seen since Kwangju in 1980. Not only students, but also other people from the middle class participated in demonstrations. The church declared officially that it urged Chun to retract his decision to suspend discussions of reform of the electoral system. In an unusual statement, the US government pressed the Chun regime to come to terms with the opposition. The US state Department urged "Korean military commanders to concentrate on the defense of Korea and allow the political process to develop in a manner agreeable to the Korean people". In addition to this shift in the US attitude from an unchallenged support to the Chun regime, there was the pressure of the risk of sacrificing the hosting of the Olympic games should civil war explode. Then on June 29, Roh made a declaration in which he promised to adopt a direct presidential system, to promote freedom of the press, to guarantee self-regulation to universities, to allow the formation of parties that "engage in sound activities and do not contravene such objectives" and finally to carry out social reforms.

These unilateral concessions paved the way for the first free presidential elections in December 1987. In July, tens of thousands of workers had begun demanding a share in the promised democratic reforms. A major target for the labour unrest was Hyundai, one of the 10 chaebols (conglomerates), and workers not only went on strike for higher salaries, but also attempted to form independent unions. The strike was settled with substantial pay raises, but workers who participated in trying to establish independent unions were arrested and sentenced to up to one year of imprisonment. According to the Ministry of Labour, there were over 3000 strikes reported until September 1987, of which almost all began after the Roh declaration in June.

On the political scene, a constitutional reform that guaranteed direct presidential elections was ratified in a national referendum in October 1987. The opposition failed, however, to agree on selection of one candidate who could unify the opposition against the Chun regime. Only weeks before the election, Kim Dae Jung decided to run for the presidency as candidate for a new party (Peace and Democracy Party - PDP) against Kim Young Sam, Roh, the DJP candidate and Kim Jong Pil (leader of the party in power in the days of the Park regime). Roh won

36% of 23.1 million votes cast, more than 2 million votes more than Kim Young Sam (28%), with Kim Dae Jung in third place (27%). While it is true that the opposition would have assumed victory if only one candidate had been selected, the margin of Roh's victory was surprisingly wide and sufficient to negate the opposition claims that the victory was due to massive voting fraud. The opposition could 'only' point to about 1000 cases of fraud, a figure far less than the 2 million margin.

We will use this long, detailed description of the contemporary history of the Korean democratic movement to raise a few essential questions in regard to the substance of the process.

1) Why did the opposition not win the presidential election? Was it purely the result of the split between the two candidates?

2) Why did the opposition not agree to initiate a parliamentary system to replace the winner-takes-all presidential system?

3) Why did the mass movement's struggle for democracy become simply a matter of rules for presidential elections?

4) What was the role of the working class in this struggle?

Kim Young Sam and Kim Dae Jung were both severely criticized for failing to come up with a single candidate, an event which most oppositionists regarded as the main cause of the opposition's defeat. But beneath the division itself, it is difficult to ignore the fact that in the months prior to the presidential elections the entire struggle for democracy turned into a mere matter of personality cult. What became of the demands for independent unions, for example? And what was the rationale behind the rejection of a shift to a parliamentary system as proposed by the Chun regime? The opposition failed to distinguish its candidates from Roh, and the regional distribution of the votes revealed that, with few exceptions, a candidate's origins seemed to be the central explanation for why a given province went to a given candidate.

Yet another issue was overlooked in the aftermath of the elections. When the opposition was still united, a platform and policy statement was issued by the RDP. The insistence on the establishment of a free-market economic system probably scared many potential supporters. Korea has been forced in the last few years to open up its domestic market, primarily to American goods and services. Many Koreans fear the repercussions of the liberalization process in regard to employment, and it is likely that the clear statement from the RDP that it would promote or accelerate this process has exacerbated its chances of winning the election.

Returning to the regional distribution of the votes, it is striking that the opposition did not win with an overwhelming majority in any of the typically troublesome industrial towns (Kwangju being the only exception, where Kim Dae Jung received 94% of the votes). Each of the three candidates came first in one and only one of the three big towns (the capital, Seoul, the shipyard town Pusan, and Taegu). Even the industrial town, Inchon near Seoul, went to Roh. The workers as a bloc seem not to have supported either of the two opposition candidates; this is likely to stem from the widespread opinion that an opposition winner would not automatically secure advantages for workers. The RDP policy platform was ambiguous in regard to labour union rights when it affirmed, "We actively encourage the normal operation of the Federation of Trade Unions structure" (the government controlled trade union). Furthermore, no protests were published by the two opposition parties at the time when worker activists engaged in forming independent unions were arrested in October-November 1987.

To label the new era when Roh took office on February 25, a parliamentary democracy would be an exaggeration. Political prisoners, approximately 1000 in number, are still detained by the police. It is still illegal to form independent unions; applications to start new daily papers and magazines wait for approval by the Ministry of Culture and Information; and no socialist political party can get official authorization to participate in elections. It is difficult to credit the political system under the supervision of former general Roh for more than a parliamentary oligarchy.

Public anger, initially aimed at the government, has shifted focus to the two opposition candidates. In response to this, Kim Young Sam decided to step down in February 1988 as leader of RDP in order to pave the way for a reunification of the opposition before the forthcoming elections to the Assembly. But even if the opposition should win the elections, they are trapped in the solution they, themselves, fought for; a president-run political system. The fact that the outgoing military regime could claim the victory in the presidential election underlines the fact that the prevailing status of the political system will presumably be maintained even after the stage of the Olympics.

The democratization movement supported by the middle class and the summer strike wave in 1987 were quite separate events with fundamentally different aims, and it is likely that the failure to combine these objectives lies at the core of the success of the former regime in the first free elections ever in the history of the republic. Maybe the workers are those who come closest to have their demands fulfilled with the passage of the first minimum wage law in October 1987.

Should parliamentary democracy really emerge in Korea one day, it is inevitable that a new mass movement for democracy must be designed. A mass movement aiming at the accomplishment of various goals, including a parliamentary system and independent trade unions. In a short perspective, at least until the next presidential elections, parliamentary oligarchy and some reduced form of fordism (minimum wages) are on the agenda.

Taiwan

Since the late 1970s and especially during the last two years, Taiwan has entered a process towards a less authoritarian political structure. This transitional process, however, should not be equated with the far more radical political change that has taken place in South Korea.

In relation to **the state institutions and the party**, there has so far been no substantial change. In early 1988, Chiang Ching-kuo died and was followed by Lee Teng-hui as president and acting party chairman. As the first local Taiwanese president Lee's appointment is just the most prominent event in the ongoing process of "Taiwanization" of the political system. The policy of the Nationalist has for some time been to co-opt local Taiwanese leaders in order to macerate the ethnic conflict between the Mainlanders and the local Taiwanese.

As regards **elections**, they have since 1977 been open for non-KMT candidates and the Dangwai opposition and later the Democratic Progressive Party has obtained 17-22 per cent of the votes. The opportunities of campaigning have been restricted in' various ways, and local election fraud and the buying up of votes have been reported several times.

In September 1986, DPP was formed in defiance of martial law and the party was de facto allowed to campaign as a party for the December elections. In July 1987, the martial law was lifted and a new National Security Law came into effect. The main consequence of the lifting of martial law was symbolic because most of the provisions in the martial law were duplicated in other laws and because the new law itself was fairly stringent. The opposition, therefore, calls it martial law under a new guide. Among other things, the law prohibits political parties from challenging the constitution and it enables KMT to ban public meetings and political groups. However, the law plays down the role of the military, as civilians no longer can be prosecuted by military courts and as the right to screen and confiscate publications is transferred from the military to the Government Information Office.

As part of its democratic opening, the KMT has submitted two new law proposals - the Law on Assembly and Demonstrations that empowers the police to ban rallies and demonstrations under certain conditions and the Amendment to the Law on Civic Organization which sets the rules for party registration. The two laws contain three basic principles already developed by Chiang Ching-kuo last year. They are: respect for the constitution (including the present political anomaly), rejection of communism, and acceptance of the status of Taiwan as a part of China (thus rejecting independence).

A ban on newspaper publishing has been removed on January 1st 1988 and the constraints on the freedom of press has become weakened during early 1988. The new president has also promised a rejuvenation of the parliamentary institutions, dominated by old deputies elected four decades ago from mainland China constituencies. However, this revitalization does not mean that KMT will compromise on its claim to represent all China, and so far there has been no indication of KMT's readiness to give up its monopoly of power. The authoritarian regime, however, has become and in the future is going to become even softer. The regime has already been transformed into a parliamentary autocracy. The Nationalists want to co-opt the local Taiwanese elites and want to legitimize their rule by means of more democratic elections. On the other hand, there are no signs that this process will move towards a parliamentary oligarchy, not to mention a parliamentary democracy. Calls from DDP for new elections at all levels of parliament and popular election of the president have so far been met by silence.

Therefore, the question arises: Why has the process of political democratization been more restrictive on Taiwan than in South Korea?

At the economic level, the present capitalist development could undoubtedly, as in South Korea, proceed under a more democratic form of political regime, the more so as a large majority of the population in fact supports a capitalist road of development. Further, Taiwan generally is developed in a less heterogenous manner than South Korea which should lead to less economic determined potentials of conflict here. However, Taiwan is faced with a set of serious restructuring problems. As in South Korea, a combination of external and internal constraints forces the country to diversify, deepen and upgrade its industrial structure and export. However, such a change towards high-tech industrialization requires a fundamental change in the island's capital structure. Taiwanese capital will have to go through a process of concentration and centralization. To a larger degree the state must then support a big capital against the interest of tens of thousands of small non-capitalist and capitalist small-scale enterprises that for a long time have made up the backbone of Taiwan's light industries. This in turn will bring the state into an open confrontation with a large part of the working class because this class one way or another has based its long term reproduction on that sector. Such a conflict can only be eliminated if an alternative source of reproduction security is developed in the form of an effective social security system. Thus, in order to carry forward a high-tech strategy, the state must be strong and autonomous but such a strategy in itself seems to weaken the position of the state unless a new social coalition is developed. Recently, the state has shown willingness to improve the working conditions but at the same time there are indications that it will be more difficult for independent workers to launch their own free unions.

On the economic level, Helmuth Asche (1985) takes up a quite different argument for the KMT monopoly of power. According to Asche the present autocracy must be explained by the role of the state for the Nationalists. The state sector is the most important channel for upward social mobility and an important revenue source for the KMT members.

Although important constraints could be identified at the economic level, we think that the main explanation of the limited prospects for democracy in Taiwan is to be found in the relationship between Taiwan and the Peoples Republic of China. As stated earlier, the Chinese Communist Party finds itself in accord with the Kuomintang party as regards Taiwan's status as a part of China. The two parties, however, disagree on the development path to be followed and on who should be in charge of the development. The discussion of democratic transformation, therefore, cannot be isolated from the broader **security issue**. During the last 10 to 15 years, the security issue has grown in importance due to three changes. First, United States has changed its policy towards "the two Chinas". Second, Taiwan has been confronted with a growing international isolation, and third, the agreements between Britain/Portugal and China, concerning the future of Hong Kong and Macau, respectively, have brought the China-Taiwan relation in focus.

While the KMT claims sovereignty over all China, the Democratic Progressive Party has independence as its long term goal. In the resolution from the first congress in 1986, the DPP called for "self-determination for the people of Taiwan". The second congress in 1987, however, strengthened the radical fraction of the opposition, and DPP passed a resolution which said that "the opposition people have the freedom to advocate Taiwan independence".

The Nationalists, therefore, have brought themselves into two serious dilemmas. First, due to the emergence of a large and highly educated middle class no longer fearful of political activity, the process of Taiwanization and democratization cannot be stopped altogether. The Nationalists, however, fear that this process might lead to a call for a unilateral declaration of independence from the mainland. Second, the official policy in relation to Peking has followed "the three no's policy - no contact, no negotiation and no compromise. Such a policy unfortunately works against people's identification with China, and the KMT particularly fears that the young people are beginning to identify less with China.

In the light of these dilemmas, it is not surprising that the new president Teng-hui Lee will follow the political will of Chiang Ching-kuo "to combat communism and press for greater democracy". During this process the Kuomintang party will have to take into account the tensions between a more responsive and representative government on Taiwan and both the enduring claim to sovereignty over all China and the perceived threat to national security.

It is, therefore, most likely, that the parliamentary autocracy will persist in a softened form. Civil liberties will be extended as far as possible without interfering with the basic foundations of KMT rule. As the regime fears the social demands from the island's majority of workers, one should expect improvements in the social security system but there is no indication that such "fordist initiatives" will be combined with a revitalizing and democratizing transformation of the national trade unions. In the long run a transformation towards parliamentary oligarchy can not be excluded if the liberal fraction in the KMT and the moderate fraction in the DPP find a modus vivendi in relation to the independence issue.

Compared with South Korea, the leading political elite in Taiwan still has good possibilities to find support for a strategy towards a softened parliamentary autocracy. The capitalist class is more committed to the island's future than to the issue of political democracy, and the KMT can probably get continued popular support both due to its merits in relation to economic development and due to the widespread fear of Chinese unification under communist sovereignty.

Conclusion

At first, it should be noted that there has been no simple relation between capitalist accumulation on the one hand and democracy on the other hand. We have found no support for the hypothesis that strengthening of the national bourgeois in itself leads to a process of democratization. The position of the capitalist class in the two countries rather supports the view that the interest for democracy in the capitalist class is limited when capitalist development takes the form of a close alliance between state and big capital. We have demonstrated that the main class force behind the democratic transformation process has been the middle class. The middle class, however, is very heterogenous and it is still doubtful whether this class will fight for a wider democracy including freedom to organize for trade unions

232

and socialist forces. Further, it still has to be seen whether this class will carry forward social economic reforms.

Although both South Korea and Taiwan has gone through a long period of dynamic capitalist accumulation, we have shown that the prospects for democracy are different.

In recent years, **South Korea** has developed into an parliamentary oligarchy under the leadership of general Roh. Further, we have argued that a transformation into a parliamentary democracy is an open possibility on the assumption that a wider and new mass movement press for free party participation in elections, freedom to organize and respect for civil liberties.

In defiance of the lifting of martial law and the de facto existence of opposition parties, **Taiwan** still is an autocracy. Taiwan falls into the category of parliamentary autocracy, although it changes into still softer and revitalized forms. A shift towards a parliamentary oligarchy should not be excluded but such a process would have to develop inside the overall framework of: rejection of independence, rejection of communism and respect for the constitution. Such a process would presuppose a new alliance between liberal KMT members and moderate opposition forces. If we take into account the present serious economic restructuring problems and the peculiar relations between the Nationalists and the state sector, a soft parliamentary autocracy appears at the most obvious short and medium term form of regime.

BIBLIOGRAPHY

Amnesty International: **Menneskerettigheder i Taiwan (Republic of China)** (Copenhagen, 1981).

Amnesty International: **South Korea, Violations of Human Rights** (London, 1986).

Amnesty International: **Amnesty International Briefing no. 6. Taiwan (Republic of China)** (London, 1980).

Asche, Helmuth: **Industrialisierte dritte Welt? Ein Vergleich von Gesellschaftsstrukturen** (Hamburg, 1984).

Asche, Helmuth: "Über junge Industrieländer und Schwellen-länder in Ostasien", **Politische Vierteljahrschrift**, Sonderheft 14/15, 1985.

Carter, Adian Foster: "Korea - from dependency to demo-cracy", **Capital and Class**, no. 33, 1987.

Casse, Thorkild: **The non-conventional Approach to Stabil-ity: The Case of South Korea. An analysis of Macro-economic Policy 1979-84** (CDR Research Reports, no. 5, Copenhagen, 1985).

Chai, Trong R.: "The Future of Taiwan", **Asian Survey**, vol. 26, 12, 1986.

Chou, Yangsun and Andrew J.Nathan: "Democratizing transi-tion in Taiwan", **Asian Survey**, vol. 27, 3, 1987.

Clough, Ralf: **Island China** (Cambridge, Mass. and London, 1978).

Development States in East Asia: Capitalist and Socialist (IDS Bulletin, vol. 15, 2, University of Sussex, April 1984).

Deyo, Frederic et al.: "Labor in the Political Economy of East Asian Industrialization", **Bulletin of Concerned Asian Scholars**, vol. 19, 2, 1987.

Economic Planning Board: **Annual Report on the Economically Active Population Survey.** Seoul.

Far Eastern Economic Review - various issues.

Gold, Thomas B: "The status quo is not static", **Asian Survey**, vol. 27, 3, 1987.

Haggard, Stephan and Tun-jen cheng: **State Strategies, Local and Foreign Capital in the Gang of Four,** (mimeographed, University of California, 1983).

Hofheinz, Roy J. and Kent E.Clader: **The Eastasia Edge,** (New York, 1982).

International Labour Reports, various issues.

Korea Report (publ. by North American Coalition for Human Rights in Korea) - various issues.

Launius, Michael A: "The State and Industrial Labor in South Korea", **Bulletin of Concerned Asian Scholars,** vol. 16, 4, 1984.

Lauridsen, Laurids S: **Smallness is no longer appropriate. The political economy of industrial adjustment in Taiwan** (Paper presented to the 5th EADI General Conference, Amsterdam, September 1987).

Menzel, Ulrich: "Die Ostasiatischen Schwellenländer. Testfälle für die Entwicklungsteoretische Diskussion", **Prokla,** Heft 59, 15.Jahrgang, 2, 1985.

Menzel, Ulrich: **In der Nachfolge Europas. Autozentrierte Entwicklung in den Ostasiatischen Schwellenländern Südkorea and Taiwan** (München, 1985).

Menzel, Ulrich und Dieter Senghaas: "Schwellenländer: Ein Neues Entwicklungsteoretisches Erklärungsproblem. Indikatoren zur Bestimmung von Swellenländern. Ein Vorschlag zur Operationalisierung", **Politische Vierteljahrschrift,** Sonderheft 16, 1985.

Ministry of Labor: **Labor Laws of Korea** (1985).

Olsen, Gorm Rye: **Politics and Development. Consideration on forms of Regimes and Change in Periphery Countries** (mimeographed, Aarhus, 1983).

Petras, James and Dennis Engbarth: "Third World Industrializations and its Implications for the Trade Unions", **Development and Trade**, vol. 7, 1986.

Shorrock, Tim: "The Struggle for Democracy in South Korea", **Third World Quarterly**, vol. 8, 4, 1986.

Shorrock, Tim: "South Korea - Chun, the Kims and the Constitutional Struggle", **Third World Quarterly**, vol. 10, 1, 1988.

South, June, 1985.

Wad, Peter: "Industrialisering, förtryck och arbeterklassen", **Zenit**, no. 86, 1985.

Wad, Peter: "Politiske regimer, legitimeringsproblemer og demokratisering - en oversigt over politisk udviklingsteori og politiske forandringer i Øst- og Sydøstasien", **Den ny Verden** (Copenhagen), vol. 20, 2, 1987.

Warren, Bill: **Imperialism: Pioneer of Capitalism** (London, 1980).

Winckler, Edwin A: "Institutionalization and Participation on Taiwan: From hard to soft Authoritanianism", **China Quarterly**, no. 99, 1984.

Yi, Guk-Yueng: "Zur Politischen Ökonomie der exportorientierten Industrialisierung: Ein Vergleich zwischen Korea und Taiwan", **Politische Vierteljahresschrift**, 27. Jahrgang, Heft 2, 1986.

Yoo Jong-Yaul: "Policy Processes in Developing Countries: The Case of the Republic of Korea", **International Social Science Journal**, no. 108, 1986.

WOMEN IN SOCIALIST REFORM POLICY
VIETNAMESE TEXTILE WORKERS

Irene Nørlund
Institute of Economic History
University of Copenhagen

Introduction

After several years' research into various aspects of
Vietnamese development, the question inevitably arises
how to estimate the standard of living of the various
social classes and within the different economic sectors,
especially in comparison with the standard of living in
other developing countries, including those under the
influence of socialism. Although this might seem an
obvious topic of study there are certain difficulties due
to the fact that our knowledge about the actual living
and working conditions is rather limited. In Vietnam the
research into living and working conditions and the
family[1] has started late, and it has been difficult for

---

[1] The first step in the development of women's
research was to the set up the Center for Women's
Research in 1984 with a permanent staff of 8 researchers.
The purpose of this Center is to study the structure the
female labour force, working and health conditions of
women in various sectors of the economy. The head of the
Center, professor Le Thi, has among other things written:
'The role of the State and the Changes in Family Life' in
'The Life of Women in Vietnam' (Paper to a conference on
'Women and the Household', New Delhi 1985) and 'Les
Activites de l'Etat de la Republique Socialiste du
Vietnam et le Progres des Femmes Vietnamiennes au cours
de la Recente Decade (1975- 85) (Paper presented at a
seminar in Hanoi, March 1985).

foreign researchers to study, as the possibilities for field research have been restricted.[2]

In connection with a research project on the development of the textile production in Vietnam during the colonial period from 1880 to 1954, I have had the opportunity to work in the country for longer periods[3] and to visit quite a few textile enterprises and handicraft cooperatives. These visits contributed to an understanding of some aspects of the present socialist reform policy. I decided to carry out a pilot project in order to find an appropriate method to study the social transition in the contemporary Vietnamese society.[4]

[2] Some of the rather few studies done by foreign researchers are connected to the largest Swedish aid project, a paper mill and a connected forestry project. Birgitta Sevefjord: Women in Vietnam - Women in Bai Bang. An Evaluation of the Effects of the Bai Bang Project on the Lives of Female Workers. SIDA, Stockholm 1985. Katarina Larsson and Lars-Erik Birgegård: Socio-Economic Study of Factors Influencing Labour Productivity in the Forestry Component of the Vinh Phu Pulp and Paper Mill Project in Vietnam, SIDA, Stockholm 1985. Lisbeth Bostrand: Living and Working Conditions for Forestry Workers in Vietnam. A Follow-Up Report. Stockholm 1986. A general presentation of Vietnamese women is found in Cecilia Molander: Kvinna in Vietnam, SIDA, Stockholm 1978.

[3] I visited Vietnam in 1983, 1984 and 1986 and stayed about 1 - 2 month each time.

[4] I would like to thank my colleagues at the Social Science Committee in Hanoi, especially mrs. Phuong, mrs. Nhanh, mr. Ngoc, mr. Dinh and mr. Ku, for their support and assistance during my work in Vietnam. The research was financed by the Carlsberg Foundation, Copenhagen, and special funds for the visits to Vietnam were provided by the Research Council of Development Research, DANIDA, and the Danish Research Council for the Humanities.

Research focus and method

The pilot project had three main objectives. First, the actual development of Vietnamese textile production since 1954 and an estimate of the interaction between craft and industry after 1954. In the first decade after independence the main stress in the development strategy was on heavy industry. Because of this the textile branch, which belonged to the light industrial sector, did not receive much attention from the government not in the officially declared policy at any rate, and not much has been written about it.

The second area of study was the concrete results of governmental policy in the textile branch, although it is often difficult to tell when, where and to what degree the policy were carried out.

The third area of concern is the working conditions in the three sectors - industry, handicraft and home production. The role of women within the various sectors is of special interest, because very little research has been done in this field. (Research into women's work in agriculture has been more extensive). Subjects concerning the work of women in the three sectors, the position of women and the division of work within the family were illuminated through questionnaires. Furthermore the pilot study also included questions related to organizations of women, women's self-conception and the society's conception of women.

Obviously it is the third area of research that illuminates the conditions of the women. It is important, however, when comparing the results with the method applied, to remember that this study was part of an investigation of broader scope.

The method applied was to collect three types of information. First in accordance with traditional historical methods, printed and written source materials (including statistical data) were collected. Secondly, efforts were made to obtain information from various institutions and organizations such as the various ministries, the planning commission, textile organizations, trade unions, and women's unions. Thirdly, information was collected through interviews with managers of factories and cooperatives and with a limited number of female textile workers.

To sum up, the purpose was empirically to follow the development of textile production, to outline the governmental policy in this field and to see how far reform ideas penetrated into the local level and into the enterprises, and especially to see how these policies influenced the women's living and working conditions.

Reform policy in Vietnam 1979-86

The reforms started at the 6th plenum of the central committee of the party in 1979. At first they were mainly aimed at the agricultural sector, which was not able to fulfil the planned targets and so supply the population with sufficient food. But very quickly it developed into a general reform policy for all the economic sectors. A new packet of reforms was decided upon in January 1981, and reform adjustments have continuously carried out since then.

The 6th plenum liberalized small production and trade and introduced a new management system for the individual enterprises. The reforms aimed at solving some basic problems of the economic crises, which the state had not been able to solve in this society of low level development plagued with prolonged wars: insufficient production; the distribution of the means of production and consumer goods; unemployment and underemployment; and incomes insufficient to sustain daily life. The liberalization of small production and trade supplemented the official incomes of the population, and filled a hole in production and distribution.

Petty production has to a certain extent always existed, but has expanded considerably since 1979, so much so that the state several times attempted to limit it before it got out of control. The general policy in Vietnam has, since 1954, aimed at organizing the small producers in cooperatives, which the state provides with raw materials. The cooperatives deliver their products through state-trading channels in return. Since the introduction of the reforms the government has also attempted to provide extra work for the employees of the state sector. Administrative personnel can through various forms of supplementary jobs earn extra income. In the cooperatives and factories the workers can for instance take home extra work, which has to be delivered back to the cooperatives and factories. The result was longer working hours and higher production. Along with these organized forms of extra work, non-organized production and trade also developed outside the control of the state.

Family economy

The traditional opinion of the party has been that the private sector was a potential source for the revival of capitalist relations of production and therefore has been regarded as opposing the development towards socialism. However, the family production in agriculture has been accepted as a supplementary source of income to the collective work efforts all the way through. After the 6th plenum the family economy was fully accepted and directly encouraged as one way to ease the acute problems of the general economic crisis and a situation characterized by low wages. The party also acknowledged that in a situation with shortage of energy, raw materials and spare parts families could produce the necessary com-

241

modities at a lower costs and in a more flexible way
that the industrial production was able to. Hoang Tung,
secretary of the central committee of the party, said in
1983 about this matter: "We encourage the peasants to
exploit the family economy, but also in the cities it is
necessary with new activities, The family is a complementary force, not the central one. The family can only
solve the problems of how to get enough for the stomach.
Only two orange trees will provide as much money as the
wage income of the whole family ... However, we will not
reach a communist society through a family economy where
craft production is rudimentary, but we will have a
higher output. When we reach a certain stage, this
production cannot be expanded. Therefore we must also
develop heavy industry."

Trade is also a troublesome problem. At the summit
of the crisis in 1979-80 many daily necessities were not
available, whereas in 1983-84, the free or open markets
were well supplied with elementary consumer goods. The
Hanoi scenery had changed because of the numerous small
street traders on every corner and along the roadsides
selling all kind of foodstuffs and market places were
blossoming all over the city. But the prices were extremely high compared with the official prices in the state
stores and food shops.

Prices

Since the start of the reforms trade problems have become
still more complicated because of the existence of several
price systems and of increasing inflation. The state has
acknowledged the problem and set up several commissions
to analyze the difficulties and establish guidelines for
the price system. For a long period, however, no solutions
were found, and when the reforms finally were decided on
in 1985 the result was that the situation in fact became

242

even more difficult. There existed, for example several exchange rates. The official one was in 1984 11 dong to a dollar, but on the black market the rate was 180 dong to a dollar. Between these two a shadow-exchange-rate of 60 dong to a dollar also was used, for instance in the ministries. The last one was probably the one closest to a market-rate.

Since 1979 the rate of inflation has risen. In 1981 it was estimated at 90%, while in 1983 it had slowed down to 'only' 55%. The consequence of the high inflation has been severe, because it has undermined the attempts to implement a state income policy for the various social groups. Since 1954 a system of state allowance of rice and provisions to all state employees (workers and functionaries) has been in operation, which has enabled this group to buy very cheap rice and some other basic commodities up to a certain amount in special shops. One kilo of rice costs in the state shops 0.4 dong, a price that has not changed from 1954 to 1985! Before the reforms, members of handicraft cooperatives were also able to buy cheap rice, but they were excluded from the state shop system during the reforms. Some special systems are arranged in the various cooperatives to provide their members with rice at a fixed price, lower than on the free market. In 1984 they paid 5 dong per kilo. This whole system provides a considerable part of the population with the most basic necessities, although there are complaints about the quality of the rice. Therefore a part of the ration is usually exchanged in order to buy rice of better qualities.

The state system of fixed prices pushes inflation on to the free and black market. Rice prices on the free market increased from 15 dong per kilo in February 1983 to 45 dong in May 1984. The price paid by the state to the peasants per kilo of rice has gone up considerably. Accordingly the subventions for rice to the state employees put a heavier burden on the state budget. On the other hand the reforms resulted in new sources of state income because of increased production. In 1981 a tax on private production and trade was furthermore inaugurated. The following year a new agricultural tax was imposed, and a system of state-bonds was set up to mobilize local resources.

The 8th plenum in 1985

The 8th plenum of the central committee held in June 1985 was of special importance, because new measures were taken to cope with the continuing economic problems. For the first time the questions of prices, wages and money were on the agenda. One of the main decisions was that the economy no longer could be built on state subsidies and on a bureaucratic organization of the economy. The aim was to increase the productivity by an economic plan where the individual enterprises should be able to manage their own economy without state subsidies. One of the methods should be a more work-promoting wage system, including piece-rates and bonuses.

One important innovation of the 8th plenum was the cancelling of the state shops system with fixed prices on rice and other goods. The gap between the controlled state market with low, fixes prices, and the free market with quickly increasing prices had been growing. This forced petty commodity production and trade even among state employees to expand, especially because the low wages only allowed people to buy very little on the free market.

The resolution of the 8th plenum states that 'aboli-tion of bureaucratism and subsidization in terms of prices, wages and money has become a pressing demand. This requires that production costs include all rational expenses, and that prices cover the actual expenses so that the producers earn an appropriate profit, the state is able gradually to build up its capital accumulation, and that an end be put to a situation in which the state buys and sells at low prices and subsidizes irrational business losses.' (editorial in Nhan Dan, Summary of World Broadcast, June 24, 1985).

The purpose of the price reform was an increased productivity which both workers and factories should benefit from and, at the same time, should enabled the state gradually to accumulate capital. Until that time prices were fixed by the state in an irrational way, since raw materials and other inputs to the factories were supplied, often with subventions, and the prices of the final products from the factories did not reflect the real costs. Prices should from now on reflect actual expenses an the attempt to rationalize the whole economy.

The other intention was to increase the wages so much that the wageworker was actually able to live on it. The resolution says: 'Actual wages must ensure that wage-earners can live <u>chiefly</u> (author's emphasis) on their wages... They should, however, be closely related to productivity, quality and the efficiency of work. 'The principle of "to each according to his work" must be observed, and egalitarianism must be ruled out.' (SWB. June 22, 1985).

The 8th plenum pointed out that the new system is a more correct way to apply democratic centralism and socialist accounting, which is necessary to increase production and trade in an efficient way in order to develop the national economy. The central committee further pointed out that the abolition of bureaucratic centralism and the subsidies system was a fundamental necessity. The reforms 'demonstrate a profound and vigorous change in our Party's approach and policy, not only in the domain of prices and wages but also in

245

commerce, finance, money, and to the mechanism of planning and economic management.' (SWB. June 22, 1985).

The context of the reforms

The reforms inaugurated by the 6th plenum in 1979 showed that the Vietnamese communist party had become more open to experimentation with new forms of economic planning. It was, on the theoretical level, recognized that the law of value also functions in a society during socialist transformation. But the party also recognized that Vietnam, with its rather limited industry still primarily on agricultural society, had to plan on the basis of its actual resources, and not on the potential resources of the country nor on the aid and the support that might be available from outside.

Several reasons led to the start of the reform period. First of all Vietnam was in an acute economic crisis, caused both by internal economic and political problems as well as by the international isolation which had begun with the US embargo in 1975. After the Vietnamese invasion in Kampuchea in January 1979, the embargo came to include almost all Western countries and China. However, we must remember that Vietnam had been through a very long and destructive war in the 1960s and 70s, and before that through another wars against the French colonialists. This is one obvious reason why economic planning in Vietnam relied so heavily on subsidies. Subsidies were essential in war-time planning. Only after 1975, could peacetime planning - though complicated by the transformation of the south and by the new conflicts with Kampuchea and China - be implemented, but experiences in rational and systematized planning were obviously limited.

The 6th plenum had concentrated on changes in the work-process. The collective work in the agricultural cooperatives was changed to a combination of collective and individual processes. Earlier the peasants were paid according to the work points they acquired from their various work tasks in the coop. Now the individual families are responsible for certain parts of the agricultural production, i.e. transplanting of rice, the daily care of the rice in the fields and the harvest. This had the immediate result that they felt themselves much more responsible for the daily tasks. This was combined with a new contract system with the state. Previously the peasants had to deliver half of any surplus above the contracted level to the state at low prices. Now they were able keep all surplus for their own use or sell it on the market.

The change of work-process in the industrial sector was meant to increase the overall production through a system which should benefit both the state, the collective and the individual. If both production and productivity were raised everybody would benefit, and to achieve this work-promoting incentives were essential, as in the new system in agriculture.

Continuity or Break?

At first glance the reform decided on at the 8th plenum in 1985 looks like a continuation and extension of the 1979 reforms. Probably this is the case as far as the work-process and the labour-promoting wage systems are concerned. It seems, however, that it was also the intention to do away with the system of subsidized prices and the widespread system of payments in kind. This was substantiated by the abolition of the special state shops and the fixed price-system. The cancelling of the fixed price-system necessitated of course a new reform of the wage-system, the aim of which was that the wage-earners should be able to live chiefly on their wages. A substantial wage-increase took place.

No doubt, an economy based on payments in kind and the household economy had "saved" the country from an economic collapse during the very critical years 1979-81. In 1986 a certain stabilization took place with a more generalized and less centralized national planning, based on the economic profitability of the single economic unit. A hypothesis is that the national planning in fact has been extremely weak and without proper coordination. The 8th plenum was an attempt to do away with this situation, and the concept of the household economy was maintained in the political resolutions of the 8th plenum. The fifth point of the resolution calls for giving 'impetus to socialist transformation, increase state-run and collective economies; to develop household economies.' (Communique from the 8th plenum of the Central Committee, June 21 1985, SWB June 22). From this it seems obvious that from the official point of view - the transformation towards socialist economy - is not at all incompatible with the household economy. The latter has the purpose of supplying the household with the basic needs, which the formal economy is unable to provide under the present circumstances. On the other hand, it seems that the widespread phenomena of paying employees in kind will be abolished, and a more rational planning based on 'socialist accounting, planning and trade' should be the fundamental principle of the economy. Undoubtedly the severe economic crisis during 1979-81 led to some very unorthodox experiments for a socialist state, although some of them were probably more spontaneous than planned.

How far did the reforms penetrate?

After the reform of the 8th plenum in 1985 the wages were raised several hundred percent to compensate for the increased prices of rice and other consumer goods which before the reforms had been available in the special state shops. In September 1985 a money reform was suddenly carried out where 10 old dongs were exchanged with 1 new dong. The purpose was obviously to get rid of fortunes accumulated on the black market and through speculation. But the currency reform had a disastrous effect, because the prices became even more floating than before. Most people continued to count in old dong, although they paid in new dong (if new dong bills were available). The difference between prices on the free market and in the state-run ware-houses and the quickly escalating inflation made it hard to know the price of various goods. The same price in old dong and in new dong possible, and the economic situation seemed to be rather chaotic when I visited Vietnam in January-February 1986. The general impression was that the reforms of the 8th plenum were welcomed, because the double wage-system and the double market - the state shops and the free market - restrained the state employees from taking part in the general expansion of the consumption. In the beginning, after the reforms of the summer 1985 most people felt that they were better off. After the currency reform the situation changed, however, and deteriorated. It became necessary to start up the state-shops again. The price reforms were obviously a failure. Most opinions were not against the reforms as such, however, but rather that they were carried out too quickly.

In January 1986 the first political dismissal of leaders responsible for the reforms started, and most of 1986 up to the 6th party congress in December 1986 was characterized by discussions between various political factions about economic policy, which of course were accentuated by the death of the party leader Le Duan in June 1986 and the following temporary change in political leadership. The congress itself did not line up a new policy, but it severely criticized of the lack of positive results of the reforms and the widespread waste and corruption. The open and severe criticism at the congress indicates that stronger measures will be taken by the new political leadership to change obvious shortcomings. But the question arises: how far had the reforms ever penetrated on the local level? or were they only political formulations on paper?

Women in the various branches of the textile production

The data provided by the statistical yearbook in Vietnam are not very detailed, but an outline can be seen from the compiled figures about the labour force and the share of the textile sector of the total labour force in 1976 and 1982 (table 1). The labour force in both industrial and craft production made up 8.7% of the total labour force in 1976 and the share was almost the same in 1982, 8.6%. The number of people employed in the textile and garment sector had on the contrary increased both within industrial and craft production. The percentage of the labour in the whole textile sector rose from 17.4% to 20.8% from 1976 to 1982. From these figures it seems obvious that the textile sector has been of growing importance during this period.

Table 2 outlines the yearly development of labour force employed in the textile sector. These figures cover both males and females, and the share of women is only known for the handicraft production and light industry together, where it is on the increase. This indicates that the share of women may also have been raising in the textile sector as a whole. Employment has been increasing every year in the crafts, but a jump took place especially from 1979 to 1980, which should be seen in the context of the reform policy. In industry on the other hand, a jump took place in 1979 only to fall again, and the industrial labour force seems to be rather stagnant until a new smaller jump in 1982. The large industrial plants are not as flexible as the handicraft sector regarding labour. From this point of view the fluctuations are surprising, unless new plants has been brought into use, or production has altogether stopped. The impact of the economic crisis was that many plants were not able to operate, which is obvious from decreasing numbers of meters of fabrics produced per year since 1978 (table 2). Still the workers are usually not dismissed even though the plants are not operating, and they will probably be included in the statistics in any case.

Table 3 shows the number and places of visits to coops in the period 1983-86 by this author, and table 4 gives some basic data on the textile plants. It shows for instance that the work places are clearly female dominated. Finally, table 5 shows some of the information collected in the pilot investigation. The basic work was done in 1983 by interviews with seven female industrial workers and two handicraft workers. In 1984 and 86 it was enlarged by interviews with several home workers, but less thoroughly. There are references to the home workers in the text but not in the tables. The following section is a more detailed presentation of a few of the women with whom I talked, representing different types of work, geographically dispersed between city and countryside.

Women in industry and handicraft, interviews 1983-84

How are the living and working conditions of Vietnamese working women? was the central question for my research when I came to Vietnam in 1983 on a research visit. There are few facts to be found in this field, although it certainly is an interesting one. The working class has always been the core of the party policy and the political struggle since the 1930s. Textile production is the

251

largest single branch of production outside agriculture. In other Southeast Asian countries a good deal of research has been done on women's working and living conditions. How is the situation in a socialist developing country in comparison? Each interview with women working at the very different work places gave material for the understanding of new aspects of everyday life in Vietnam. But as exciting and instructive as the visit to factories, cooperatives and home-weavers were, it is just as difficult to draw general conclusions. Some illustrative excerpts from the visits and interviews are given below.

The textile factory in Nam Dinh

Nam Dinh is one of the largest provincial towns in Northern Vietnam. The textile factory there is the largest and the oldest in the country. It was founded in 1900 and enlarged several times. Nam Dinh is one of the historical core areas of the workers' movement. Today 11,000 persons are employed at the factory, and the women constitute 65% of the labour force. All the employees are members of the trade unions, and 20 percent are also members of the party.

Vu Thi Hong (informant nr. 1) was 40 years old in 1983. She is married and has three children. In 1962 she got a job at the factory, and she took part in the resistance against the US-bombardments in the 1960s. She has 7 years' education. Today she is working in the thread-producing workshop. The equipment is of French origin and goes back to the colonial period. The workday is divided into three shifts, and she works 8 hours in one shift. She is head of a work-team of 17 persons.

Hong had a basic wage of 124 dong monthly in 1983 ($ US 11 according to the official exchange rate). The basic wage tells the wage level one belongs to, but that mattered only during sick-leaves or other leave, because the factory had introduced the new wage systems. That was one of the new schemes of the reforms. In 1983 Hong had an actual income of 400 dong monthly according to a piece-work system. Furthermore she had a yearly bonus of 540 dong. In 1984 she had - except for one month because of difficulties with the equipment - an income similar to that of 1983. This meant, however, that her real income had been falling over the two years, due to an annual inflation around 60%. She was content with the new wage system, despite the inflation, because before the reform she earned about 200 dong monthly. The state ration system with the cheap goods at fixed prices meant that the inflation did not influence daily life as much as might be expected. One kilo of rice cost 0,4 dong against the free market prices of 40 dong. Hong said that almost all their money was spent on food.

Hong's husband was a state employee working in a bank where he had a monthly income of 160 dong. They had an extra income from chickens and pigs, which they kept around the house. Their house was rented from the factory. It was build in 1976 and the monthly rent was 5.5 dong. The distance from the factory is about 20 minutes by bike. They live in the suburb, which they found advantageous because of the possibility of rearing animals. There was one living room in the house for a family of five, and besides this they had both a kitchen and a bathroom, electricity and water in the house. Of consumer durables the family had one radio and two bicycles. The housework was done by Hong herself together with the two girls 11 and 14 years old. The three year old was taken care of by the grandmother or the older sisters. The workers of the factory had an annual leave of 10 days. Hong was a member of both the trade union and the party. Normally she only attended meetings once a month. She did not want more children, so she used contraceptives.

Ha Dong, a town about 20 km south of Hanoi, is situated
in an area known for a flourishing handicraft production
in the colonial period. The cooperative La Khe is situated
in the periphery of the town. The village, with gardens
and small ponds among the houses, is organized both as an
agricultural and a handicraft cooperative. Production
consists of silk and cotton cloth. 1,200 handicraft
workers live here, 2/3 of them are women.

Nguyen Thi Tan (informant no. 2) was 33 years old at
the time of the interview and had four children. A total
of 8 persons lived in the house.

Tan was a weaver. The loom was placed in a separate
room in one end of the house. It was a hand loom with a
cord driving device which she operated with both hands
and legs. She worked about 8 hours a day and was able to
produce 13 meters of unbleached cotton. Her father-in-law
also operated the loom, when Tan was doing other things.

Tan was able to earn 99 dong for 40 meters of fabric
in 1984. The raw materials were provided by the cooperative, and the finished materials were returned. She
estimated her income to be about 1,000 dong monthly.
After the start of the reforms the payment per meter of
fabric rose, but she could not buy food as cheaply as
before. The cooperative had its own shop with a rice
price of 5.4 dong a kilo. Tan's husband worked in Hanoi.
Most of the income was spent on food, but she did not
know exactly the total income of the family. 'We spend
the money, when it is there' she said. The family had
radio, TV, a big tape recorder and three bikes. The house
was built of stone with three rooms, and had electricity
and water.

Tan was born in the village and she started to weave
when she was a child. She went to school for 7 years.
Women are more suited than men for weaving, she thought,

because they can take care of the children and take part in the harvest at the same time. Tan was not a member of the party, and she did not attend meetings. There was not much time left after the housework. Sundays do not exist, and if she had any time left, she played with the children. She had no wish for more children and used contraceptives.

The handicraft cooperative Phuong Thanh, Ha Nam Ninh province

Nam Ninh is a district in the Red River delta close to the coast in the province of Ha Nam Ninh with Nam Dinh as capital. The cooperative Phuong Thanh is based in the countryside, far from the provincial capital and 5-6 km from the main district town. The coop produces cotton, silk and jute fabrics, including fabrics and towels for export. This cooperative is solely a handicraft cooperative. 600 persons work here, 88 percent are women.

Dinh (informant no. 3) is a weaver, 32 years old in 1984 and unmarried. She lived with her two brothers and a sister-in-law in a newly built house. She was born in the village. She worked 8 hours a day, but they shared the looms in the household and worked in shifts. Two looms were set up in the house, but altogether they had three looms shared with the rest of the family who lived nearby. Dinh was able to produce 20 meters of unbleached cotton fabric daily. Each meter gave her 2,15 dong from the cooperative, and in a normal month in 1984 she would earn about 800 dong. The loom was a hand loom (i.e. non-mechanical loom) operated with the legs only. The house had no electricity. The loom was a much newer and improved model compared to the one Tan used in Ha Dong and it demands much less human power.

The cooperative had organized a shop where Dinh could buy 15 kg of rice monthly for about 5 dong a kilo.

There were four adults in the house, but no children yet. The construction of the house had been a major expense. It was built because the parents' house had became too small. It was build with modern materials, but not very big, with two rooms, a larger and a small one, outside was a large cemented courtyard. Dinh's mother prepared the food for all of them and she was also doing the shopping. Dinh went to school for 7 years, but she started to weave when she was only 12 years old. Now she was one of the best weavers in the coop. The house had neither water nor electricity, so the household had no electrical appliances, only one bike. The nearest well was about 100 meters away. Dinh is a member of the Women's Union and the Youth Union, and she attended meetings about once a month.

Viet Thang textile factory in Bien Hoa

Bien Hoa is about 10 km from Ho Chi Minh-city (Saigon) in the south of Vietnam, and this region is the most in-dustrialized in Vietnam. The textile factory Viet Thang employs almost 5,000 of which 75 percent were women in 1983. 84 percent of the employees were members of the trade union, but only 4 percent were members of the party.

Nguyen Thi Hue (informant no. 4) is a weaver. She was 34 years old, married and had three children. She operated a Japanese machine. In 1966 she was employed at the factory at the age of 21. In 1983 she had a basic wage of 142 dong. Since the change of the wage system with a better piece work-rate she earned about 650 dong monthly plus a yearly bonus of 700 dong. The work was organized in three shifts of 8 hours, and she was head of a work-team.

Hue was able to buy cheap food in the state shop. Her family had their own house, which was free. It had three rooms, including a kitchen and a bathroom. Electricity and water were available. Of consumer durables they had one radio and two bikes. She had no other jobs and incomes. Her husband was employed in a food-company. She and her the mother-in-law did all the house work. As in the northern part of Vietnam there were 10 days leave every year. Hue was a member of the trade union and normally she attended a meeting once a month. She did not want more children and used contraceptives.

Women, standard of living and working conditions

These short women's portraits give an idea of the variation within the working and living conditions in Vietnam among working people. Some crafts-women are able to have quite a good income, whereas others - especially in the branch of embroidery - will have to work long hours to earn enough to make a living. Therefore it is very important to have access to cheap rice and other goods. Otherwise one must buy all goods at the free market. The women working in the factories have the most regulated working and social welfare conditions. Their working hours are more regulated, however, the work in the machine hall is more dangerous, dusty, dirty and noisy than in a handicraft coop. It seems that the standard of living in the families is higher in the cities than in the countryside, except in the case of the craft-woman in Ha Dong (informant no. 2). Her family is an example of how the income from handicraft production is combined with the wage-income of the husband and with some agricultural production. She has very long working hours, but a good income. For this family it is an advantage to live in a well-established area with brick houses, electricity and water. At first glance their home did not differ from many other homes. The house was rather old and not luxurious. Still the brick house is probably the reason why they could buy more consumer goods like TV-sets and tape-recorder than families in other regions. When the economy makes it possible, the first investment will normally go to a brick house, but in the established area of Ha Dong, the house was probably inherited from the family and the surplus money could be spent otherwise. Of course there is always the possibility that a family may receive money from relatives abroad, but this is hard to judge without knowing the family better.

Follow-up interview with Mrs. Hong in Nam Dinh

In January 1986 I met Vu Thi Hong (informant no. 1) for the third time. She was still working in the same thread workshop at the Nam Dinh factory. She estimated her monthly wage-income in 1984 to be 10,000 old dong plus a bonus of 50 dong. In 1985 after the change of the price and of the monetary system she earned 700 new dong monthly (1 new dong = 10 old dong). In December 1985 she had received an extra bonus of 100 dong. She still did not find this wage sufficient, although it was better that the old income. The family had a higher income from raising pigs, which gave them 26,000 old dong per year.

The price of rice was now 3.6 new dong per kilo (up from 0.4 old dong), the price of meat was 38 new dong per kilo, up from 4 old dong, but the ration was smaller than before. Her husband, employed in a bank, had 450 new Dong monthly. The price of rice at the free market was at this time about 10 new dong a kilo. Hong said that the state shops were badly supplied and the prices had risen, but obviously the state shop system was functioning in January 1986. At Tet - the lunar New Year - they got some extra provisions from the factory, but that system has always existed.

Since I met Hong in 1984 she had procured a sewing machine. It cost her 34,000 old dong, but she said the price today would be double. She was able to make clothes for the children, and the children could make clothes to sell on the maket. This happened only when it was necessary and during summer-holidays, she said. Only the pigs could bring in any extra money for saving.

In January 1985 changes had taken place at the factory. The division of labour within the work-team was changed and attempts were made to improve the quality of thread. The work-team consisted now of fewer workers, and less qualified workers were moved to other work-shops. The quality of the thread had increased greatly. None of the removed workers are unemployed today, she said.

Conclusions

For the women, one of the most important changes brought about by the reform-ideas of 1979 was the acceptance of a new central role of the family economy in the Vietnamese economy. This form of production, complementary to the formal work, was not only acceptable to the state, it was directly encouraged. In an acute economic crisis, as was the case in 1979, each family had better possibilities to supplement the generally small income from the formal work. Furthermore reforms in the wage-system also included the encouragement of piece-rate wages in the industry. These reforms were not applied in all industries, but obviously the new system worked within the textile industry in 1983. A new system (usually called the C-plan) made it possible for the factory to use all kinds of left overs from production as in-puts either in handicraft-production, in special work-shops (C-workshops) or for the textile workers to take home for home production. The C-workshops produced for instance garments for children and cotton blankets, and in the homes thread-ends could be knotted and re-used, even garments and blankets were produced at home. Some of these jobs could be done by different members of the family, but the general tendency was that the workload of the women increased. This included both home production, trade connected with petty market-oriented production and also the selling of a share of the wage, if it was paid in kind, on the market. It is still the women who dominate in petty trade.

The on-going inflation has contributed to deepening the gap between those who receive coupons (ration cards) to buy cheap goods in the state shops and those who have to buy food in the cooperative shop or, especially, those who are totally dependent on the free market. The first category includes - in 1983 - all state employees (including workers), the last the cooperative craftspeople. From the interviews, however, it seems to be normal for the cooperative shops to provide the handicraft workers with rice at reduced prices, but that might not be the case for all town-based cooperatives. My impression from several journeys in the country sustains the idea that the petty producers and traders are numerous, but it is very hard to estimate the numbers working outside the state- and cooperative economy. Often the petty producers will have links both to the formal and the informal economy, and at any rate some members of the family will usually have access to the cheap goods.

The intention of the reforms in 1985 was to establish a unified economic system by abolishing the state shops and controlling prices on the free market. To make up for the abolition of the very cheap rice (0.4 dong per kilo of rice) in the state shops, the wages were increased substantially. This increased in fact in one stroke the buying power of all state employees and thereby enabled them to buy consumer goods at the free market. It was also the purpose of the reforms that the wages no longer should be partly paid in kind. That can be seen from the reference to ensuring that 'wage-earners can live chiefly [sic!] on their wages'. The 'economy in kind' was obviously not wanted, whereas the family economy was not touched.

The general aim of the 1985-reforms was to establish an economic system based on rationality and profitability, so that prices would reflect the real costs and the state subsidies therefore would not diminish. No doubt planning would be easier in a system working on these principles. For women, the 1985 principles would be an advantage, because higher wages would level off some of the extra work. In reality it has not changed the system much, however. The very quick changes of prices and wages and later the currency-reform made the economic system more chaotic than ever. Prices were floating, and inflation had eaten up the surplus of the wage-increases.

The abolition of the old institutionalized system with state shops lasted only a few months. Then it came back in a modified form. State prices of rice went up in 1985. One kilo of rice is in 1986 3.5 (new) dong per kilo, and the rationed amount of fish, meat and sugar smaller than before.

The supply of daily necessities has become less secure for workers and state employees since the 1985 reforms. After some years of growing wealth after the economic crisis of 1979-81, the situation in early 1986 seemed to be critical. The dissatisfaction was not directed towards the 1985 reforms as such, but more at the way they were carried out. The situation does not seem to have changed much during 1986 and the party congress criticized severely the political leadership for its inability to manage the economy. Seemingly only limited parts of the 1985-reforms were actually carried out, and the problem is how to obtain the wanted results. On the other hand the reforms starting in 1979 seem to have had a thorough-going effect on the daily life both for the industrial, the cooperative and the home workers. Not so much because of changes in real incomes, but because of a response to new possibilities in the economic system.

From the information collected during my three visits in Vietnam in the period 1983-86 and from visits in 1974 and 1978, it is my impression that a certain increase of wealth seems to have occurred. There has been a rather explosive increase in new private houses in the suburbs of the cities and towns. Clothing has changed much during the last few years both regarding fashion and colours, and the numbers of bicycles and mopeds are increasing year by year. From talks with various people, however, the impression was that to them the situation had not changed much over the last five years. An inter- pretation of these two contradictory impressions could be, that the new mobility in the economic system also increased expectations, which might have run quicker than the actual improvements.

One of the few women, I have had the chance to meet three times is Vu Thi Hong. The economic situation of her family can be seen as an example (Table 6).

Based on this partly constructed example the basic food, rice, took up an increasing share of the formal income of two adults in a family. It is assumed that the two adults had rice rations of 13 kilos a month for a state employee and 19 kilos for a worker which can be bought at cheap state prices. If the yearly consumption for a family of five persons is about 680 kilo of husked rice, the real income had fallen after the reforms, mainly because of inflation. This is correct also for Hong's family, even if she had an income higher than an average worker. In 1984, and probably also 1985, the family had to spend more than the formal income on rice. The formal income had to be supplemented with other sources of income if the family were to survive. Hong's family had an extra income from pig-raising and they grew vegetables for own consumption. An increase of wealth could only come from the expansion of the family economy and from petty production and trade.

After the 1985-reforms the situation ameliorated for Hong's family for a while, but inflation quickly changed the situation. Hong mentions that their only source of extra money came from the pigs. Actually, she had also bought the expensive sewing machine, which might be a source of considerable extra income. If only one person in the family had been connected to the public labour market or the well organized cooperative sector providing the family with cheap rice, they would have been comparatively worse off. After all, the percentage of labourers with no connections at all to the state or coop-sector is fairly small. No doubt the state-shop system encourages labourers to be employed within these two economic systems. It is probably mainly smaller producers and successful business people who stay outside the state or coop organizations.

Since the reforms both the formal and the informal incomes have increased, but so have also the daily working hours. The role of the women under the reform policy is especially important in Vietnam, because the female participation rate on the labour market is higher than in many other Asian countries. Official figures say that women constituted 51 percent of the labour market in 1985. Divided into various sectors, women constituted 66 percent in handicraft and light industry in 1985 and state trade 63 percent (1979). To this should be added family production, which often is various kinds of domestic crafts carried out by women. Based on the official Vietnamese statistics, 42 percent of the new jobs in the state and cooperative handicraft sector in 1976-82 was created within the textile branch. This branch is heavily dominated by women, and more women have probably been included in the informal labour market during the reform years.

One of the aims of this pilot-investigation is to gather some basic information about women's working and

living conditions in industry, handicraft and home
production. The preliminary conclusion cannot be defini-
tive though. The sample used here is far too small to
provide adequate comparison of conditions of the country
as a whole, and income distribution is not clear either.
But it could be said that women in formal industry have
more secure working conditions and better social security
than the craftswomen. On the other hand the work is not
very attractive because of air and noise pollution, and
therefore some women prefer to work within handicraft.

New tendencies concerning the role of women in Vietnam

According to official statistics, the share of women in
the total labour force has decreased a little from 53
percent in 1975 to 51 percent in 1982. This should be
compared with the increasing numbers of jobs within the
female dominated areas like textiles and garment. In this
context the question could be raised, whether the Vietnamese government has taken the problem of the role of
women in the development, especially in the reform period,
seriously enough. In the existing research concerning the
role of women in the development in Vietnam, Christine
White has, among others, asked, if the party and the
government in Vietnam, which mainly consists of aging
males grown up with an orthodox marxist orientation, have
been able to acknowledge the depth of the conspicuous and
special role played by women in society.[5] Several signs

---

[5] Christine White: Women and Socialist Development:
Reflections on the Case of Vietnam. PSA Conference,
Exeter University, April 1980; C. White: Reforming
Relations of Production: Family and Cooperative in
Vietnamese Agricultural Policy; C. White: Socialist
Transformation of Agriculture and Gender Relations: The
Vietnamese Case. IDS Bulletin, vol. 12 no. 4, 1982; C.
White: Thoughts of Kinship, Gender and the Socialist
Transformation of Agriculture. Paper for a conference on

indicate that this has not been the case. The Women's Union, the only women's organization of importance since independence, has been fairly conventional in its ideas, although all laws related to women's conditions will pass through this organization which has a seat in a legislative committee under the national assembly. Recently, however, it seems that certain changes are under way among organized women. This can be seen in some important although still limited initiatives: A Centre of Women's Research has been set up[6], which means that women's research is starting now in Vietnam, and initiatives are taken in respect to international cooperation. Another result is a collection of laws accepted in January 1985, including the prolonging of maternity leave from 2 to 6 months. Research about women is still in its childhood, however, and much work is needed before a sufficient basis of empirical knowledge about women's conditions can be provided.

The labour market and the informal sector: a new field of research

The labour market has to be defined very broadly to include both the formal registered work in industry and handicraft, and the informal work has to be defined differently than is done in most market economies, which

---

'Kinship and Gender in Laos, Cambodia and Vietnam', Northern Illinois University, July 1986; Jayne Werner: Socialist Development: The Political Economy of Agrarian Reforms in Vietnam. Bulletin of Concerned Asian Scholars, vol 16, no 2, 1984, pp. 48-55; J. Werner: The New Household, The New Family and the Sexual Division of Labor in Post-War Vietnam. Paper presented at Northern Illinois University, July 1986.

[6] Irene Nørlund: Nyoprettet center for kvindeforskning (New Center for Women's Research). Vietnam 1/87 p. 12-14, Copenhagen 1987.

official international definitions in statistical collections are used. In Vietnam handicraft is included in the official statistics (see table 1) which is not always the case in other countries. As regards informal work and family work, no statistical data is available like that collected by the ILO.

To include the informal work as a focal point in research therefore demands new kinds of research methods. The collection of data for the present pilot-investigation has mainly taken the formal work as a point of departure. Visits and interviews with home weavers, showed that they were all organized within the frames of handicraft coops, even in the countryside, and this type of domestic work should not be included in the definition of informal work. But a wide range of other productive and reproductive activities contribute to the family income.

The material collected for the pilot-investigation can contribute to a better understanding of the various production forms and their potential development perspectives, and the very complex situation in Vietnam with regard to the attempts of the government to regulate the economy. The material also provides an opportunity to discuss the role of women in the development. Women have a specific place in production through a combination of formal and informal work, which will be hard to regulate by legislation. Their daily life is not only burdened by a double work like that of most other women, but they often have to take on much extra work to make ends meet. This can be a major obstacle to their further education and career. The present methods of collecting information are not sufficient, however, when it comes to work and income in the informal sector. Only small glimpses could now and then be seen in this sample, although its actual size must be substantial. Other missing points are the family situation, division of work within the family, and the women's understanding of their own role. This would entail that information should be collected within the household.

If the household is to be the core in further research the method of research applied in this pilot-project has to be reconsidered. On the other hand, if the core continues to be the state labour market as the point of departure, the present method might be useful. But it should be followed up by investigations concerning the household, division of work in the family, the total work and incomes of the household. The purpose of the research frame is <u>both</u> to understand the contents and realities of the socialist reform policy <u>and</u> the role of women in this type of transition, and thus a focus solely on the household might be too narrow. With such a focus it will not be possible to examine and understand the seemingly conscious use of the informal sector in the development, after all a quite unorthodox policy, which contains perspectives in relation to the Third World development debate.

Table 1. Labour force in various branches in Vietnam 1976 and 1982

	1976	1982
Population	49.160 mill.	56.065 mill.
Social labour force	22.631 mill.	26.631 mill.
In productive sector	92%	92%
Industry	10%	11%
Construction	6%	5%
Agriculture and forestry	69%	69%
Trade, material supplies	5%	5%
Transport and communication	2%	2%
In non-productive sector	8%	8%
Total	100%	100%

Employment in state, state/private and handicraft production in industry

	1976	1982
Productive employment in state and state/private industries	462,700	644,100
Professional handicraft labour	1,514,200	1,656,600
Total	1,976,900	2,300,700
Percentage of social labour force	8,74%	8,64%

Employment in the branch of weaving, leather, sewing and dying

	1976	1982
State and state/private	95,700 (20.7% of all in state and state/private sectors)	116,300 (18,1% of all in state and state/private sectors)
Handicraft labour	248,500 (16,4% of all in handicr.)	362,600 (21,9% of all in handicr.sector)
Total	344,200	478,900
Textile sectors in percentage of total employment in industry and handicraft	17.4%	20.8%

Source: Số liệu thống kê nước cộng hòa xã hội chủ nghĩa Việt Nam, 1982. (Statistical Data of the Socialist Rep. of Vietnam. General Statistical Office, Hanoi 1983.

Table 2. Features of employment and production within textiles and garment

	Employment within all types of textiles, garment + leather industrial employment (1000)	handicraft employment (1000)	female employment in percentage of total workforce	women employed in handicraft and small industries	state investments in weaving, sewing, leather, dying % of total invest.	production of cotton fabrics mill.meters	cotton fabrics pr.capital
1975	-	-	-	-	-	140	-
1976	96	249	53%	51%	8.3%	240	4.9 meters
1977	104	276	53%	54%	-	299	5.9 -
1978	106	297	53%	58%	-	238	6.6 -
1979	109	309	52%	62%	7.9%	287	5.4 -
1980	111	349	51%	66%	-	175	3.3 -
1981	112	343	51%	68%	11.4%	158	2.9 -
1982	116	363	51%	65%	12.5%	223	3.9 -
1983	-	-	50%	66%	-	287	-
1984	130	402	50%	66%	-	365	6.2 -
1985	137	470	51%	66%	-	374	6.2 -
1986	144	446	-	-	-	358	5.8 -
						370 (1987)	

Source: Số liệu thống kê, 1979, 1981, 1982 and data from the Centre for Womens Research, Hanoi 1986; Niên giám thống kê 1986, Hanoi 1988; Light Industry Ministry 1988.

Table 3. Visits to handicraft cooperatives 1983-86

Nam Dinh	embroidery, lace, knitting	townbased	1983
Nam Dinh	footwear, sports equipment	townbased	1983
Hanoi	garment	townbased	1983
Ha Dong	weaving (silk and cotton)	countryside	1984
Ha Dong	weaving (cotton)	countryside	1984
Ha Nam Ninh	weaving (cotton and jute)	countryside	1984
Da Nang-Quang Nam	weaving (cotton, silk, sacs)	countryside	1986
Da Nang-Quang Nam	weaving (cotton, carpets)	countryside	1986
Hanoi	weaving (cotton, carpets)	countryside	1986
Hanoi	weaving (cotton)	countryside	1986
Da Nang-Quang Nam	weavers (cotton) Hoi An	townbased	1986
Ha Son Binh	weavers (cotton/silk) traditional	country	1984
Ha Son Binh	weavers (cotton) Muong-village	country	1984
	Thai-village	country	1984

Table 4. Industrial textile enterprises, visits 1983-86.

	Nam Dinh textile combinate	Hanoi 8th of March	Hc Chi Minh Viet Thang	Da Nang Hoa Tho	Da Nang 29th of March	Hanoi Winter-spring	Hanoi Thread factory no 1	Nam Dinh Silk factory
Number of employed	11 155	6 157	4 826	1 450	700	2 000	2 000	2 000
Women in per-centage of employed	65%	75%	75%	73%	82%	85%	85%	70%
Sex of director								
Production	spinning weaving dyeing blankets	spinning weaving dyeing blankets	spinning weaving dyeing	spinning weaving dyeing blankets	towels weaving dyeing	jersey and underwears	spinning	weaving and dyeing of artifice silk
Purpose of production	national market small export	national market 8% export	national market small export	national market export?	50% export	up to 70% export	mainly export	up to 80% export
Fixed anets 1981	330 mill. dongs	86 mill. dongs	82 mill. dongs	21 mill. dongs	-	-	50 mill. US $ invest-ments	21 mill.
Capacity of production	62 mill. meters cloth 14 200 tons thread	34 mill. meters cloth 6 500 tons thread	26 mill. meters 1 800 tons thread	8 mill. meters 1 800 tons thread	1986 pro-duction = 12 mill. towels	9 mill. pieces of underwear	8 000 tons thread	8 mill. meters cloth
Trade union organization	100%	100%	84%	-	-	-	5%	90%
Party members	20%	15%	4%	-	5%	-	-	15%
Years of construction	1900	1960s	1960s	1962	1976	1959	1983	1904
Visits	1983, 84, 86	1983	1983	1986	1986	1978, 84	1984	1984, 86
Year of information	1983	1983	1983	1986	1986	1984	1984	1984

Table 5. Interviews with 9 female textile workers. 1983

Employment and income

9 workers interviewed:	1	2	3	4	5	6	7	8	9
Place of employment	textile factory Nam Dinh	textile factory Nam Dinh	8th of March Hanoi	8th of March Hanoi	8th of March Hanoi	Viet Thang Saigon	Viet Thang Saigon	handicraft cooperative Nam Dinh	handicraft cooperative Nam Dinh
Household	6 pers. 3 kids	5 pers. 3 kinds	3 pers. 1 kid	5 pers. 3 kids	6 pers. 3 kids	6 pers. 3 kids	8 pers. 7 kids	2 pers. - kids	8 pers.
Family status	married	married	married	married	married	married	unmarried	married	married
Job	weaving-machine	spinning-machine teamleader	spinning-machine	weaving-machine	weaving-machine	weaving-machine teamleader	spinning-machine	embroidery	venice lace
Years of education	6	7	9	7	6	-	6	7	7
Yearly income (1983) (estimation from individual information) in dongs	10 720	5 340	5 400	6 660	7 260	8 620	6 550	2 616	1 200 (in training)
Household income (formal wages) in dongs	12 520	7 260	7 200	-	27 600	-	-	4 416	-
Informal income	no	chickens pigs	-	chickens pigs	chickens pigs	no	no	no	no

Living conditions

9 workers interviewed:	1	2	3	4	5	6	7	8	9
Number of rooms	1-2	1	1	2	2	3	1	1	3
Kitchen, bathroom	sharing with others	x x	x x	x x	x x	x x	x x	x x	sharing
Electricity, water	x -	x x	x x	x -	x x	x x	x x	x -	x -
Consumer goods in household	radio 1 bike	radio 2 bikes	1 bike	TV motorbike 2 bikes	TV 2 bikes	radio 2 bikes	radio 1 bike	1 bike	-
Ration cards to state shop	x	x	x	x	x	x	x	-	-
Support during sickness (of basic wage)	100%	100%	100%	100%	100%	100%	100%	-	-
Number of sickdays (yearly)	5-6 days	rare	rare	some days	2 weeks	rare	7-8 days	never	rare
Maternity leave (months)	2	2	2	2	2	2	2	2-3	?
Child care	kinder-garden	grand-mothers sisters	kinder-garden	home	in school	grand-mothers	no kids	no kids	no kids
Holidays	10 days	10 days	10-15 days	10 days	10 days	10 days	10 days	-	-

	1	2	3	4	5	6	7	8	9
Housing expenses (dongs)	5.5	5.5	3	6	5.4	6	owner of house	owner of house	?
Periods of un-employment	-	-	-	-	-	-	-	-	-
Use of contra-ceptives	x	x	-	x	-	-	-	x	-
Division of work in the household	no	sharing with the daughters	no husband employed as soldier	everybody take part	everybody take part husband certain tasks	sharing with grand-mother	sharing with sisters and brothers	eating in parents home	brother help a little

Social relation

	1	2	3	4	5	6	7	8	9
9 workers interviewed:	1	2	3	4	5	6	7	8	9
Family background	-	-	peasants	peasants	peasants	peasants	mother invalid	-	small trad-ers
What employment would you like for your children?	workers	univer-sity gra-duates	own deci-sion	study medicin	workers cadres	univer-sity gra-duates	workers	-	-
Organised in: Party	x	x	x		x	x			
Trade union	x	x	x	x	x	x			
Women's union ..	x	x	x		x		x	x	
Youth union									x

Table 6. Formal income in the rice-prices 1983-86. (1983-85 old dong, 1986 new dong)

Year	Hong's income	Husband's income	Total income	State/market	5 persons' rice expenses	Percentage of income spent on rice
Before reforms	2,400 d	1,920 d (estim.)	4,320 dong	0.4 d/5 d	380 kg a 0.4 d 300 kg a 5 d	= 1,652 d = 38%
1983	5,340 d	1,920 d	7,260 dong	0.4 d/15 d	380 kg a 0.4 d 300 kg a 5 d	= 4,652 d = 64%
1984	like 1983	1,920 d (estim.)	7,260 dong	0.4 d/40 d	380 kg a 0.4 300 kg a 40 d	= 12,152 d = 167%
1985	10,000 d					
1986	8,500 d	5,400 d	13,900 dong	3.6 d/15 d	380 kg a 3.6 d 300 kg a 15 d	= 5,868 d = 42%

CONTRIBUTORS

Antlöv, Hans - B.A. (social anthropology); Department of Anthropology, Gothenburg University, Sweden.

Brun, Viggo - Cand.mag. (Thai studies); assoc.prof., East Asian Institute, University of Copenhagen, Denmark.

Bråten, Eldar - Cand.polit. (anthropology); dr.polit. student, Department of Social Anthropology, University of Bergen, Norway.

Casse, Thorkil - M.Sc. (economics); project economist, Rambøll & Hanneman, consultancy, Denmark.

Gravers, Mikael - Mag.art. (anthropology); assoc.prof., Department of Ethnography and Social Anthropology, University of Aarhus, Denmark.

Lauridsen, Laurids S. - M.Sc. (political science), Ph.D. (geography); ass.prof., International Development Studies, Roskilde University Center, Roskilde, Denmark.

Long, Litt Woon - Mag.art. (social anthropology); senior executive officer, Department of Immigrant Affairs, Ministry of Local Government and Labour, Oslo, Norway.

Kalland, Arne - Dr.philos. (anthropology); research fellow, Nordic Institute of Asian Studies, Copenhagen, Denmark.

Irene Nørlund - M.A. (history); assoc. prof., research fellow, Nordic Institute of Asian Studies, Copenhagen, Denmark.

Rudie, Ingrid - Mag.art. (anthropology); assoc.prof., Institute of Social Anthropology, University of Oslo, Norway.

Sison, Jose Maria - M.A. (arts); prominent politician of the revolutionary left in the Philippines.

Wad, Peter - Ph.D. (cultural sociology); senior lecturer, Institute of Cultural Sociology, University of Copenhagen, Denmark.